Joan Colebrook grew up in North Queensland. From 1937 to 1940 she lived in London; since then she has lived in Truro, Massachussetts. Her books include *All That Seemed Final*, *The Northerner*, *The Cross of Lassitude* and *The Innocents of the West*. Parts of *A House of Trees* were first published in the *New Yorker*.

A HOUSE OF TREES

Joan Colebrook

CORGI BOOKS

A HOUSE OF TREES
A CORGI BOOK 0 552 13487 2
Originally published in Great Britain by Chatto & Windus

PRINTING HISTORY

Chatto & Windus edition published 1988
Corgi edition published 1989

Copyright © Joan Colebrook 1987
Maps of Australia by Joseph P. Ascherl

Conditions of sale

1. This book is sold subject to the condition that it shall not, by way of trade *or otherwise*, be lent, re-sold, hired out or otherwise circulated in any form of binding or cover other than that in which it is published *and without a similar condition including this condition being imposed on the subsequent purchaser.*

2. This book is sold subject to the Standard Conditions of Sale of Net Books and may not be re-sold in the UK below the net price fixed by the publishers for the book.

This book is set in 10/11 pt Ehrhardt

Corgi Books are published by Transworld Publishers Ltd., 61–63 Uxbridge Road, Ealing, London W5 5SA, in Australia by Transworld Publishers (Australia) Pty. Ltd., 15–23 Helles Avenue, Moorebank, NSW 2170, and in New Zealand by Transworld Publishers (N.Z.) Ltd., Cnr. Moselle and Waipareira Avenues, Henderson, Auckland.

Reproduced, printed and bound in Great Britain by
Hazell Watson & Viney Limited
Member of BPCC Limited
Aylesbury, Bucks, England

FOR ROBIN AND HAZEL

Contents

I stand in a house of trees.

–LES MURRAY

'The Away-Bound Train'

A HOUSE OF TREES

1

On the Veranda

In Australia we used to sit on the veranda. It was hot – at least, it was hot in the dry season – and in moments of leisure – that is, in the afternoon – we would automatically gather there, under the overhang of the roof, and look out over the cleared spaces of the paddocks to the wall of the rain forest (we called it 'the scrub') which ringed us around. Sometimes, through the drowsy silence we would hear the whistle of the little train as it rounded the bend, and we knew that the world, represented by the gray canvas mailbags, was approaching us. If no passengers wanted to get off, the bags would simply be tossed from the train as it passed, and the stationmistress, a short woman with small, obscure dark eyes, her hair drawn back tautly from her forehead, would rush out, arms pumping, to pick them up.

So the news of the world reached us, not in great headlines or in the loud voices of modern communication, but slowly, slowly, over the vast oceans from England, creeping up from the south of Australia by boat, and inching along in the small train that crossed the coastal strip, negotiated the steep ravines and the spidery railway bridges, and at last, like some brave panting animal, mounted steadfastly to our northern plateau, the Atherton Tableland, on the edge of the Great Dividing Range.

I grew up in the 1920s on these ranges of the northeastern seaboard of Australia, which were the product of the great upward thrust formed during the Pliocene Epoch (a movement of earth that shuddered like a wave from New Guinea to Tasmania), born into a world different from the large

13

and mostly desertlike areas so typical of the continent – of the Center, of South Australia, and of a large part of the west. The rain in my native North Queensland, drawn by the divide of mountains, watered the fertile soil eroded from basaltic lava and created – subsequent to the arrival of the pioneers – a brilliant landscape, where the grass grew to a vivid emerald and the reddish roads veined the earth as capillaries vein flesh. Everywhere, in those days, there was a backdrop of rain forest, nourished by the rich fifty-foot-deep topsoil and watered by the misty rain of the yearly monsoon. The sound, the feeling, the envelopment of such constant light, swirling rain has been with me always, like one of those primordial lullabies we are supposed to carry with us from an earlier world.

The lullaby would rise to a crescendo when the cyclones swept in, raging in a circular motion, clawing at the waves and piling them up along the continental shelf until glassy walls of water rushed inland to break against headlands or foothills, to sweep away the broken timbers of the rain forest and fragments of boats and masts and docks, of houses and men and animals. One of my earliest memories had been of a cyclone that pounced from the north, swept up to the high tableland that lay inland from the port of Cairns, and circled the jungle with its wind and torrents of rain. It still had enough energy left then to lift the tin roof off the small room, recently attached to the house, where I slept; I awoke, crying, to feel the rain on my face, and my father's arms carrying me to safety.

To the north of us, although then I didn't think about it, were the myriad islands dotting the waters of the Torres Strait, where the warriors of New Guinea – the sails of their canoes, plaited from coconut fronds, glittering in the sun – still sang their head-hunting songs as they paddled from shore to shore. To the south and west extended a whole broad continent, its shape cut out in bold antique form and its surface leveled by aeons of stability and freedom from geological movement. Long before the Himalayas, the

14

Andes, and the Rockies built their heights, this Australian surface, part of it among the oldest such stretches in the world, had remained static – stretching out with an air of permanence, shimmeringly deceptive with its grasses of light gold, its ragged and weary-looking trees.

Our veranda on one corner of that continent was the extension of our lives – and hemmed in here, in this boundless and free pioneer's world, by the very narrowest of possibilities, and by the edge of the property which my father had helped to cut out from the virgin scrub, and by the distances which had to be crossed (not rapidly, but in places at a snail's pace) before contact could be made with the rest of settled Australia – such an extension had an incalculable psychological value. By it we were rescued from the prisoner's mentality. And when the mail came up, was sorted out, discussed, and exclaimed about, and when the tray-mobile was trundled from the kitchen carrying tea (ceremonial drink) flanked by a sponge cake fresh from an oven that had been stoked by aromatic jungle woods, the atmosphere became one of expansive contentment. A letter was a mark of the world's favor, a scrap of newspaper something to be pondered over, news from a passing traveler cause for wonder and exhilaration. My father would read the red page of the *Bulletin*, that all-Australian weekly which in the past had done so much to encourage and establish the first poets, writers, and cartoonists, and which still, in spite of its die-hard 'dinky-di' nationalism, was de rigueur in every bush household. My mother would sew. My quiet unselfish brother would gaze at us affectionately, then excuse himself and go back to work. My three older sisters would carry on conversations about local affairs, or about immediate or future amusements:

'Let's get our togs and go to the falls for a swim.'

'No, it's too late.'

'It's not too late – there's mobs of time.'

'We'd have to round up the horses,' someone might object lazily.

'Anyway, I'd rather finish my book,' someone else would chime in.

Perhaps the conversation would peter out as the somnolent claims of the veranda dominated again. The very form of the veranda expressed a triumph. Had it not been built as a leisurely afterthought – almost as an expression of affluence – and tacked on to a smaller structure which, in its turn, in defiance of the power of the rain forest, had been built after the first house across the creek had proved impractical? Along with the veranda, two small rooms with tin roofs had been built at the back of the house proper, and the dining room had been extended into nature itself – that is, into a fernery, where delicate plants, such as begonias and spider lilies and cunjeboi, bloomed under the ten-foot-tall tree ferns, whose roots were entangled in piles of basaltic rocks. Thus, on one side of the house the jungle was suggested, and on the other, where the veranda was, cleared land stretched toward a horizon bisected by a road, down which in the distance some horses or vehicle might travel, surrounded in the dry season by a cloud of red dust. Then we would shade our eyes, as did the two sisters in the story from *The Arabian Nights* ('Sister Ann, Sister Ann, what do you see? Who is coming?' 'Nothing, dear sister, I see nothing . . .').

Now I realize that the great distances separating us from the heart of the Empire of which we were supposedly part had been deeply impressed upon us always. Vastness and a doubt of belonging make us all seem small, and here we swam in a vacuum – aware of the sky, of the silence, of the slow journeys which faced us before arrival; possessed by that doubt which is the inheritance of those born in lonely places. ('What is that behind the sky?' asks one of the characters in *The Sheltering Sky* by Paul Bowles, and the answer is a little frightening, in that it is that there is *nothing* behind the sky – nothing at all.)

We, at least, never having known civilization, were conscious that we breathed nature. Where the wall of the rain forest rose up, there stood impressive trees – palms and lianas; trees such as the red cedar, so valuable and now so rare; the fig tree, sometimes strangling its host tree, sometimes dangling roots in a heavy curtain twenty feet to the ground; the Queensland bean; the candlenut, with its smooth, broad nuts; the maple; the immense kauri pine; and the fire wheel, which at flowering thrust its scarlet against the somber green. Some of these rain-forest trees were not only tall, stretching skyward for several hundred feet, but immensely wide and solid, their strutted roots so ponderous that they were difficult to climb over. They were trees to worship – sacred groves, like those in Europe through which the Germans at the time of Caesar traveled for months without coming into the open; or like the wealds of Kent and Surrey, old remnants of the great forest of Anderida. The beliefs of the Australian Aborigines in certain places centered on trees: the Warramunga tribe in the middle of the continent believed that in some gums (eucalypts) disembodied human spirits lived, waiting to be born again, and other tribes thought that trees had souls – that they could feel pain, as humans did, and would cry out if they were cut by an ax. The planters who cultivated the coconut plantations on the shores of Queensland's Gulf of Carpentaria, northwest of where we lived, told how Aborigine workers believed in this jungle sensibility, and would act out around the campfire the drama of the tree's pain as the ax bit into its trunk: mimic the creaking and crashing of the great trees successfully felled, let out roars of wild anger, leap into the air, and finally throw themselves screaming to the ground. And we as children felt a similar sense of identification, when the jungles spangled with light or dark, with rain and mist, seemed linked to a past life that we no longer knew, and accepted us between the pillars of great trunks into what seemed temples, smelling eternally of sweet leaves and of the disintegration of wood.

In spite of that shadow of mortality which so often haunts the tropics, it did not occur to us to fear any part of the nature around us. All that had to do with the earth seemed natural, for we had known no other life. Sometimes when the cows of our herd – having worked their way into the enclosure near the house in the middle of the night to eat the rich uncut grass at the corners of the fences – woke me with their hoarse, heavy breathing, I would be afraid at first to get up and peep out of the window, where they loomed out of the darkness, their horns silvered by the moon. But soon I would see them as harmless shapes – just as harmless as when they were safely stalled in the dairy and I could hold my head against their necks and smell their milky breath. Nor did the snakes which we had been taught to fear seem evil, having so bright and beautiful a pattern on their backs, and often lying coiled up innocently on the grass in the sun, warming themselves after the rain. And in the evening, when the lamps had been put out, great tropical cockroaches flew into the kitchen, but they did not fill me with the horror I was to see later among my friends in their grimy New York apartments: ours were creatures in their own context, no more to be feared than the velvety, thick-bodied moths, of marvelous shades of rich red, crawling from their pupae between the stems of the grasses the pioneers had sown to take the place of the felled timber. Yet a certain wariness had been instilled in us from babyhood. The men in the scrub wore heavy leather boots, partly because of the mud, but also because of the common poisonous snakes and stinging plants.

'Be careful,' someone would call as we rode our horses along the paths of the rain forest.

'Stinging tree here,' the rider at the front would call back, pointing with his whip.

'Stinging tree,' the second rider would repeat to the one behind. The fruit of this tree, ruby-colored and especially beautiful, hung like glowing bunches of raspberries against the dark leaves, as if to seduce us. But the toxic hairs of the leaves and stems would, at the slightest touch, send their detachable heads into the skin to inject a painful, long-lasting

18

poison. Once, as a child, I brushed my bare shoulder against this dreaded tree, and for weeks I suffered pain whenever my skin came in contact with water.

'Do you remember,' one of us would say, 'how that school teacher's horse got stung and bolted off down this path? The teacher was nearly killed when he got struck by a heavy branch. Do you remember?'

'Of course we remember,' the others would chorus.

This general awareness of danger was at variance with the sense of exhilaration which the environment suggested, with the sense of a joyful dawn of life which urged us on to follow behind our father as he cut a path through the scrub with a cane knife; to swim in a certain cold torrent where great basaltic rocks, as smooth as skin, stood out of the foaming water; to race our ponies along the homestretch as if to the beat of the ballads of our Australian poets which we had all learned by heart. Songs accompanied us to the clatter of the hooves and the creak of the saddle, and although we didn't think of this then, to familiar rhythms hammered out by Browning and Swinburne and Byron – but with a special Australian jingle and a special Australian simplicity:

> 'Twas merry in the glowing morn, among the gleaming grass,
> To wander as we've wandered many a mile,
> And blow the cool tobacco cloud, and watch the white wreaths pass,
> Sitting loosely in the saddle all the while . . .

There were other sensations of joy and they all seemed to be related to that physical body, pressed toward danger and exultation, so that in this perilous effort the self could be forgotten and time could stretch out and become a satisfactory continuum. That we were observers of a vanishing world was obvious, but the acceptance instinctive to childhood told us that everything had still to happen – that we lived in a bell of creation, which if tapped gently would ring forever. Yet the reality of the situation was that, in the interests of survival, beauty and emotion must take second place. No one told us this; we gradually learned it, nonetheless. But initially, how could we believe that, as the roads branched and multiplied, as still another acre or two of rain forest crashed to the ground and a new building or two rose in its place, the radiance of living might be tarnished? It was a knowledge to come only with the fullness of experience. We were like the great hideous-looking black lizards, the *Amblyrhynchus cristatus*, that Darwin observed adapting themselves to the rocky shores of the Galápagos Islands. Had not our parents, inheritors of Western civilization, adapted themselves to this untouched country, from which, in self-protection they sheared the rain forest, so that they could exploit its soil and live the good life of modern men?

Not that our parents were the first, by any means. A quarter of a century earlier, explorers had penetrated the upland ranges, had discovered gold and tin, had swum flooded rivers to get their claims in to the mining offices, had made the harsh rocky gullies resound with the striking of picks and shovels, the blasts of dynamite, and the jangle of bells from the mule packs bringing in supplies. But down in the thick scrub of the tablelands progress had been slower, with paths nonexistent, or at least narrower and wetter and harder to follow. One story has it that when an early group of settlers tried to find easier access from the steep ranges to the coast, the leader burst out: 'Stone the crows! Our flamin' horses will have to sprout wings!'

Wild blacks had attacked the teams as they struggled upward, had plundered the packhorses plowing their way through the thick mud; had hurled spears at the rough huts in the clearings – those clearings which still continued to reverberate with the sound of ax and saw and gun. In 1900 a group of men brought a load of half-green wood, a tin of kerosene, and a case of whiskey to a favored pocket in the scrub. They piled up the wood, poured the kerosene over it, started a bonfire, drank whiskey, and made speeches. They then called the town Atherton.

A few years after the turn of the century, my father, still a young man, made the slow journey north to the fertile tablelands. Living for months at a time in jungle clearings that through the wet season were lost in mist and rain, he mapped, with the help of a government surveyor, scrub blocks solid with trees.

When I asked him what it had been like in those days, he said, 'It was very wet. And very chilly.' And I imagined the tents under the canopies of trees, and the red earth around them a sea of mud, and I fancied the campers' attempts to open tins of beef and to boil the billy over spluttering fires of green wood. 'We were glad to get any kind of house built,' he added. 'Especially when it was ready enough for us to put in an iron stove.' We knew a good deal about the virtues of that iron stove, around which in the early damp mornings we would gather to keep warm and to watch the oatmeal, which was eaten with brown sugar and with cream from the dairy, slowly bubble and thicken. Never then did we consider that we had been among the first to destroy that sacred covering of trees and vines, and I found when I returned years later that I had kept this knowledge from myself with such success that I could only feel anguished surprise as I looked out upon the almost denuded tablelands, the vanished shrine of my childhood.

We sensed, perhaps, that the destructive side of our activities could not be debated, for although we were British we were Australian first, and to be Australian meant that one had to survive. The whole 'English thing' as seen from the sultry Australian schoolrooms, that sense of ordered and thoughtful beauty in cottage gardens as in noble estates, that 'manageability,' was foreign to us – we who, except in the scrub, had gone barefoot for much of our childhood, our feet and legs daily plunged into the rich earth of the sacrificed jungle (even though our orderly heritage warred against that earthy stain as it crept from the door to room after room, kept at bay only by a good deal of patient scrubbing). To us, who had listened to the savage, lonely, and ululating cry of

21

the wild dingo, and had thought of the story of the solitary settler with a broken leg who lay helpless all night as the dingoes came closer and closer, until a passing rider found him at dawn and the circling dogs melted into the scrub – to us, nature meant the overgrown and tumultuous. Perhaps there were even dark gods we knew nothing about – rather like those set up farther north, in New Guinea, where the longhouses of the Sepik River were turreted with human skulls, and where the headlands and the coasts of nearby islands were adorned with propitiations to shark deities notorious for their love of human flesh. It was against such barbarity that we saw the railing of the veranda as a protective ledge, behind which we pragmatic Anglo-Saxons, inheritors of the British Empire, could safely shelter. The truth was that we did not really know *what* we were, for no one had yet told us, and we certainly did not see ourselves as playing a part in a drama of conquest.

But the stories we listened to gave this impression – stories we heard while sitting in the stark white moonlight or in the firelight at picnics, or on the veranda after dinner, or on the long rides we took together, when the horses moved slowly along narrow tracks. The stories were always of men who performed heroic deeds against deadly antagonists, and the heroes always won in the end. My uncles, who loved to 'yarn,' told tales so strange that we found them hard to believe – tales that often seemed dark, as if shadowed by the great jungle-clad heights that loomed up from the tropical coasts of North Queensland or New Guinea. Through these stories ran a thread of gold, a thread of dauntless courage and good luck, woven by heroes more athletic than ordinary men – horsemen, swimmers, runners, marksmen – as patient as beasts of burden, as clever as amateur doctors, as reckless as tightrope walkers.

Our uncle Anthony Linedale, our mother's brother, who had run away from school at sixteen and had traveled as far as the goldfields in New Guinea, had a soft humorous voice that went on and on – not always grammatically, for he had left scholarship far behind when he chose the life of a wandering explorer and miner, and had picked as companions those who followed similar professions.

'Oh, yes, we done it all right, we done it, and we didn't think twice of it,' he would say as we settled down to listen to him. 'I remember one time on the Mámbare River, in New Guinea, when the savage tribes attacked us, and speared poor George Clarke – that was a bad time, a very bad time . . . But I was lucky. Although I came down with a fever that rattled my bones and turned my nostrils and the lobes of my ears black. Long afterwards, that fever would come on in the night, and my camp bed would shake and slide around.'

His stories were full of the atmosphere of those rough, desperate older days. As a boy, he had seen 'pacification' campaigns in the north after the Queensland government created a Native Police Force armed with guns. Sometimes these guns, in the hands of the new black recruits, were used to kill old tribal enemies. 'There was one time,' my uncle said, poking at his pipe, 'in the ranges back of Herberton, when I sat on my horse for a long time, watching the pile of black bodies which the police boys had set on fire, perhaps thinking that we white fellers wouldn't know what they had done. The pile smoldered there in the bright sunlight, and I sat sadly watching it. One group had attacked a tribe that had broken the accepted laws, and that was the end of that. People'll tell you that the whites massacred the blacks, and this is true, sadly true: but the blacks massacred too, by hang. We came with our guns, and they learned with terrible results to use them instead of their spears and nulla nullas . . . but it was up in the wet desert – Cape York – that the blacks were worst. Big cannibals, these men were. Over those ranges you'd walk miles and see no one, but they were there behind you all the same.'

He went on to tell a nightmare story of cannibalism, concerning a faithful Aboriginal boy called Yarry, who belonged to a distant tribe. On one occasion he took Yarry to Innisfail, on the coast, and left him to mind the horses until he returned from the races. While my uncle and his friends were away, a group of wild blacks carried Yarry off with them, and when it was discovered that he was missing, my uncle hired a black tracker and went to look for him. They found him at last in one of the camps, which had been deserted at the approach of the white men's horses. Yarry lay there with both of his legs and all of his fingers broken, so that he could not possibly escape. His arms and legs were strapped to a pole with lengths of lawyer vine. 'Like any other game of the country, he was trussed up ready to be eaten,' my uncle said. 'It was a long time before he could feed himself, poor fellow. Fierce warriors they were in the far north. You'd not think so many white men would wander around alone, as they did, sometimes from necessity but often from choice. The old bushmen I knew were funny chaps – all they wanted was the stars and the campfire and what they call in the west a bit o' Kimberley mutton [roast goat] or a pigeon or two . . . Yes, I had an old mate back there on the Upper Clarence and he was quite a "hatter" [a solitary]. When we came to some pub and were shouting each other drinks, he didn't like it because he didn't drink, and someone called him a wowser – that's about the worst you could call someone in those days. Well, he went out o' that pub and we never seen him again. He wandered off and later they found his body. Something had happened to him; he'd done a perish . . .'

There was a pleasing simplicity about my uncle, and to watch his big, dark, expressive eyes was to understand his kindness, and to know more about the men of that time. Although he had little formal education, his knowledge, especially of mining, was extensive, and later on in his life he traveled through Europe to explore new mining methods. He understood human things, too – the fear and distrust of strange tribes which so many of the Aborigines felt, for instance.'One day,' he explained to us, 'I sent a wild runner from Chillagoe to Irvinebank, and he didn't want to come into the house, and when he did he frightened your mother and your aunt by standing behind the window curtain, so that when they came in they could only see his big dark feet. He wanted to keep hidden because he was so sure that the local blacks would eat him, and for that reason, even after his long run, he left without rest and just disappeared into the bush again.'

The women of that time were supposed to be as brave as the men, and I heard my mother describe occasions when spears had been thrown at her as she watered her pony at the crossing in Irvinebank, and recall how at Tolga, our first home, she had sheltered her children under a table covered with wet sheets while a bush fire raged outside.

These stories were like books to us, with the pages turned over again and again. We listened without thought of how long the stories took to tell, or of whether or not we had heard them before. It was a time when hours were not measured. But eventually the more sophisticated world intruded and brought with it worldly confusions. We all read by electric light until nine o'clock, when the home generator was turned off, and later by lamplight, and even later, clandestinely, by a solitary candle – and a profound split in our values became apparent. For while books were a bulwark against isolation, those we read came from far away, and we could accept the active, sociable lives their characters led only in the way we accepted fairy stories.

Naturally, it did not strike us then that as members of the human species, born at a certain time and place, we were subject to laws which governed a good deal of our behavior – as other circumstances governed the behavior of other human beings.

But whether or not we were aware of it in plain terms we did know that it was absolutely necessary to put the self aside if emergencies arose, and we learned early what was serious and what was not, and that, when disaster struck, it was almost by reflex action that the settlers would form a lifeline, taking over one from another, held by a strong rope woven of effort and loyalty. If a man cut himself felling timber, that was serious. When a woman drove wildly in a buggy into our yard, her hair flying, the horse lathered, and cried to my mother, 'Come quickly, come quickly, Mrs Heale! Dick's real bad! Up at the corner of the scrub near Henson's place,' one of us would speed off to find the men in the paddocks, and my mother would gather bandages together and get the little medicine box, and we would imagine how the ax, honed at the end of each day to an ever finer edge, had come whistling down through the air and at the last moment slipped a little to slice the man's leg at the knee. (Shuddering, we could imagine how the man, like other men we had seen, went white under his tan, and sat groaning and biting his lip, staring at his leg covered with blood, the bone showing white through the flesh. We knew that he would try to control his fear and pain, because that was what men – big men, pioneers – did.)

My mother, who was knowledgeable about illnesses and accidents, had large, dark, intensely sympathetic eyes, like her brother's. When she stood in the yard listening to someone's troubles, she was like an angel of mercy in a straw hat, which she wore to keep the sun off, and with feet planted in rubber boots like my father's, but smaller. 'The family is so poor,' she said to my father as they returned from helping the man injured in the scrub. 'There's almost nothing in the house, Ted. They're sleeping in sacks. We must take them up some sheets and some bandages, and a pillow to make him more comfortable.'

'How many children are there?'

'Three now,' said my mother, 'but soon there will be four.'

She sometimes helped a woman in labor before the doctor arrived, or a family with influenza in the wet season, or a man who'd spent time in the northern islands and now had a recurrence of dengue fever – fever so bad that his skin had grown horribly sensitive, his headaches were unmanageable, and he had become delirious, raving alone in some small, dirty hut two or three miles from the nearest scrub track. Once I tagged along behind my mother to such a hut where an old man needed help, and found that the walls of rough bush timber were plastered over with pictures cut from magazines: there were beautiful girls in very modest bathing suits and early cars and smart people attending the races. I remember climbing onto a stool to gaze at them. Another time it was a curly-haired Irish girl whom my mother helped. 'God love her,' the girl said about a year after the accident, her eyes uplifted under her bangs. 'It was on the veranda of the dairy cottage on your father's place, and there was a big tub of scalding water, and it was in the dark, and I fell into it. If your mother hadn't known what was best to use, I don't know whether my face'd be here today.'

So life went in the shadow of the scrub, with the creak of the great trees falling, with the monsoon rains fertilizing the new grass and corn, with the cows multiplying and their poddies sucking our fingers as we taught them to drink milk from buckets instead of from their mothers. None of the novels we had read about English life prepared us for what we were actually experiencing – these books which talked about rivalries in Parisian courts; pirates who strung people up and looked for treasures of gold; squires impregnating farm girls without fear of revenge; English villages where manners were restrained, if somewhat waspish; and gentle heroines who waited dutifully to be wooed!

Behind what we read lay the questions of customs and morals, for although Australia had no state church, and in theory gave equal acceptance to all religions, the Anglican Church – to which we as a family belonged – held the dominant role, both numerically and socially (it being, of course, the ruling church of England). At the same time, I think that there existed in Australia some sort of natural prejudice against the 'respectable' view. Far away from the mother lode of stern English propriety, there had grown up a desire for less restrictive social rules.

'In Australia,' someone later said to me reprovingly when I mentioned the convict influence as something which must at least be reckoned with, 'it is believed that human nature should have a second chance.' Implicit in this Australian philosophy was the suggestion that after all it might be better to be descended from a convict or a ticket-of-leave man or an impoverished rural immigrant or a lower-class industrial worker than from some effete second son of an old British house, although this notion did not quite jibe with the warm attachment to the 'old country' or with the strong middle-class respectability which many Australians strove for (as if to offset any accusation of coarseness of origin). 'Well,' as my father said, laughing a little, 'we all love England, but even if Englishmen are our brothers they're also bloody pommies!'

When visitors came, it was rather as if they were castaways who had been thrown ashore by the tide after a shipwreck, and our house sometimes astonished them, in spite of the fact that it was only a medium-sized sprawling structure of wood (set up on stilts painted with creosote as protection from the ravages of termites, and half disguised, half flattered by the tropical plants and flowers which blurred its edges). Nothing much was expected here on the borders of a jungle where survival was everything, and it often happened that visitors arrived at the end of a long journey to find a small four-room place of unrelieved ugliness, or an echoing wooden bush hotel noisy with the voices of half-drunk men and with the clucking of wandering fowls in the kitchen. Our house, by contrast, was a place that at least represented civilization. There were a few books in the bookcases, some old prints on the walls, simple furniture made by an immigrant carpenter, and a number of improvised household additions, such as the little bureaus my mother had conjured up by tacking cretonne around the edges of raw packing cases. At tea time, the cups would be spread out on a starched cloth, and at dinner the candles in the ancestral silver candlesticks – faithfully transported after each change of residence – would illuminate the platter of rare roast beef and Yorkshire pudding and the quivering Victorian desserts which my mother knew so well how to make and which would delight visitors who did not expect to be so nostalgically welcomed on the 'fringes of Empire.' That old British idea of dressing for dinner 'come what may' ruled on such occasions. It was like the attitude of the nineteenth century explorer who, after a wearying trek through African terrain, would demand the lighting of fires, the heating of water for his portable canvas bath, and the bath itself (with the black porters exclaiming at his curious white skin), and, finally, dressed again and with hair suitably combed, would sit down to toast the sunset with a peg of brandy. We, in the wilds of Australia, would see these guests who arrived at dusk, red from the dust of the roads – or, if it was the wet season, with mud marking their shoes and the hems of their raincoats – and dazzle them with lively talk about local affairs, along with casual and generally quite innocent references to the fifteen-foot snake found only that morning in one of the cupboards.

'I do *relly* think, Mr Heale,' one tall and dignified English Member of Parliament said as my father – consciously or unconsciously – played up to the idea of the indomitable Anglo Saxon exerting his will and his humor under the last lonely flutterings of the Union Jack, 'it's *relly* extraordinary what you and your family have done out here. By Jove, you've made a reality out of this Garden of Eden. It's *frightfully* exciting. I *relly* mean it. We can't thank you enough for the way you hold your end up out here.' At which my father looked astonished, because he did not look upon his life as a hardship. In fact, if any of us sensed deprivation in our environment we might also have had some slight scorn for the British visitors who came with their pink cheeks and white hands, their good manners and their knowledge of the world, and who by making passing reference to licensed pleasures (shooting in Scotland, and fishing in Ireland, and yachting at Cowes) suggested both the lighter side of life and they themselves in the center of things. Perhaps it was natural for us to feel that the English were not of the *new* world, and so for all their charm and politeness did not belong to the future.

But who *did* belong to the future? In the kitchen my eldest sister, Hazel, getting the afternoon tea for our parents and for the new young man from London (who had come out to Australia as part of the Queensland Immigration Worker's Scheme, and hence up to the tablelands), was emphatic as to who did *not* belong.

'They just don't seem to fit in.'

'Who doesn't fit in?'

'These pommies they send out.' (We always called Englishmen 'pommies,' although we were not encouraged to call Australia 'Aussieland,' or Brisbane 'Brissie,' or Tasmania 'Tassie,' or claret 'clarrie wine,' or a Communist a 'Commo.')

'Why doesn't *he* fit in?'

'He's a bit cheeky if you ask me,' laughed one of the girls from the dairy, who was helping my sister to clean the kitchen.

'What did he *do?*' I asked curiously.

'Nothing.'

'*Nothing?* Is he ugly?'

The girl who was helping looked at my sister and laughed. They were two older girls confiding in each other.

'He's got a red nose,' she said.

'He's got a cockney accent,' my sister added. 'He said, "'Ow I've been *wyting* to meet a pretty *Austrylian* girl!"'

Later that night we heard the sound of a gun, and it turned out that the new immigrant was so frightened of animals that he had shot at a possum which was scrambling harmlessly across the tin roof of our kitchen. The shot had woken us all and my father had been irritated, partly because he had come out ready to deal with an intruder. 'What a bloody idiot!' he said angrily. 'He's trying to be an Australian,' my mother explained. The gun, after all, was a symbol and it wasn't so long since guns had been necessary to the settlers. These pioneers – hunters, fellers of forests, breakers of horses – were the product of an ongoing process; to them it seemed natural to be poised for action. A certain sense of danger and dread had entered into their souls.

Apart from the books and the visitors, it was a close-knit little world we lived in, a circle so narrow that variety was thought of only in terms of going far, far away – to Egypt, perhaps, to see the Pyramids, or to New York, where the skyscrapers were. When the tall brown farmers, swaying their hips a little awkwardly, would come into the local hotel with their wives, it was as if they were coming to the hub of the world. A few had electricity in their houses but many didn't, and the hotel at the tiny nearby settlement of Malanda must have seemed ablaze with light to them. Their wives, scrubbed clean and rosy and wearing fresh cotton dresses, stood just inside the door of the hall and stole glances at themselves in the spotted mirror set into an old silky-oak umbrella stand, which was like some clumsy Victorian animal transported unchanged from suburban London to a series of rank tropical clearings.

The hotel, a two-story slab of a place with an upper veranda and a lower overhang, was painted a dull reddish brown, and its everlasting purpose seemed to be to enclose and hold the strong smell of beer, wafted – as the louvered door swung to and fro – from the sacred MEN ONLY bar. Everyone came on Saturday night, men and women and sometimes children as well – the stationmaster and his wife, the butcher, the grocer, the bachelor in charge of the branch bank, the men who worked in the scrub and on the railway line, and the few available young women. At the Saturday-night entertainment, a woman from 'down the line,' her blond curls tight on the top of her head, her jaw determined, pounded out tunes on the jangling piano, her hands flying like ponies over the keys – crashingly and at full gallop – while a thin wizard of a man with a fiddle would get drunker and drunker through the long evening, until at last, like the Pied Piper, he was leading the dancers with his enchanted fiddle all around the room and would have, had they wanted to follow him, led them outside and up and down the solitary street.

Sometimes after these entertainments we would feel more isolated than ever. Perhaps there was some slight uneasiness in the Australian social position. We could not feel that the British immigrants or the British visitors were truly associated with Australia. The expatriates, of course, were more kin to us in some way, because although they might have been of British origin, they were still from our half of the world. They were from an empire not yet diminished but with its foundations quaking as if in premonition of the cataclysms of World War II. Their skins were brown like ours, but would often have that deep-dyed look of having been subjected to years of tropical heat. These expatriates would tend to be thin and restless, and the women would invariably wear pastel dresses of tussore silk or shantung, with heavy necklaces of crystal or ivory or lapis lazuli. Lighting up their cigarettes, the women would talk with animation of their lives in various parts of the East, of their tennis tournaments, their rubbers of bridge, their gay goings-on in that universal holy of holies – the 'club.' There would also be endless talk about servants; their number-one cooks, their amahs, their taxi wallahs, their garden boys – and, if they were plantation people, their coolies. The men might have come from rubber plantations in Malaya or Java, or been D.O.'s (district officers) from Borneo or India, or even businessmen from Hong Kong or Singapore. Occasionally, especially if they were originally Australians or New Zealanders, they might be military men or special policemen who were serving out their time in the East, or even in New Guinea just to the north of us. Again, they might be mining men, harsher and more adventurous, either going restlessly from field to field or obsessed with some special rocky hill or ridge from which they intended to make their fortunes – on their way to or from London or Berlin or Johannesburg with the intention of trying to raise suitable capital.

Some of the British visitors might have been prisoners in the past – that is, prisoners of their environment (something which became clearer to me later when I myself traveled by train and bus through dreary London suburbs) – and it certainly seemed that their accents were less of Oxford than

32

of various provincial universities. My father said once that many of them had entered the Colonial Service because in the stiff British hierarchy this was the only avenue open to them. They were psychological exiles then, somewhat as the Australians were. What I didn't think of was how the isolation and the heat, the bitterness and the loneliness, might have affected them in their exile, or the strangeness of the cultures to which they had to adapt. In other words, I didn't know how dearly they might have paid for the liberty they had gained by leaving their native land. I don't think it occurred to us either that the pioneers on the newly opened-up tablelands had also paid for their freedom.

I knew as I grew older that my parents were brave, that my father, who always protested loudly against anything that he felt was an injustice to others or to himself, only protested because he was trying to keep on living – that is, acting and working and, if possible, conquering.

I remember that material objects suggested a certain pathos. The harness room at the back of the house held saddles on wooden props, and the saddles especially seemed to be alive as if they were part of the animals from which they had been taken. Whips and bridles hung on the walls. On the floor stood a long row of leather and rubber boots, stained and caked with red mud. Old battered felt hats hung on hooks. And the door closed with a wooden peg on a string, smooth and familiar to my hands. These things were the manifestations of life, but where was the life itself?

I could only think that life was a part of the things I looked at and touched; that life was mostly action; that life was a kind of courage.

2

To the Schoolhouse

The details of the life lived by our parents before we were
born seemed to us always romantic and elusive. When my
mother and father were married they settled at Tolga, a small
settlement close to Atherton, where my father had bought a
share in a timber mill. The soil at Tolga was not spectacularly
fertile, and there was always the lure of rich earth farther out,
so that eventually he bought land at what was to be called
Kureen (derived from an Aboriginal word meaning 'little
creek'), and for this property he chose the name Fleetwood
(taken, according to the nostalgic Australian habit, from a
country place owned by his English ancestors).

In 1909, therefore, and while it was still the wet season,
our father and mother drove out from Tolga in a covered
buckboard to this virgin property at Kureen with Hazel and
the two babies – that is, the twins, Margot and Helen – and
also with an immigrant nursemaid who was for some time
in a state of astonishment at what life could really be like in
faraway Queensland, and who said also, as if in reproof, that
she had once worked for the Lord Mayor of London! That
first arrival, traveling in the manner of ancient wanderers,
happened to be accompanied by a frightful storm, with wild
lightning and rearing horses, so that the last mile or two
had to be managed on foot. In spite of this, our mother
said, a splendid meal awaited them – 'roast chicken, and
bananas and pineapples grown in the rich mold of the just
cleared rain forest.'

The house here was the first I knew, and I associated
it with a world of play among the bleeding stumps and
fallen boughs of the cut-down jungle trees that lay flat

on the ground among the inkweed and Cape gooseberry bushes, which had sprung up from the earth charred by the clearing fires – we called this game Bridges. There was another game we played (with a little Aboriginal boy from the camps) and this was called War – it consisted of running about shrieking and throwing handfuls of red and black earth into the air.

And for me at least, this first house was important because it was so close to the jungle that ever afterwards it seemed to me natural that one should be awakened at dawn to a chorus of birds; just as it seemed natural that as the sun dropped down again and night fell, those bird voices should be muted and die away one by one. Less natural seemed the enormous tree which leaned near one of the walls of the house close to my room and was in its turn embraced by a thick mottled greenish vine which twisted around its branches so that as a small child I feared that it was a snake and about to come into the house. How lucky I had been that after the haughty first nurse deserted us, Jessie, the new immigrant mother's helper, had come to us from Scotland, and would reassure me about this vine, lifting me in her strong arms and holding me against her ruddy cheek to murmur, 'It's only a plant. Don't be afraid, my bonny wee lassie!'

Soon after the arrival at Kureen, a shed for cows was put up and supple-hided black-and-golden jerseys wandered in the paddocks, eating the soft green grass which sprouted between the stumps of felled trees. But eventually there came the ringing of the hammers of our grandfather and our father, who were working together on a better and roomier house on the other side of the creek. It would be not only more centered on the property but closer to the red road which wandered away for two miles to Malanda, which was also small and primitive, although it had a butcher's shop and a smithy for shoeing horses and mending plows, and eventually a cooperative butter factory built and managed by the nearby dairymen.

***

World War I was over, but Australia was assessing her losses. It was said that the government had hesitated to tell her citizens the full story of the country's casualties, and had only announced the death list slowly and circumspectly, for the highest percentage of casualties among all the British forces had been Australian, and our soldiers – perhaps because of their reckless heroism – had been used as entry forces in a number of dangerous operations. After the war ended there was some turmoil about the way the Australian troops had been employed, and families began to relive their grief.

Visitors had come to our house from a distance, and there were buggies and horses hitched up to the nearby fences. I remember clinging to my mother's skirts, enfolded in a world of riding boots and riding habits, all stained with the red mud of the rainy season. There were people crying – crying for memories of Gallipoli and for the Somme, and Ypres, and Amiens. Auntie Bea was crying again for the death of her two sons; and someone else was crying for one of the heroes of Hill Sixty. They were all embracing each other as their tears fell, and I was frightened. Soon they sat down at a table, and again I was in a world of semi-darkness, and I put out my fingers timidly to touch the marks of mud and water on their boots and riding habits; the words of war, not yet understood, echoed in my head: Gallipoli – Hill Sixty – the Somme – Ypres – Amiens.

At that time buildings and fences were being put up, and the rain forest was being pushed back further each day. Life was sketchy and improvised, but the herds were increasing, and year by year we were conquering the essential simplicities. Year by year we also took a firmer grasp of the earth. As children we were put to sleep wherever there was room for us, but we were secure in this wooden castle built from the living trees.

It was after this very early time that a one-room school-house was put up near the road to Malanda. Small and square, it was set up on stilts, so that the termites could not destroy the building too rapidly (and as a bonus, the pupils could play games underneath the building when it rained). The land on which the schoolhouse stood had either been given or sold to the Queensland government by my father, and was not far from the slight rise on which he had chosen to build the new house for his own family. So we looked across at it from our veranda, and could see that point on the horizon where the white skeletons of dying trees marked the place where the jungle cutters had temporarily ceased their work. On school days one could hear from our veranda the rhythmic nasal chanting of tables and spelling, and sometimes the sound of students singing such songs as 'Waltzing Matilda,' its meaning only half absorbed, but its chorus always shouted out with patriotic fervor.

My teacher had red hair and pale skin, and she would sometimes lift me up and stand me on one of the long wooden benches and have me read aloud parts of our first-grade book to the smaller children while she herself set tasks for the older pupils, or wrote sums on the blackboard, or even sat for a moment with her red head bent on her hands, as if she could scarcely bear any longer the confusion of so many children of different ages. Then we would guess that she had a headache, and when there was a pause in the lessons we younger ones would crowd around her with a certain inarticulate distress. Sometimes during the monsoon rains (which in this part of northern Australia enveloped the tablelands in moisture for three months of every year), some of the bigger pupils, who generally rode their ponies to school, bareback, and perhaps two or three to a pony, would not appear. So in that tin-roofed box of a place, even with the rain dripping onto the metal and drifting against the window, it would be quieter than usual, and the teacher would tell stories and let us go home early, because it had become so damp and mysterious, the mist creeping up and wrapping its long, eerie ribbons around the edges of the scrub.

This school was an integral part of our early lives. Among other things, it acted as a screen through which were tested aspects of our reality – through the school view we were

37

forced to look at the world in a more complex way. My first clear memory of the Aborigines, for instance, had come from an earlier time, when – as a very small child and holding my father's hand – I went into a dark part of the scrub where an Aboriginal family had built their gunyah under the jungle trees. It was an arched shelter of rough boughs curved over into a semicircle and roofed with the fronds of scrub palms. This was during the monsoon, I remember, but the soft rain was deterred by the thick screen of trees overhead. In front of the little shelter, a tiny fire smoldered, sending up its smoke to drift across the dark faces that looked out at us with a sense of infinite patience. There were the glowing eyes of the old man, set in the hollows of his face beneath a fringe of white hair, and the eyes of his two women, and of one or two children, and the eyes of the half-dingo dogs – all those eyes, dark and shining, and staring out at us from the heart of that passive, curling intimacy of bodies, as if they could not think why we were there but accepted us all the same. My father must have gone to offer them something – or perhaps to ask them to work for him – but I only remember the sense of waiting, and their staring at us as we stared at them. I remember also that I thought them strange and beautiful, like something out of one of my most treasured picture books. At school, however, a different view had been propagated. To my simple thought that they were beautiful and rather thin and fragile was added the theory that they had no proper tools or clothing or cooking utensils and no means of transportation, and that they were very lucky, therefore, that we (white Australians) had come to teach them the importance of living properly.

Much of the knowledge attained at school was of that kind – suggestive rather than concrete, but with the didactic power of an organized idea. When we played games such as 'Oranges and Lemons, the Bells of St. Clement's,' or chanted (as we seesawed on the big planks from my father's timber mill placed there conveniently for us):

38

See saw, Margery Daw,
Jenny shall have a new master,
She shall have but a penny a day,
Because she can't work any faster . . .

the words meant little, having come to us from so far across the seas. We did perhaps wonder why the one game should end with heads being cut off, and why the other should suggest such cruelty to children, but our speculation went no further than this. In the meantime, while we listened to the scanty outlines of our own history we were adjusting ourselves to pay tribute to the great virtues of the British. When we were told to put our shoulders back and march in line, or to stand silently and wait for the teacher to tell us what to do, the implicit understanding was that it was necessary to learn to obey – that we were in fact small soldiers of the great British Empire. Sometimes, as the harsh, bright light of the north pierced the aureole of jungle, or when the flat, slightly demonic laughter of the kookaburra disturbed the stillness, we were aware of a sensual difference in our state, but we could not grasp what that difference was. Already in the school of reality, where we learned how to handle horses and other animals, how to encourage crops to grow, and how to move with caution but without fear in country not yet tamed or completely understood, we accepted as well a purely exotic emotional world which harked back to disciplines worked out over centuries on a small, fertile, sea-surrounded island. These disciplines enfolded us still. They had been modified, of course, in various ways, having been transferred to Australia originally in those creaking ships which carried the convicts and the first settlers, and carried not only the spirit of an adventurous past but also the conflicting passions of an industrial society.

He was playing at Plymouth a rubber of bowls
When the Great Armada came . . .
But he said, 'They must wait their turn, good souls,'
And he stooped, and finished the game.

And no matter if one of the older boys, long-legged and shambling as he rose to his feet at the command of the teacher, and already with the wrists and hands and feet of a man, thrust back his mop of wild hair to pronounce, in the true colonial way, 'playing' as 'plying' and 'wait' as 'wite.' His emotions were aroused by Drake's pride and independence, and he was likely to try to translate these qualities into his own life.

> *Fifteen sail had the Dutchmen bold,*
> *Duncan he had but two,*
> *Yet he anchored them fast where the Texel shoaled*
> *And their colours aloft he flew.*
>
> *'I have taken the depth to a fathom,' he cried,*
> *'And I'll sink with a right good will,*
> *For I know when we're all of us under the tide*
> *My flag will be fluttering still!'*

These ballads of courage and steadfast bravado, in our case and in this primitive school, concentrated on action of some kind, especially on war and defiance and belief in victory. The issues of principle were not dealt with. Yet the impulse to doubt and to question must have existed all the same.

One rainy afternoon I did not go to school, and the next day I explained that my mother had kept me at home to help her plant verbena in the garden. The teacher refused to believe me – or at least she reproved me in an authoritarian tone.

'You do know that you must come to school *every* day? That it is your *duty* to come to school?' she asked.

'Yes,' I answered, knowing that duty was something difficult, but not sure just what it was.

'Then why didn't you come to school?'

'Because my mother said I could stay,' I hastened to explain.

'To help her in the garden?'

'Yes.'

'But it was raining,' the teacher protested.

Unable yet to rationalize aloud, to defend myself, I simply hung my head (although I could have said that it had been raining only a little bit and that this was the best time to transplant baby seedlings) and remained, as I sensed it, condemned for not being entirely truthful.

Perhaps I knew that I wanted to stay at home anyway, because now that there was a new little girl in the house, a brown-eyed plump creature with a very small and yet curved nose like the beak of a baby bird, I found it hard to gain my mother's undivided attention. The new baby was suitably called Robin, and when my mother asked me to help her while the baby was asleep, that had seemed like a special privilege, and I had hastened to obey.

But this was not the end of the matter. I felt guilty, and the word 'duty' was obscurely linked to that even more delicate word 'honor.' I did not know then that it was more than authority I was encountering – that it was that tension which had shaped so many solid citizens of the Empire, so many much-abused Tommy Atkinses, so many long-suffering Jack Tars, and, here in Australia, so many intrepid explorers, patient settlers, and reformed convicts. In short, it was only because of such imported educational methods (passed on by the more responsible and better-educated descendants of the English gentry, by the pick of the 'younger sons,' and by those who had special talents and special resistances to having those talents stifled) that this raw new culture had become tenable. But if I didn't follow the actual process – didn't understand that it was by such imported educational disciplines that good colonies are made, and that here was the germ of an order which would create a future prosperity – I did at least know that any hint of lack of a sense of 'duty' suggested the deepest reproof. Yet Australians of my own generation also made fun of work, and had absorbed a philosophy which derided what they did – partly because of their need to protect themselves from arduous conditions,

41

and partly because of the special ironic turn of their humor. In fact, they developed a glossary of expressive statements (for instance, 'I'd have been here before, but I was too busy doing nothing') to forestall accusations of laziness; and it was not by accident that one of the first great outback novels – *Such Is Life*, by Tom Collins – begins with the sardonic words 'Unemployed at last!'

Sometimes in hot weather, luncheon picnics would be held at the school. Parents and children from miles around gathered, bringing great wicker baskets filled with food, with fruits and salads and freshly baked scones, and cakes spread with thick cream. Games were organized for the children, and the adults sat under the sparse shade of a group of umbrella trees. The farmers, with their weathered faces, and wearing their best trousers and shirts, all sat together, in a phalanx of masculine solidarity, and the women sat together, too. ('Australian women gather together,' my cousin in Sydney would say, 'like a lot of hens.')

It seemed to me remarkable that my mother mingled easily with the other women from the district, some of whom, I realized, did not speak as well or as clearly as she did. Many of them had that look of hardworking farm women who are out in all weathers, saddling the horses, milking the cows, tending the vegetable gardens, and they seemed shiny-skinned and coarse beside my mother, though she, too, was a working woman, her hands as worn and brown and cracked as any. It was her speech and manner that set her apart, and the colors of the clothes she put on, and the slight dusting of powder she wore on her small nose and high cheekbones. But in the drowsy heat they all sat there together, half lying on the grass, the women's big hats tilted against the sun, while the smoke from the men's pipes floated in and out of the light-speckled shade. And we, the younger generation, played our games or hovered restlessly on the perimeters of the group and waited for the high point of the afternoon, when someone would open the lid of the wooden churn and serve the delicious ice cream inside it – but without understanding that this little box of a schoolhouse had been built for us and for Australia. Nor did we realize that all these suntanned and splendid but slightly worn men and women saw us as the justification for their efforts, and wanted to send us out as emissaries into the void of time – not only those of us considered the best but also those considered the worst, even the little girl with the harelip, for instance, who might or might not have Chinese blood; and the small freckled boy who dropped all his aitches and was so terribly adenoidal, and wore his big brother's cut-down pants to school, and was thought to be the one responsible for spreading lice through the heads of the pupils who sat next to him. Pride and hope were reflected so often in the conversation of the adults that it seemed to be boasting.

'I've never 'ad ink and pen in me 'ouse before,' one old farmer said, in a rusty grating voice, 'but now the nipper's in school 'e gets orl upset if it's not there when 'e wants it! By crickey, 'e's a real little worker and when the lamp's lit 'e's at 'is books in 'arf a mo.'

'And that's how it should be,' his neighbor agreed. 'As we used to say in the old country, a penn'orth o' learning is better than a pound o' show.'

A woman addressed my father, her plump shoulders spreading down toward her waist as she slumped in the grass in her black-and-white cotton dress, for all the world like the speckled leghorn hen ruffling her feathers with which my cousins might have compared her:

'And don't you know, Mr. Heale, when all of us come up here, we didn't think of schools then – it was only the blacks and the stores and the wagons and gettin' the land cleared that we set our sights on. Now even this school is too small fer us.' She went on to compliment my father on his enterprise in providing the government with the land for the school.

My father, who was even then thinking of sending some of his own children on to the Church of England boarding school which was soon to open up in the mining town of Herberton, some hundreds of feet higher up in the ranges,

43

smiled and nodded his thanks. He must have felt that slight discomfort which egalitarian Australians were doomed to feel as religious and social differences were deepened and widened in their still young society. The school in the ranges, primitive as it might prove to be, already carried the cachet of the Church of England, which represented, by its ministry, schools such as Westminster and Eton and universities such as Oxford and Cambridge, and which, by tradition at least, upheld the theory of a superior English classical education. In other words, the dominant religion (dominant in the sense of numbers and in the sense of the reflected glory of the Anglican British ascendancy) was thereby emphasized. Naturally we knew about Catholicism, too, and we felt, insensibly, that Anglicans were a little worried because Irish Catholic migrants were flooding into Australia, according to the prejudiced view, in 'unchecked numbers.' We might even have heard around us, though certainly not from our parents, remarks about 'the errors of the Catholic Church' or the 'evils of popery.'

If my father was silent about his decision to send his children to this not yet established school, it must have been because there were so many Catholic families among the tableland pioneers, and he felt too much sympathy with them to mention the fact. My paternal grandmother – in her black dress with its high lace collar, and with her white hair piled around her regal and somewhat heavy-featured face – must have been absent from this particular picnic, since she openly supported the Church of England in all its projects.

She would probably, in fact, have cheerfully served up all her grandchildren upon the church altar that she felt was permanently situated in her own drawing room. In reality, every second week a rather high sideboard there was transformed with a white embroidered cloth and pink and white tropical lilies in slender silver vases, and the cross and the chalice brought by one of the newly arrived Brothers of St. Barnabas, who came riding to the door of her little

44

wooden house, exhausted from bumping up and down for so long a distance.

My grandmother's spirit dwelt in her small wooden house in what seemed a strange amalgam of British rectitude (one upheld the old British values, come what may), colonial fortitude (no self-pity, a cold bath every morning, and castor oil if one was ill), and Church of England ritual (a perfumed presence of sanctity and concentration, with rustling silk dresses and petticoats, and kneeling to the rhythms of splendid prose to receive the sacrament). All this suggested a relationship of which as children we were only slowly aware, a relationship between that ritual and my grandmother's actual life, which was passed not far from her son's house, it is true, but in a rather lonely manner. Her solitude was broken only by the church services, by our own visits, and by the monotonous repetitions of her second husband's rather riotous returns from the local hotel. Through the mists of the monsoon and the dusts of summer evenings – while keeping herself busy with her cooking and her gardening and her books and sometimes with her piano – she no doubt listened for his footsteps, as she had so often listened for the footsteps of her grandchildren.

We had never known our real paternal grandfather, who had died when we were young, but we knew our grandmother's second husband, whose name was Walter Thompson and who was a rather dapper and neat person, with a gray mustache and a joking manner. He would sometimes on social occasions recite long poems in the Victorian way, especially Longfellow's 'Excelsior,' with its refrain at the end of each verse about 'a banner with a strange device,' the key word always being pronounced with a rising tone and suitable gesticulation. Very interested in the tricks done by our grandfather's pair of fox terriers (Punch and Judy, one of them, presumably Punch, wearing a small straw hat set on the back of his head), we were, I think, at those long-ago community gatherings of local settlers and their families, just slightly embarrassed by the recitations.

On the other hand, I remember feeling pity for this grandfather, especially when I was staying at our grandmother's house, and we listened late in the evening for his faltering steps, so that soon I would hear her breathless and cajoling voice begging him to be careful: 'Come, Walter ... No ... No ... *don't* sit down *yet* ... Come, darling ... *Come.*'

And then I knew how it had been. Hadn't he proceeded from his work at the mill office, and gone into the hotel near the railway station (where I had never been allowed to go) and had a drink or two at the darkish glittering bar; and, after that, happy and expansive, stumbled noisily out of the swinging doors, walked down the red earth road, and along the fence under the umbrella trees toward the glow of the lamp with the roses painted on the bowl, which my grandmother always kept in the front window of her bedroom, so that it should safely guide him home?

My grandmother and my schoolteacher were friends, and sometimes in the late afternoon the teacher, her red hair making a splotch of color in the lowering sun, her arms curled around a small parcel of books, could be seen cutting diagonally across the paddocks toward the patch of jungle trees which had been spared by the timber cutters to shadow my grandmother's house. The teacher was served afternoon tea (finely cut bread and butter, pikelets, and sponge cake with whipped cream and jam) and she returned the books and selected new ones from the crowded bookcase which stood in my grandmother's cramped little hall beside the Victorian plaster replica of the Laocoön. Perhaps my grandmother and the teacher talked about books. There is no doubt that in this loneliness – where the cleared paddocks were like the sea, upon which the rare houses, their windows glittering in the sunset, were thrown up like passing ships – their voices stretched out toward each other in a mingling of greeting and appeal.

'Mrs. Thompson, how lovely it is to see you.'

'Come in, come in, Miss Newman. I have been expecting you.'

The matter of religion, like that of human contact, was then too pervasive to be much spoken about, but I myself viewed it with great interest. I knew that my grandmother believed in something, and this aroused a curiosity that has never been satisfied over all these years – not because a similar belief seemed necessary to the third generation, but because belief is attractive in itself. By what values is it that we judge such things? Alluring as was my grandmother's house, I sensed that we judged things differently in our own house, across the way, where something more worldly ruled, but where, all the same, my father would often suggest that the whole family cross the paddocks to be present at the evening service given by the Bush Brothers. Why was it that, as if to negate his suggestion, he would then lie down on the sofa with the pink page of the *Bulletin* over his face and rapidly fall asleep?

And what was it that gave me such a sense of satisfaction on those rare evenings when he did rouse himself (from the well-earned rest of a man of the land who'd been out under the tropical sun since six in the morning) and marshal us together? Taking a lantern in his hand, he would lead us over the paddocks to the service and later – with the lantern lit, and with the grass wet with dew and the moon haloed with mist, and the smell of cows in the air – lead us home again, a patriarch illuminating the path of his family. Undoubtedly my relief at his action had something to do with the recognition that the faith of my grandmother, even if it was not quite shared by my mother and father – and even less by the rest of us – still constituted a landmark, as a track does in the jungle.

The question of leaving the old schoolhouse in the paddocks and going away to the church school in the ranges was somehow related to all this. As far as my grandmother was concerned ('The more religion those children have, the better' was what she might have said), the issue was less the education than the Mother Church. But in our own house

47

the matter could not be separated from worldly arguments. After a long discussion, our two Sydney cousins, who in deference to their age and sophistication were always listened to, said, in effect, 'At least the girls won't learn to talk about Shykespeare and Jyne Austen.' And my mother confessed to her own particular sensitivity, which was that she did, of course, want us to learn as much as possible, but that as well she hated the fact that at the little schoolhouse across the way we had all got lice in our hair. 'It's so much trouble getting rid of the ruddy things,' my father agreed, with a laugh. In other words, we did not enlarge upon the possibility that the decision had something to do with the conflict embedded in Australian society, or the need to recognize the nature of the country we were in – not only the newness of it, not only the deserts and forests and, in our case, the wall of dark jungle that seemed at first to repel human hands, not only the unremitting toil needed to keep abreast of the earth's demands, but also the sense of a heathen image which we could not worship and must therefore charm away with a martial front. It was for this reason, surely, that we accepted so readily the old shibboleths bestowed upon us by the English – the prows of the Norsemen, the spirit of Neptune, and the banners of the Church Triumphant (as we also accepted the prisons of Newgate). We thought of God as a source of help, as a towering barrier between us and physical or economic disaster. It was the voice of God which drove us to become educated, and drove us also to believe blindly that we could thereby control our future.

On that afternoon when all the families gathered at the little school and when the smoke from the men's pipes rose into the air and mingled pleasantly with the scent of grass and flowers and the perfume of a big platter of ripe pineapple that was ignored by the well-fed picnickers, one knew, too, that it was a holiday. The signal had been given to relax, to laugh, to overeat, and to invite the indulgence of adults. For a short while we could forget the heavy responsibility which going to school had cast upon us. Even the women tended to loll on the grass with their babies beside them – including the latest baby in our own family, flushed and rosy on a blanket beside my mother, her little legs thrust out at an angle, and already nut brown from the sun. The northern (here in Australia) tropical climate was claiming us, and southern (in the global sense) blood was being mixed with that universal strain from the cold pale-skinned world across the seas; because of that alone we were bound to encounter conflicts in our search for grace. And as we grew up, deeply steeped in nature as we were, we inhabited a place where natural creatures predominated, and seemed to provide us with justification for our own wild state. (Such creatures were so long isolated that they retained the innocence Darwin noted on a rock in the ocean where hundreds of noddies and boobies, never having seen humans before and not being aware that they were dangerous, could so easily be killed by the blows of sailors striding among them with wooden clubs. So, too, the kangaroo when hunted paused, occasionally in full flight, with a frank, gentle turning of the head, making itself a perfect target for its hunter.)

If we ourselves found an occasional possum or snake in the house, seeking warmth in the wet season, curled up in one of the cupboards, we were not surprised – especially if it was one of those rather rare verdant pythons for instance, which might grow as long as twenty feet and whose wrinkled lip seemed to curl upward in a half smile. When in the path of our horses the small wallaby known as the paddy melon hopped away, appearing to wear black gloves on its paws like a Victorian lady, we never had to check the horse's stride. Even the green possum, so rarely caught – its fur not exactly green at all, but simply giving the impression of being so, exquisitely molded as it was in three layers of whitish beige and brown and gold, one on top of the other, nature having thus mysteriously managed through long years of adaptation to approximate it to the leafy world in which it lived – went half hidden, and not seen. It was this natural world, the product of such exquisite and ancient evolution, which provided us with some of our spontaneous satisfactions.

We were not apt, in such an environment, to weary ourselves with thinking, and only later, in the gloom and severity of the scrublands, and through the long, brooding wet season, did we learn to consider some of that moral beauty which constant effort urges upon men.

3

Going North

Pioneers are not generally particularly sophisticated people. In fact, they are accustomed to accept without question their role as 'shock troops' in the great battle against the undiscovered, and to face their experiences without completely understanding them.

In our rain-forest heaven – at least externally it appeared a Garden of Eden – we found exploration a primary occupation. When our father, diverted from a familiar track, plunged into the unknown with his scrub knife in his hand, we would imagine as we followed him in single file that we were 'overlanders,' intent upon something more serious than a Sunday picnic. I suppose we thought that the danger of snakes and the pain of the vines with their long backward-curving thorns were necessary accompaniments to the explorer's life, and so must be encountered with good grace. We absorbed the fact that great discoveries were made by the pioneers, but not without cost! And we were never surprised to hear that X had recently been swept away when swimming his horse across a river, or that Y had been murdered in a drunken brawl on Cape York, or that Z had taken a trip to the Center and walked down the Birdsville track and never been seen again. This sort of thing was as native as the gum tree.

> *No game was ever yet worth a rap*
> *For a rational man to play,*
> *Into which no accident, no mishap,*
> *Could possibly find its way.*

Behind all of this, of course, was a certain state of ignorance. Not only did we children not know much about the

51

tableland's early history; we did not know much about our immediate forebears either. Our parents had 'gone north' and so effectively cut us all off both from southern affairs and from southern relatives.

Just as it was hard to believe, when we made butter out of cream from our own cows, by shaking a jar of it laboriously to and fro, that there had *ever* been a time when there was rain forest only and no cows *at all*, it was also quite hard to believe in relatives in the south – cousins, uncles, aunts – whom we had never seen.

When we asked our mother to talk about the past, as we so often did, perhaps we might have been trying to find out how we were expected to behave. But we were also trying to educate ourselves, for our instinct was to ape our parents, to try out our expertise. Perhaps the shadow of the rain forest increased the sense of being landbound, and we knew that, in spite of our love for it, we also had a feeling of pleasure when we could see at last, through those vistas cut into the tangled trees, to refreshingly open land – land that produced succulent grasses for cattle, and heavy crops of corn and sorghum, lucerne and peanuts.

But none of us had seen the country as our parents had seen it – with the rain forest almost untouched and the routes to the coast still primitive, with even the coastal transport irregular, and the boats small and ill equipped to cover that distance of nearly a thousand miles which lies between Brisbane, the capital in the south, and Cairns in the north. Here we were at the very crux of fertility in North Queensland, on those rich basaltic tablelands which lie between the edge of the coastal range and the Great Divide, but we knew little about the arduous history of its exploration. As far as we were concerned, we stood on the horizon of the world.

Our mother stressed the fact that, in the past and after the first settlement, there had been a pressing need to get packhorses up the ranges with supplies for the tablelands. Again and again men battled their way to the end of the ranges, and then made it on foot and by compass through the scrub. Such rough tracks were the forerunners of a spiderweb of primitive roads, so that long before our family came into existence the stamp of civilization had already been put upon the wilderness. The rest of the British world was busy with industrialization, but for North Queenslanders it was still the time of explorers and prospectors: still the time of confrontations between two groups of human beings – the Aborigines and the Europeans. 'There was James Venture Mulligan, the great prospector of the seventies,' our mother said, 'and Dalrymple, and Christie Palmerston, and George Clarke ... Oh, we suffered sometimes, but for us it was never like it was for the first settlers. Most of the early settlers traveled with animals. Think what that means! There would be blacks following them; they would have to swim the horses and cattle over the rivers. Sometimes they had to camp waiting for the rivers to go down, and then they'd run out of food. Yes' – she would shake her head and give a deep sigh – 'I remember a little woman who told me that for nearly a year she and her husband and baby had to live almost as the blacks did. Their stores were lost "in the wet," and slowly what remained gave out – tea, jam, tinned meat, sugar, flour – one after the other!'

'But what did they *eat?*' we asked.

'Seeds,' our mother said solemnly. 'They rubbed nardoo as the blacks did, with pieces of volcanic stone, and made a kind of flour. Roots, water-lily bulbs, and other roots. Game.'

'I wish I'd been there,' I said romantically. 'I wish I were there *now.*'

'I *don't,*' one of the twins said with horror, and the other chimed in with 'I don't *either.*' (My twin sisters, Helen and Margot, were older than I was, and therefore considered knowledgeable. I felt that in some mysterious way they really existed together, with their hearts beating as one; and whenever they stood together like this, I knew that, in the end, I would have to defer to them.)

53

'Long, long ago,' our mother said again, 'the living conditions were quite shocking.' She had not of course known what the old roads had been like, when even steamers didn't run, when the bullock teams had toiled laboriously out of Bowen, the sunburnt squatters with revolvers ready and long knives stuck in their belts, the port they were leaving crude beyond imagining. British travelers used phrases like 'brute force,' 'savage debauchery,' and 'disgusting language' to describe this early society. Because she had been able to take the boat straight to Cairns in the north, our mother hadn't actually visited those ports in the very early days – but she did know all the folklore. 'They said that the competition for land was so keen,' she added, 'that rivals would race each other to the nearest land office to register a claim.' She thought a while and said reflectively, 'You know that Rockingham Bay, which they finally called Cardwell, is backed by those horribly high and broken mountains. Dalrymple finally managed to get behind the mountains, and discovered the Valley of Lagoons, a valley starred by lakes with blue ranges behind it.'

Absentmindedly, she murmured, 'Your uncle was there,' not telling us which uncle. 'He said the lagoons were covered with pink and white lilies . . . I always loved water lilies,' and we saw her at once arranging a great glass bowl of water lilies with her dexterous fingers and placing it in the middle of the round table in the breakfast room.

The original union of their parents seems a deep mystery to children, and often we would interrupt our mother's stories and try to discover exactly what impetus had driven our parents north in the first place, and how they had come to marry. Why did people do things? That was the question. And what was the real story? We wanted to know the beginning, the middle, and the end. Who came before us? And what had *they* wanted, and what had they *found*?

'Did you like Daddy from the *very* first?' Margot had asked. Margot was the one in the family who believed in, and hoped for, utter faithfulness; just as she was the one who always wanted to put a rose from the garden in a small vase on the tray of anyone who happened to be sick.

'Well, yes,' our mother would say. 'I think we got engaged on the very day after we met.'

'And what did your mother say?'

'And what did Uncle Tony say?'

She would smile at these naïve attempts to find out the exact status of the marriage. 'I think they were pleased,' she would say modestly.

Our mother, Robina Linedale, had been born in the south at Newton Boyd in 1872, close to the New South Wales border – an area where granitic rocks had been eroded for millions of years and cassiterite, or tin, had been buried in the watercourses. It was these tin lands that had brought my mother's parents at first to Stanthorpe, and then to nearby Tenterfield, where miners in high boots worked the sluice boxes and large numbers of Chinese came to screen the creeks for what remained of the alluvial metal.

'*My* mother,' our mother said, 'that is, Isabel Buchanan Reid, had pretty wavy hair, and gray eyes, and an attractive skin. The family lived in a house which you could describe as comfortable, with a large garden and fruit trees. I remember the grape trellis in the orchard standing among the fruit trees; it was a family custom to preserve the fruit each year and pack it in wooden boxes. Every Sunday we [the Linedale family] would go to our grandmother Reid's house to have dinner.' This story would be told when she was busy cooking, or sewing, or doing her hair. Rather absentmindedly she would tell about how her father, Anthony Theodore Linedale, had come to Tenterfield because he was offered a contract to build wool sheds at the town station; and how, because he had passed through Trinity College in Dublin, he was also able to train groups of young men for English universities. 'He was an engineer,' she would add. 'In those days people moved around, always looking for new opportunities. Once we went to Boorak, where a new mine was opening, and a horse wagon came for the clothes and the furniture, and I remember they put in a big Dutch oven . . . meat tasted so *good* in that oven. We loved Boorak because it was tropical and there were orchids in the trees, and Aboriginal boys and girls to play with, and to help with the work . . . but unfortunately the mine failed!'

In Tenterfield the Linedale family had first encountered John Moffat, the outstanding man in our family tree, the one who was later so important in Queensland's mining history and, in a narrow sense, in international mining. He'd been at the outset that loneliest of all Australian workers – a shepherd on a sheep station; but he had brought with him some intellectual baggage (he called himself a Sweden-borgian), and it was this man, John Moffat, who was to marry my mother's sister Margaret. I was to be named after him, the John perforce being changed to Joan.

'He had his puritan side, I suppose,' our mother said. 'He didn't like the Australian pubs, to which the workers rushed the minute they stopped working. You know how it is when everyone streams into the pubs, and you know how it is with early closing?' We all nodded, because we knew very well.

'Then he liked the town to be clean . . .'

'Did he *make* everyone be clean?' someone asked in bewilderment.

'He didn't *make* them. He just liked the houses to be painted white, and he suggested it and encouraged people. You see, John Moffat was used to an older way of doing things. He came, after all, from Scotland . . .'

She would pause as if she didn't know what to say. 'He was very . . . idealistic . . . he had *inner* reasons for everything. In Tenterfield he set up the general store, and he bought tin concentrate to send to the Brisbane smelters; and one day he got the idea of building a real smelter on the borderlands where there were such quantities of tin. Before long he fixed up a partnership with John Holmes Reid, and this John Reid was my uncle and he always used to say that John Moffat mesmerized him, because he was so convincing . . . You know that everyone expected the Scots to be good

56

businessmen as well as *absolutely* honest. You've heard how much they expect of the Scots, and if a Scot is involved in anything dishonest here in Australia, they always say, "He's a *disgrace* to the Scottish race!"'

At this we would look at each other and smile, for we knew very well that the Scottish schoolteachers had a reputation not only for great severity but for not hesitating to use the cane.

The northern connection which our mother talked about was now clearer to us: we understood that William Jack and John Newell, early friends of John Moffat, lured by the goldfields, had found their way north, and that eventually they had encountered the dense primeval scrubs near Tolga (very close to where our father would eventually settle and build the house we were living in). Explorers had written about the well-thatched gunyahs of the Aborigines in these scrubs and the huge stands of untouched cedar and kauri pine. Later these two men, who were also to become relatives, located the Great Northern tin-field, in present-day Herberton, and sent the news to John Moffat down in Tenterfield.

'This was in 1880, when I was only a small girl,' our mother said. 'Willie Jack and John Newell had seen tin in more than one place, but then they struck the Great Northern lode, which could be traced for more than two miles, and they tried out a sample of the ore in the stump of a tree, using a felt hat for a draft, and it proved so valuable that John Newell decided to spend all night riding across country, via Watsonville and the Walsh River, to file a claim. They said that in all the shanty bars on all the fields there was nothing but talk of this tin on the Wild River.

'When John Moffat heard about it, he caught the steamer to Cairns and bought into the Willie Jack–John Newell claim – up to one-fifth of its worth. Later he bought a majority interest in the mine.

'You see, Herberton's tin lodes went deeper and were more valuable than the alluvium. Your uncle worked for stability; he gave this stability to Herberton, because he not only put money into the Great Northern lode, but he built an efficient tin mill and smelter nearby at Irvinebank, and then he spent his smelter money on searching for new lodes. Your uncle came here before the wet set in, and he put out an order for crushing material – it took four days to move the heavy load only three and a half miles through the deep mud . . . and that was with fifty bullocks!'

'*Fifty bullocks!*' we would echo.

We were all fascinated by this uncle, and I was especially fascinated because, after all, I had been born in his house, and named after him as well; it was a little like a fairy story to me. He was the Prince: the youngest son who went looking for treasure and found it, although it was under the earth, and waved his hand, and all at once there were hotels, and stores, and miners, and policemen, and a town!

Telling the practical version, our mother added that John Moffat went off to Cornwall and to Germany and Belgium to learn the modern methods of tin smelting, and when he came back he and Tony moved a few miles from Herberton to Irvinebank, which was an even richer field, and there they lived for months in six-by-eight tents in front of the new dam they had built. That dam attracted all the birds, and it was alive with black-and-white ibis. 'In fact,' our mother said to us, 'your uncle became the most successful promoter in Queensland, and at one time Irvinebank produced more tin than any other place in the world.'

As children, of course, we took the point of view that Atherton was the hub of the world, because Atherton was a central point and close to Kureen. But actually Herberton had come first. Many of the families we were to know later had struggled up the old Robson track from the coast, with their infants on the packhorses – in boxes or the woven baskets of Chinese market gardeners – and had made that epic trip to Herberton not even daring to light fires at night, lest they attract the blacks. But for us Atherton was the center, although even the main street, wide in the Australian way, had had to be spread with mullock to prevent teams from getting bogged down there en route to the great mine.

Herberton was taken for granted – that was the place where it all began; where the hotels were dark and had numerous passages; where the big mining men went; where the large wooden School of Arts was commodious enough for the pupils of St. Mary's to put on *A Midsummer Night's Dream*, with proper footlights and real costumes made by the school dressmaker. (I played the fairy Cobweb, wearing a shiny gray neck-to-toe affair with gauzy appendages, and was humiliated when, on opening night, I fell asleep in the wings and missed my cue!)

'At the time of the Herberton rush,' our mother explained, 'I was still in Tenterfield, at one of those small ladylike schools which girls went to then. Life seemed to have changed. John Newell and Willie Jack, those old friends of John Moffat, had gone north, and then John Moffat went north too.' Eventually both of Willie Jack's daughters, Janet and Beatrice, were to follow their father, because Janet was to marry John Newell, and Beatrice was to marry Tony Linedale. So friendships led to friendships, and mines to mines, and marriages to marriages. When our mother's sister Margaret married John Moffat, our mother followed the rest. She, too, 'went north.'

'I rode up the ranges, and over the Bump,' she said. (The Bump was a particularly steep grade on the Port Douglas–Thornborough road.) 'Ladies were supposed to ride sidesaddle, so that is what I did, in long skirts, and with a revolver strapped to the suitcase on my saddle. When the party reached what were known as the Big Scrubs, I felt how restless the horse was ... The horses always knew when blacks were hiding nearby, and they would tremble and their eyes would roll. By that time the Aborigines were not attacking so much as in the past – although once or twice they threw spears at Hova, my little black pony – but they would make traps of lawyer vine to catch the hooves of the pack animals, and in the ensuing panic

59

they would lead a few horses off and kill them and rifle the packs.

'We were all very happy together in the old house at Irvinebank. Tony had become prosperous and sometimes he would give me sixty gold sovereigns all at once, and Margaret and I would send south for new dresses, and riding habits, and cabbage-tree hats from Mountcastles, a London firm with a branch in Brisbane. We loaded our petticoats with miles of Valencia lace, and we would dress up and have dance parties. Then on Sundays we would play tennis, and there would be music in the evenings. Spirituals from the U.S.A. were fashionable in those days; we would sing "Steal away to Jesus" and other American gospel songs.'

The big Irvinebank house was built in 1884 on eight great red cedar posts, with a cool lower floor for offices and an assaying room and storeroom. Upstairs it had a sixteen-by-fourteen sitting room, two bedrooms, and front and side verandas. It was a man's house, of course; women didn't have much to do with the architecture of those days. But by Irvinebank standards it was grand enough. When I went back there with my cousins a long time later, I tried to imagine which room I might have been born in, and how the sitting room had looked when the walls were of natural wood polished with oil, and the rosewood piano stood in the corner where they had all gathered on Sunday nights to sing 'Steal Away to Jesus.'

In that small Irvinebank settlement – new from the ground up, set in the eucalyptus-smelling hills, and focusing on the silvery expanse of the dam, home to wild birds – the idea of making a quick fortune and then getting away with it did not seem to occur to John Moffat or to his close associates. He thought in terms of a community, and plowed part of his profits back to stabilize every new center. But being modest, and disliking public relations which boosted false values, he tried to suppress unnecessary publicity when floating a new company; indeed, later, when his Chillagoe mines floated into a big Melbourne company and his own free shares commanded high prices on the stock exchange, he, alone of all the directors, refused to unload them – thus losing a paper fortune but saving hundreds of shareholders from losses.

All sorts of stories were told about John Moffat – one of which was that when I was tiny, and demanding a lot of attention, he would wander around the house with two teaspoons of jam, looking for my twin sisters, who he thought might be feeling neglected. Other people said that long ago, on the sheep station at Pickinjinnie Plains, he had been too kindhearted to kill a sheep for his rations, and had had to pay someone to do it for him. At Irvinebank also, even after he had been such a success because of the international reputation of the great Vulcan mine, he had been genial enough to chat with the old fossickers in his office downstairs, but too shy to want to entertain all the important foreigners and mining magnates who came to see him.

His daughters said that he carried gold sovereigns around in his pockets in case he should meet old mining men down on their luck, or families in trouble, and many of the women and children in Irvinebank experienced his charity, as was demonstrated by the stone set up when he died which read: 'In memory of charitable and philanthropic John Moffat – the children ended their prayers each night with "God bless John Moffat."' But perhaps his most useful contribution in that time of desperate pioneer endeavor and reckless physical courage was his effort to guarantee public crushing for the independent miner, for metal prices were falling and there were increasing problems with transport and labor. He was forty-nine years old, and had taken the trip to Sydney to get married, and he spoke then about the anxiety he felt for the shifting fortunes of the mines and the dependency of the miners. Worried by the strain of management, he sent his cousin George Young along with Tony Linedale to London to sell the Montalbion mine to the London brokers.

It was close to this time (1895) that Uncle Tony, perhaps with John Moffat's encouragement or suggestion, had gone to New Guinea – the bird-shaped island that lies on the other side of the Torres Strait, almost pressing down upon Queensland's Cape York, like a large hat on a small head. A certain kind of bom-bom (white man) was drawn to New Guinea as by a magnet – to this large mountainous island, once part of Australia, to this remnant of Gondwanaland, this tangle of wild gorges, ragged razorbacks, and high fertile valleys. Such country was deceptively beautiful, its peaks lost in a constant damp mist. But swaths of rotting moss covered the trees and the crevasses, so that in breaking through this slippery gelatinous undergrowth, travelers could hurtle to their deaths. Confusing, conflicting, and often warring groups of dark human beings lived their lives out on this island – in settled communities, in village stockades, in groups of houses built on stilts in the swamps. These peoples cultivated gardens, fenced them, and built sacred longhouses, unlike the nomadic Australian Aborigines who wandered over the face of the continent to the south. Some of these New Guineans were small and wiry, some tall with strongly marked features and beaklike noses. Warriors and brides were much decorated, with glimmering shell ornaments and dazzling paints. Most tribes grew taro and cut sago and kept pigs, the subjects of complex rites.

At all events, Tony Linedale went to New Guinea at a time when very little was known about it – or rather, when what knowledge there had been filtered down through the stories of sailors and explorers, prospectors, gold miners, and missionaries. Scientists saw the island as of prehistoric interest; the religious saw it as a source of souls; the Queensland government (which in 1884 persuaded the British government to assume sovereignty over the southern area) looked upon it as ripe for development; and miners who had been through the gold rushes at Rockhampton, Charters Towers, and the Palmer River (and seen these rushes pale, like stars on the horizon) yearned toward it as a new source of gold.

We scarcely knew, as we talked to Uncle Tony of his visit to New Guinea, anything about the history of that rare island. In fact, only after I married and found myself in the

United States in 1940, when the Allied soldiers were being pressed by the advance of the Japanese, did I think much about its actual geographical nature. New Guinea was the 'India' of Australia. It represented a dream image. The Torres Strait islands to some extent, and especially New Guinea, were Shangri-las to be won for, or at least enjoyed by, Anglo-Saxons, and they meant escape for certain kinds of Australians.

Uncle Tony had gone to this New Guinea – one of the largest islands in the world – long before we were born, and he had looked for gold. We therefore, absorbing the family folklore, thought that when *we* were big enough, we, *too*, would go to look for gold.

'Is this gold?' we would ask, returning flushed and dirty from scrambling around old mullock heaps and pressing rocks into his hands.

'This is gold, isn't it, Uncle Tony?'

Later we got to know that gold is not so easily found, although at that time mineral specimens were everywhere – on the dusty shelves of the School of Arts buildings, passing as decorations in the hotels and offices of little towns, reposing on crocheted mats on the tops of pianos in the local houses – rare ruby tin and black-and-white feldspar, and of course milky-white quartz with the telltale golden veins.

If our uncle, his aging voice cracked by numerous bouts with tropical fevers, began to speak of the Mámbare River, we would be hushed into silence, and, leaning against his thin knees encased in immaculate white duck, we would listen to him with fascinated attention.

'That coast up there in the north was very close to the German border; it was indented like the fjords of Norway . . . but very blue the water was! The station of old Champion, the explorer, had been somewhere there, at Ioma, I think it was – the white man's grave . . . What we done was to go there . . . we didn't know what to expect. *Nobody* knew! . . . Everyone set off to the Mámbare – boats, luggers, canoes,

63

outriggers ... but I can tell you some of them only got as far as T.I.' (T.I. was Thursday Island, just to the north of Cape York – a small island but important – and here the Australian government had set up a residency. Our uncle did not tell us directly that the initials T.I. also stood for 'Thirsty Island.')

'What happened to them?'

'Well,' he said, 'some of them stopped to take a little drink ... but long before we got to the river there were rumors already about gold in other places – rich alluvial it was. Gold everywhere, gold on the creek bottoms, gold on the rocky bars of the rapids, gold even in the roots of the trees where the water swirled around ... so if we failed on the Mámbare, there was still gold to be got. You had to be careful of the natives all around. They were cannibals, you know.'

We listened wide-eyed. He spoke of killings as casually as he spoke of death from dengue fever; he explained how one tribe held another to account with what they called 'payback.' He told us of the famous missionary Chambers, who was murdered on an island when he went to save souls, and was cooked and eaten with sago. He described the tall cold ranges, as high as 17,000 feet, and the nearly naked warriors who decorated themselves with the brilliant red plumes of the scarlet bird of paradise, and wore tiny aprons of beaten and painted bark.

In 1895, at the time of the expedition, when Uncle Tony's group reached forty miles upriver, the leader, George Clarke, sent him downriver with one of the carriers to try out for gold, while the others – all except George Clarke, who remained in the boat – got out and tried to haul it up over some rapids, using long ropes. Apparently, at this point the local natives surprised them; they cut the ropes, surrounded the boat, and killed George Clarke. When my uncle returned he found that the expedition carriers were being attacked on the towpath, and he went to help them. Afterward he swam out to the boat, and found that Clarke had been speared. 'A good old mate of mine,' Uncle Tony would say sadly.

The resident of New Guinea at the time, MacGregor, appalled by the murder, came to the Mámbare later to investigate the Clarke incident, and discovered that villagers on the riverbank had in their possession articles belonging to the expedition. Eventually he took six men back to Port Moresby to try them for murder; but before that there were two small earthquakes on the riverbanks, and the natives were so impressed by the power of the bom-boms to make the earth move that they rushed out with their hands up, calling, 'Peace . . . peace . . .'

As the new century got under way, John Moffat, already thinking of retiring from active management, was saddened because the Vulcan, deepest of all Australian tin mines, reached blank ground at 1,220 feet, and it took extra investment to keep returns coming in. By 1914, the year of the Great War, Chillagoe was shut down, and a rapid, almost unbelievable exodus began from the town – it seemed like the end of an era, and of course it was. But, in any case, the story of Uncle Tony's biggest mining adventure, fascinating as it was to us, was not after all about our 'own North.' So we would say to our mother, 'Go on . . . you didn't finish. Tell us about when you met Daddy.'

Naturally it was after my mother had gone to stay with her sister Margaret and John Moffat at Irvinebank that she met my father – Edward William Hesketh Heale, to give him his full name – who had been trained at Dookie, the Victorian Agricultural College, and was drawn north by tales of the fabulous soils on the Atherton Tableland. (It was said that this land would grow anything, and when grassed, would support two animals to the acre.) Part of his purpose had also been to help the government surveyor to mark out blocks of scrub in the Atherton rain forests. It was the most natural thing in the world that in Irvinebank he should have met John Moffat; and on that very day there happened to be a dance in the local School of Arts, with its big stage and blue embroidered and painted curtain and its rows of cane chairs standing against the walls. That night he danced with my mother.

I could imagine my father dancing, because on such occasions he was always smiling, and kept his head up, and sailed around the room with an air of genial enjoyment. My mother, petite and dark with pink cheeks and big brown eyes, would probably have been smiling also. Later, when asked what happened on this first meeting, my father would say cheerfully that he sang the song 'Prithee, Pretty Maiden, Will You Marry Me?' which came, I think, from the Gilbert and Sullivan opera *Patience*, and had in it the words:

> *I would fain discover*
> *If you have a lover*
> *a'dangling after you.*

At all events, they were married, and went to live in Tolga, where the big trees were being drawn on bullock wagons to the first sawmill. And eventually they went out to Kureen, which at that time had no name and was almost at the end of the track, with its thick lonely scrubs and its deep, rich soil.

I don't know how it was that our mother and father managed to tell us so much, but I realize now that this was the way we lived in those days – we were entertained by other people's memories.

It was in the family tradition that our mother would let us worry her when she was resting. We would selfishly not allow her to sleep and would clamber all over the bed, and sometimes implore her to let us brush her hair and pin it up on top of her head. She would seem to like these play and question-and-answer sessions, but would often sigh as if the past were all too laborious to remember, however much pleasure and camaraderie there had been. She told us about the first flowing of the pastoral tide, which had made familiar names like Kangaroo Hills, Firth's Lagoon, Mount

Surprise, Cashmere, Maryvale, Lammermoor, Lyndhurst, Carpentaria Downs, Bluff Downs, and if we didn't recognize those places by the names of their owners (whom our parents might have known), at least we knew some of the children, or the grandchildren.

Nor were the station houses what they had been at first – just simple cabins of logs and saplings, with roofs of bark or cane grass; the outside kitchen under the lean-to. Gradually these cabins carved out of the isolation conformed to a certain bush beauty, with pillared verandas hung with creepers; wooden floors and terraces of stone or handmade brick; living rooms with flounced chair covers; mirrors with gilt frames; and also pianos, which carried on the shining tops great bowls of roses. From these houses a delicate network of human relationships spread out, radiating warmth and friendliness. My mother repeated the familiar litany of names: Atkinson, Atherton, Anning (the Annings came north in a covered wagon with 'Melbourne Ice Company' painted on the side), Collins, Christison, Cunningham, Curr, Chisholm, Fulford, Garbutt, Hann, and White – names synonymous with effort and adventure, names representing confrontations with wild nature and wilder blacks.

After these stories we would always find something to joke about. For instance, because our mother was active in an organization called the Country Woman's Association, popularly known as the C.W.A., we would make fun of it a little, and – even when a rather hurt look appeared on our mother's small sensitive face – we loved to stretch out our arms and chant in an exaggerated way the words of the C.W.A. song:

> *Stretch out your hand*
> *To the woman on the land,*
> *From the out-ba-a-ack to the se-e-e-a!*

At the same time we knew very well what it meant to be a woman out there in those distant places, with their large acreages and inadequate communication, with the men sometimes gone with the stock for weeks at a time, and no one for company but children and Aborigines.

Perhaps there was a serious side to all these long talk sessions – as if our parents were the teachers and we were the pupils. Were we not, after all, trying to learn how to behave, and to learn what life had in store for us? In this saga extracted from our mother with such persistence and over so much time, we may or may not have found that crucial information. But it was surely from these early predecessors that we obtained some essential truths – perhaps, in the historical sense, dreadful truths – which could affect the rest of our lives.

I remember how hard I found it to absorb Uncle Tony's truth about his friendly Aboriginal helper and guide, Yarry, on the occasion when the myalls captured him and trussed him up to be eaten. How could it be possible that in our 'own North' – where the Union Jack flew and where Christian values were supposed to exist – such a reality should rule? And then Christie Palmerston, the romantic explorer-hero of our own rain forest, had seen worse things than my uncle had, and in areas much closer to Kureen. He once described the tableland scrubs as 'terrible jungle country where you never see the sky,' adding that here there were 'leech-infested nights' and 'cold to make the bones ache.' On his trek from Innisfail to Herberton and back in 1882, he had seen, among the quickly deserted gunyahs and among piles of red fruits and nuts collected by the Aborigines for their feast, an earth oven in which the body of a female child was being roasted. He also saw many human bodies cured by smoke, some doubled up and stored in large woven baskets. On another occasion he saw a very large human body, its head severed at the mouth so that the white teeth of the jaw were brought down over the chest.

If we thought about these dreadful customs, and of the indisputable evidence of their prevalence in the north, it was probably to dismiss them with a shudder; or to reflect briefly that they added to what sometimes seemed a somber shadow brooding over the rain forests. Christie Palmerston tempered his tales of horror with memories of an Aborigine called Pompo, who, according to Palmerston, 'followed me during the darkest scenes of my life ... through sickness, famine, adversity ... and even saved me from death.' 'Even now,' he said after Pompo's death, 'I think of him with an overwhelming sense of grief.'

Our predecessors, those early explorers and pioneers and squatters, seemed close to us because of what we knew of their difficult lives, just as our father and mother were close to us for similar, if broader, reasons. I knew that John Moffat, who had almost gone from the scene by the time I came upon it, was also a great predecessor, a man of power and imagination, who, unlike the rest of us, had a philosophical background. He had brought his ethos with him to Australia, and perhaps tried to turn it into reality, for his belief was that you must *live* your religion.

Although I had no clear memories of John Moffat, I felt that he was even more set on his lonely and thoughtful way than was my father. He spoke of himself as a 'Swedenborgian,' and afterwards this seemed logical – first because of Swedenborg's early interest in mining and metals and his anticipation of modern scientific facts, and then because of this philosopher's later desire to relate the soul to the body (through anatomical studies) and so to contend for the supremacy of what was spiritual. Although I could never talk about all this with my uncle, it still pleased me to think that he shone as a leader in the northern pantheon.

In quite another way, Christie Palmerston, who almost paralleled my uncle's time, taught us what was necessary for our survival. His diaries charted those invaluable tracks through the dark scrubs and down to the coasts, and also left us an image of how it had really been in those early days, helping us to face squarely the fact that, in this continent without carnivorous beasts, it was man who – because of his need for protein, the food of the brain – became the predator.

How valuable this image was, we ourselves did not know, any more than scientists today know how to chart the complete evolutionary saga of the human mind. All the same, insensibly, through proximity in childhood to a knowledge of man's early need to live by consuming human flesh, a complex view of good and evil was implanted. So Palmerston – struggling in these jungles, using his gun to survive while loving at least some of his Aboriginal friends – suggested to us something of the symbiosis between civilization and barbarity. He seemed to assure us that we could conquer nature, but that nature could not easily conquer us.

4

With My Father

To be a member of a large family is to share in the diversity of the world, and sometimes when we were all assembled around the circular dinner table at Fleetwood, the sense of one personality reacting to another would fill me with a certain kind of fearful pleasure. The table, painted green, stood in the middle of the enclosed porch that we used for meals on ordinary days – the porch that opened out into the fernery, where the tall hairy-stemmed tree ferns thrust out their crowning fronds to break the tropical light pouring down from above. The discussions we had would be long and rather inconclusive, and during them my father would act as umpire. It was a role he enjoyed, especially when the discussions raged out of control and showed all the ignorance and innocence of his children; he would frequently look around the table as if amazed that so much confidence and misinformation should be possible among a mere six children. When the clamor grew too loud he would call out, 'Order! Order! Point of order, Mr. Chairman!' as if we were Members of Parliament in the old colonnaded Neo-Georgian building in Brisbane – Brisbane being at that time little more than an over-grown country town, but still an important center in Australia and the capital of the state of Queensland. To gain our attention, and to carry the analogy further, my father would tap smartly on the table with the bone handle of the bread knife.

Because we had no other point of reference, the special atmosphere of our native land was somewhat beyond us all. Although we would laugh a great deal at some aspects of the debates that went on in Parliament House, I doubt that any of us, our parents excepted, really saw the joke. For them it centered on what was immortalized in the press, and what, with devastating ease, could be deduced from this about the state of local standards and aspirations. But as children we could identify only with what could easily be recognized – the general tendency toward belligerence. Long before we were even thought of, the Honorable Ratcliffe Pring had been rebuked by the Honorable Member for Warwick, Mr. Clark, for coming to the House in a 'certain state,' to which the Honorable Ratcliffe Pring replied simply, 'Come outside for five minutes – I will kick you,' to which the Honorable Member for Warwick answered, 'Anyone who knows me knows that I am not afraid of anyone in the House or out of it,' whereupon Mr. Pring pulled Mr. Clark's beard, which, if one can believe the photographs of those days, was probably a full one. Because of the long history of episodes like this, being asked to 'come outside' was always a joke among us; perhaps we liked its quiet understatement. And the old records show that some members were suspended numerous times for making the invitation – one not only for 'bellicose intention' but for kicking down the door of an office when he was shut out of it, for 'creating scenes,' for 'throwing his tie on the floor,' and for kneeling in mock submission to declare, 'I humbly withdraw the statement.' The phrase to 'withdraw the statement' also became a cause for amusement during mealtimes in our house, and, with our father as skillful monitor, we could sometimes avoid the wrath of a sibling, and drown all objections in laughter, by offering to 'humbly withdraw.'

In a household which, for all its isolation from the literary life, had a certain general interest in style, it was not surprising that we admired the unabashed vigor of the debates and wondered at the devotion to the classics which those debates showed. We felt in our element when we noticed in the weekly newspapers that someone had been compared to a 'kangaroo rat' or a 'venomous snake' or a 'lurking dingo.' (My father, living as he did in a family of five daughters, with only one boy to support him, would also use bush phrases and occasionally claim the right to go off into the scrub and 'live in a hollow log.') If we repeated with relish the latest political gaffes, it was less to dissociate ourselves from naïveté or from scrambled similes (a member once suggested that a certain bill was a 'sheep in wolf's clothing,' and another that members were descending upon the dairy industry 'like ticks, as the Assyrians descended upon Israel') than because of sheer enthusiasm. I remember laughing heartily when Randolph Bedford, my favorite M.P. and journalist, who was a friend of my parents and uncles, made sarcastic remarks about members running to the Bellevue Hotel across the street at the first tinkle of the division bell.

It was generally when I was with my father that I thought about history. I say 'thought about history' because there seems no other way to express it: this is what I was being drawn to do. The process seems to have had its origin in the manner he had of introducing into family discussions the history of the Egyptians, as if this were the sole touchstone by which the conversation could proceed. I don't think that my father knew very much about history, because he had been trained at an agricultural college, where the courses must have been so heavily oriented toward agricultural science that there was little room for more than the briefest introduction to ancient and modern happenings, with perhaps some slight attention to literature or philosophy. But the Egyptian story seemed magical to my father – a people, as we knew, who had made the enormous pyramids, developed a system of picture writing, recorded economic transactions on clay tiles, worn clothes made of flax grown in the Nile delta, used cosmetics, decorated wooden furniture with gold and lapis lazuli, and created god kings and queens who bore other men and women with them to their graves. Because all this seemed so fascinating to my father, it also seemed fascinating to us.

That his constant coming back to the history of the Egyptians pointed to the frustration of an intelligent man now solely occupied by the necessary struggle with the earth was only partially clear to us. There was no doubt that he was intelligent, but perhaps his intelligence suffered because of his frustrations. I do know that I would often find myself plunged into a dream as he spoke about long-ago achievements in a world I could not imagine – a dream which gave me a taste later for the history of that vaster world of which Egypt was only a tiny part.

What matter that the discoveries we made at the clamorous meal table were buried in the turmoil and toil of the pioneer task, that there were never enough hours to cope with the thousand and one material chores that should have been completed each day. What matter if the discussions sometimes ended in bitter quarrels, with my father forbidding us to argue any more, or my mother reciting our names in a rapid litany: 'Hazel, Margot, Helen, Joan, Tracey, Robin . . . *please* be quiet' – ending always with a phrase we knew well: 'It's a shame, so it is!'

When I accompanied my father on one of his trips with no other member of the family present, when we left the boundaries of our property behind and passed into strange territory – went down to the coast, perhaps, or to visit someone from whom my father sought scientific or political help – my experiences were hard to assimilate. Something quite new to me would be talked about – a local political problem, industrial conflicts in the south, a struggle among the northern cane farmers, or the question of the centralization of power. I would hear unfamiliar phrases or words like 'picket,' 'Australian Workers' Union,' 'go-it-alone patriotism,' or 'protectionism.' And I would find it faintly boring, even if I listened carefully, sitting on the edge of some alien chair and holding a glass of lukewarm lemonade.

Trips of this kind with my father were not like those when the family were present. Those were times when we went 'to have fun' – to picnic in some favorite spot, to swim, to climb rocks in the hot sun, to lie half asleep in the shade, to boil the billy and drink the pungent tea, to eat fried chicken or roast beef with salad, to return home, only reluctantly, after the light had begun to fade, and on the long jolting journey to sing rounds like 'Row, row, row your boat, gently down the stream' or an Australian song such as:

Back to Croa-*jinga-linga-linga*-long,
That's the place *where I* belong,
Where a sun-*kissed maid*
'Neath the gum *tree's shade*
Waits for me to go along to . . .
Croa – jinga – linga – longa
No longer *will I* roam
From my old Austral – ian – home . . .

The expeditions with my father were not demanding. He asked for no special attention or help, and sometimes, if he was occupied with his own thoughts or worried in some way, we would ride or drive in silence. If we stopped at a house, there would always be tea. Not to offer tea to a chance caller in any part of pioneer Queensland would have been the worst kind of rudeness. Then I would be allowed to wander around and to explore for myself, to play with the animals, or to climb down a hill to some small creek where there were wild birds to watch, or a platypus stretched out on a log above the brownish water, the big nostrils of its bill seeming vulnerable, and its wet fur shining a little as it dried in the sun. If the place was a farm that appeared very poor – the grass worn, the soil eroded, the house rough or dirty – my father might expatiate afterward about how hard life was for the farmer, how unfair conditions often were. 'Yes, it's hard to make a go of it,' he would say, with a faint touch of disgust in his voice, as if he were saying that it was hard for him, too, although *we* were better off, because *we* had more property and more sense of how to go about the whole farming process. But the tone also held a little bitterness.

One day we rode to what had once been the State Farm, and I was amazed to learn that this whole quite roomy house and all the outbuildings and yards had been built to show the farmers how to do things: how to look after their stock, how to rotate their crops, how to fertilize and harvest, and how to store grains. It was a windy, sunny afternoon, and it was getting late. We had ridden for some distance, and although I don't remember where we had started from, my father had ridden his big bay horse, and so he had had to wait for me, on my smaller horse, to catch up. I remember how he pointed out the queer shape of an extinct volcano in the distance, a green cone rising abruptly from the ancient-looking landscape and emerging from a deep, purplish shadow of scrub. 'That was once alive, pouring out lava,' he said. 'It has left us this rich soil we have.' As we cantered up the road to the State Farm he complained that all the money spent on the farm had been wasted, because the place was now practically closed down; the buildings were in disrepair, and there were no more demonstrations or advice for the farmers.

'It's a political matter.'

'Why is it political?'

'It means that they did it in a burst of enthusiasm, and to get votes.'

'But, Daddy, wasn't it *good*?'

'Yes, it was good – but in politics they keep looking for something new. The old things get abandoned and neglected. Look at those bricks.' He indicated bricks piled up near the fence. 'And see the roof of that barn. The whole bloody lot deteriorating ...' His voice had in it the same disgust that it had when he spoke of how hard life was for the farmer. I remember that the scene suddenly appeared melancholy as the sun lowered and the wind blew and the strange archaic volcanic cone shone in the far distance.

I didn't know then that I was looking at more than a deserted farm, but rather the remains of one phase of what people had called 'the Queensland socialist experiment.' Not that the Queensland of those days was exactly a workingman's paradise. There were still many settlers living with very little in the way of worldly goods – they fed their families on homegrown meat and milk, pumpkins and corn and sweet potatoes; on wild roots and fruit; and on what their guns could bring down. Yet the workers were so much better off, and their resistance to exploitation was so much more widely accepted than it had been in the Old World, that most of our generation never saw real poverty until we left Australia and glimpsed the hovels of the Irish or the slums of the English.

A conversation might go something like this:

'Daddy, they aren't *hungry*, are they?'

'Who aren't?'

'Those men on the line?'

At that time the railway line had pushed up from the coast and penetrated the tablelands and the higher ranges, but there was always some smaller extension being worked on and ordinary repairs being made after the wet season, so that through the years we constantly came upon little groups of men working slowly in the hot sun, or sitting under their lean-tos with mugs of tea in their hands.

'They don't *look* hungry, do they?'

I had to admit that they didn't. I remembered, too, the visits to various stations inland from the coast, where the men sat around with their long legs thrust under the rough tables and concentrated with primitive intensity upon an array of food – great lumps of stewed beef, great piles of vegetables, great slabs of bread and butter with a golden syrup we called Cocky's Joy, along with deep drafts of stewed tea.

Occasionally, on one of these expeditions, we would talk to the road workers, and once we listened to a union organizer addressing such a group of them in the fierce language and flamboyant manner that could have earned him the title of 'Red rabble-rouser from the south' (a phrase I had heard used, though not so much by my father as by others). It was on this occasion that I gained the first feeling of what 'social action' was. Although the men did not seem to take the message as gospel truth, there was still a certain seriousness in their eyes as they stood there, tanned and healthy-looking, in their gray flannel singlets and coarse, baggy trousers, seeming to welcome the chance to listen to this organizer, who from the slight elevation of an empty kerosene tin was haranguing them about their living conditions. They were in fact delighted with the interruption.

'Fair go, mate,' one reproved another, who had made some uncomplimentary noises. 'Let's 'ear wot 'e wants ter say to us.'

And as the organizer went on talking about the 'bosses sucking the workers' blood,' one man shouted out, rather jovially, "Oo sucks 'oose blood?'

'Yer own bosses, that's who. All bosses are loafers – *that* I can guarantee,' the organizer replied.

And I, who knew that the organizer was referring to people like my father when he talked about 'bosses,' and who knew that my father *did* work, and that there were more kinds of work than this pick-and-shovel labor in the ranges, felt that all the same there was something sad about the men's eyes as they listened – perhaps only a skepticism that a man's real troubles could be as easily solved as that.

There were other sights. Once we watched a young man, still dirty from his day's work, comforting his even dirtier baby in front of a small hut. His bedraggled young wife was trying to cook their dinner under a brush lean-to, pushing away a thin mongrel as it nosed the shovel upon which she was roasting a piece of meat.

'He's a new immigrant,' my father said. 'They haven't even got cooking utensils'; and, again, his tone told it all – the pressure toward emigration from the English, Scottish, and Irish cities; the long sea voyages for these lost urban souls; their poor preparation for hard country living.

Behind this stretched decades of workers' struggles, and the assumptions and methods of radical ideologies imported to Australia, first from Britain, and later from the United States – ideologies bent, in a new country, upon forcing a way out of restrictive Old World patterns. Looking at this little immigrant family, I knew that they, too, would probably have the opportunity of rapid upward mobility. To many such families nothing would seem more important than the fact that they were here in Australia; nothing more exhilarating than reaching out for communal betterment – betterment including not only a decent living but a primitive deciphering of the aspirations of their fellow men. When my father had taken me with him to see the abandoned State Farm, I couldn't have put it into the right 'socialist' context, but I had a dim idea that everyone was supposed to be happy and well fed, just as I had absorbed from such adventure-story homilies as *Swiss Family Robinson* a belief in family virtue and how it contributed to ever-increasing wealth and happiness.

In the same context my father would sometimes talk about the Irish heroes of the 1848 rebellion, men like Smith O'Brien and John Mitchel, and he would bring in the Scottish Martyrs as well and the Dorsetshire Laborers – always glorifying the Australian role to some extent, and finally updating the conversation by talking about the kanakas (the Polynesian word for 'men') who had been brought long ago to Queensland as part of a scheme to provide labor for the sugar plantations.

'But soon a stop was put to that.'

'Why did they put a stop to it?'

'A lot of reasons . . . Queenslanders didn't want black labor.'

'But they were cruel to them, Daddy.'

'Who was cruel to whom?'

'The men who brought Islanders down to Queensland were cruel men.'

'Ah, yes,' my father would answer, slowly as if he didn't like to admit it. 'Some of them were hard men. Mind you, most of them wouldn't have a bar of that bully business. But some of them would sail up to an island, and have a wongi [conversation] with the Islanders, and promise them the sky, and trick 'em into the boats . . .'

'But they killed them.'

'Yes, there was trouble like that. There was a boat come into Brisbane once, and it was found red with blood and filled with black bodies. But that was before my time . . .'

79

By 1906, when my father came to the north, it had been decided once and for all that the trade in Islanders had to be phased out. What we saw later was only the remnant of a system, and the workers still in the state were mostly those who had chosen to stay, and who had become so integrated into Queensland life, through marriage or religion, that they could not, humanly speaking, be deported. There remains a letter, later printed in various missionary accounts, written by a Melanesian teacher, who mourned the exodus for a deeper reason: 'I am only a poor South Sea Island boy,' he wrote. 'And maybe I do not know much but if white people know the true God how can they think it right to send us back to a land . . . where there is always fighting, where life is never safe . . . where there can't be schools for years yet . . .' Then came the ironic farewell cry: 'Goodbye, Cairns . . . goodbye, white Australia . . . goodbye, Christians!'

Perhaps I already noticed in myself the dislike of staying in one place, the impatient curiosity, the weakness of the romantic wanderer. But I was also to think later that these expeditions with my father, and my desire to take part in them, were more than anything else the desire to be close to him – that is, to the primary male – and so to be drawn on voyages which separated me from a family of siblings. In any case, a need to be loved and wanted often merges with a need to understand, and it was through the doors of these unseen frontiers that I shared my father's passion for the Australian distances and the Australian achievement . . .

There were times when I did not want to go with my father, times when I thought that the visits would be boring and the stretches of waiting long; when the evening hour would stretch out and I would be sitting on some veranda, my head against the back of a chair, listening to the men's voices rising and falling, rising and falling . . . but I often went all the same.

One evening a pre-election gathering was held at a little school-house in the scrub, because my father was standing for Parliament; a colleague had come all the way from the south to give him political support. There was no electric light in the school-house, and we sat on hard wooden benches, and I think my father forgot me for a time because he was up on the platform, and the man with him stretched out his arms, using phrases like 'great pioneer,' 'man of vision,' 'advocate for the North,' and 'farseeing North Queenslander . . .'

My mother had tried to persuade me not to go to the meeting: 'It will be quite late, darling.'

'You won't like speeches, will you, Johnny?' Hazel said.

'Oh, let her go,' my father said.

In the end I wished that I had stayed at home, since the evening seemed endless and I had to jerk myself awake again and again so as not to fall off the wooden bench. My father, who was opposing the Labor representative and standing for the small farmers on what was later to be called the Country Party ticket, was deploring those who wouldn't 'give the man on the land a fair deal.' His face was ruddy in the light of the acetylene lantern, and I looked up at him curiously, because suddenly up there on the stage he seemed a different person.

My father's supporter spoke again, and detailed past errors of Labor representatives, and someone in the audience interjected, 'What about 1901?'

My father's colleague replied, 'How should I know? I'm not Rip Van Winkle!' – at which everybody laughed. I don't remember the rest of the evening, but I know that Labor won again, so my father was not elected, and I remember his rueful expression when the results came in. I think my father gave up the idea of being a politician then, and perhaps this, and not the depression, was the moment in his life when his talents – greater than the sphere in which he found himself – ceased to look for a legitimate outlet.

On these itinerant travels I began to understand that I lived not only on the right side of the ranges (the side where the rain was), where we had not (as had the children in the districts beyond the Great Divide) cried because we

81

had never seen rain, but also in Queensland itself, which stretched for miles and miles beyond the mountains, to the very frontier: to the long rivers that wandered from the great Artesian Basin to the Gulf of Carpentaria – country I imagined shining like dull silver and bordered by mangroves growing in thick purplish-looking mud. This was the land belonging to the endless flocks of white cockatoos, their crests sulphur yellow as they wheeled in the sun. I didn't know that country, I had only heard of it; in fact, I scarcely thought of most of it as land at all (not land as we knew it – rich and heavy with long grass and scattered with cattle forever browsing contentedly). Rather it seemed something desolate and harsh, dark brown or red or umber, occasionally wrinkling into eroded stony hills with metals glinting on the surface, stretching out as far as the eye could see, merging with the central desert beyond the border, and going on and on for two thousand miles to the red cliffs of Western Australia, and so to the blue Indian Ocean, which finally set the limits of the land.

During some of the family discussions, unfortunately as forgotten as the language of the Tasmanians (for one generation was too young to record them with accuracy, and the other is no longer here to attest to them), I would feel that my father was more than an Australian landowner – that he was the descendant of landowners, one of those English squires who liked to work with his men, or one of those Royalists-turned-Puritan who brought the country with them to Cromwell, and to whom we were supposed to be related. I was sure that their concerns lived on in my father in some mysterious genetic inheritance, as the concerns of the sea live on in families of sailors. I felt that he could not help buying land, even too much land, and then trying to nurture it, whether or not it was economically feasible to do so. Although I realized that he did not want to be a martyr to the land, and had a strong desire to enjoy life, it was also true that he had an element of what is mistakenly called altruism – an element he shared with his fellow pioneers. They, too, not only defended their terrain but extended themselves to include the most difficult and unrewarding aspects of the terrain of others.

History was a plodding, mechanical story of people putting up shelters to keep out the wind, of planting grass and vegetables, of devising some way to bring water more conveniently from a stream. It was remarking upon what had been done and upon what had still to be done. But it was also my father looking out of the car window and saying, 'They lived in bark huts with ant-bed floors,' or 'The grass wasn't good for cattle out there, but they made it better,' or 'Someday I want to go as far as the Plains of Promise.'

I did not know what the link was between these things my father said and the storms of emotion they stirred in me. Excitement. Curiosity. Something close to pain. I understood that on the tableland we were really all cash-poor farmers, and that because of this we had to have group pride, the rewards of belief and faith. My father could not let his beliefs go because they were too much a part of his compensations. Later, I would look with wonder upon that quality in him that had dwelt upon Egypt with such interest, and that had sent him scouring the state of Queensland to better understand it. And I would look back with even more wonder upon the glimpses I had had of the significance of life lived in places I had never seen, and of fleeting pieces of information about the state of man.

These recognitions were curiously disconnected . . . they flew like brilliant flags against the emptiness of the sky.

5

In the Cubicle

The brilliant light which illuminates the contours of north-eastern Australia strikes also across a sea aswim with islands, and throws into mysterious pearly relief the longest and most complex coral reef in the world. When I finally found myself at the boarding school in the ranges, this same light illuminated a world that had a stripped and pristine quality – the rocky ranges glittering under a thin forest of gray-green eucalyptus that seemed to stretch away for miles in every direction.

The Herberton ranges, which lie behind the Atherton Tableland, were romantic to me, being the place of my birth. My mother had often told me of the night at Irvinebank – she was visiting her sister and John Moffat there – when she waited for me to arrive. Lying in the little side room that looked off toward the hills, she could see a fire built by local Aborigines who were holding a corroboree. The glow of the fire was barred by sparse, dark trees, and by the figures of the Aborigines as they acted out their dramatic pantomime, leaping into the air to the sound of chanting and the beating of sticks. Down on the tablelands, there had been a storm with a good deal of thunder and lightning, but my father had continued to ride Signal, his big bay, up the ranges to see his wife and, by then, the child who – since he had three girls already – he had hoped would be a son. He rode, he said, all through the storm, the downpour streaming like a waterfall over his head, and over the black raincape, and over the horse, making great gullies and trenches in the steep, sandy track.

The next morning the range road would have been

dazzlingly white, for the surface shone with grains of quartz, which were never whiter than after rain – unless it was at the time of the full moon, when the hills were so bright that one could read by their reflected light. Shortly after being sent with my sisters to the boarding school at Herberton, which had long been promised to the Church of England settlers by the Anglican bishop, I found myself in one of a row of green-painted cubicles in a two-storey wooden building. Each cubicle held a narrow white bed, closed off by a white curtain in place of a door, and had its own window. There was a wide ledge to the window, and on it the moon would pour down its dazzling light. When the moon was at its zenith, long after we were all supposed to be asleep, I perched on that cubicle ledge and – sometimes shivering with cold, but intoxicated by the romance of the world – read my way through such books as *Les Misérables*, *The Count of Monte Cristo*, *The Black Tulip*, and *The Scarlet Pimpernel*. If these books were a delight to me, they were also strangely involved with the radiance of love which the moonlight suggested, with that deep current in the lives of some women – an idealized sensuality that made convent girls like George Sand beg the moon to guide them, even if to death: 'My dreaming soul is drawn to you/Moon, mournful lover of the tomb/Guide my steps . . .'

The night reading sometimes made it hard to get up in the morning. In winter we would be called early: bells would clang, and feet would run to the shower rooms, where the lead on the floors, which had been wet the night before, was rimed with ice. (Herberton's altitude was about 3,500 feet and therefore its climate was cooler than that of the tablelands.) In the hysteria bred by a British kind of discipline, which married so well with the traditional cult of Australian toughness (and, in my case, was reinforced by the thought of my hardy grandmother), we would dip ourselves under the cold shower, thrust ourselves with still damp skin into white underwear and navy-blue cambric uniforms laced at the neck and sides with tan cords. Tumbling over each other, we would then try to catch up with the 'leaders,' who were bent upon sprinting before breakfast to a culvert called the One Mile. The broad white road to the One Mile was lined with pale green gums tipped with red, with shaggy she-oaks – Australia's most melancholy tree – and an occasional blackboy, or grass tree. We all knew that we must not fall down, because the harsh quartz-covered surface of the road tore the skin off knees and shins. The sun rising above the hills would already be glittering warmly on the iron roofs of the small scattered houses; the chapel back at the school would wait in its emptiness for our first prayers; and the tables in the refectory would be laid out with plates of bread and scrapings of butter, with bowls ready for the saltless and slightly burned porridge, with the dark wells of golden syrup that served a universal purpose in early Australian cookery. Our rushing to reach the One Mile before prayers and breakfast had, or seemed to me to have had, a lot to do with a senior mistress known as Miss Andrews – the common belief being that Miss Andrews was really Lady Andrews. This seemed doubtful to me, who at that time associated nobility only with glorious names such as Mountbatten, Churchill, Windsor, Buckingham. In our minds some mystery centered on this ash-blond, rather young-looking and serious woman, who seemed interested in sports rather than scholarship but had come all the way from Scotland to teach us. She generally wore a pleated tunic of oat-meal-colored holland, a white shirt, spotless white sandshoes (sneakers), and – as her only ornament – a sports whistle that hung on a black ribbon around her neck. It didn't seem particularly logical that a sports teacher would be a necessary addition to our curriculum. She must have come to encourage us yet again in that chastisement of the flesh by arduous physical programs and cold baths about which we were already well informed.

Like most children we were not particularly aware of the economic and social situation in which we grew, and it didn't occur to us to wonder where the money came from to build the barnlike buildings in which we lived, or to question how teachers such as Miss Andrews were paid or whether the new order of Anglican Sisters, the Sisters of the Sacred Advent, were paid at all. These last could be seen with a crocodile of girls in the streets of Herberton, or hastening about the school grounds from building to building and back again, their pale faces shadowed by white starched coifs and collars, their sexless dark serge habits flapping in the wind. Nor did it occur to us to wonder why some lessons were held in the quarters of the Brothers of St. Barnabas, the center for those traveling priests who at this time were fanning out all over the tablelands and ranges – sometimes by horse, sometimes by train – visiting houses, preaching, and perhaps hoping to demolish that old North Queensland adage 'There is no God north of Rockhampton!'

We scarcely realized how great an effort these Bush Brothers had had to make – how upon their graduation from the great English universities they had prayed for grace to serve in the slums and in deprived areas of the Empire; how some had come to Australia, where they had not experienced the comparative comfort of the urban dioceses but had gone straight to a bush community; how they had learned to ride, to camp out, to cross flooded rivers ('I was shy and always sunburnt,' one of them confessed later), to wait for the occasional train, to beg the farmers for horses, to sleep on bags behind shanty bars, to preach to unwilling audiences in mining camps, and to deal less with cases of spiritual confusion than with cases of delirium tremens. These unusual men did not seem unusual to us, for we had little scope for comparison. We had always known them, and it did not seem strange that they practiced such self-denial, because it was considered that men of the church were as accustomed to poverty as they were to prayer. It was only later that I was told how the first Bishop of North Queensland, George Frodsham, on a visit to England to make known the difficulties of the Australian Church, had been allowed at Oxford to deliver a spirited appeal for more priests. He had stirred the hearts of his listeners when he said, 'Let us have men who will preach like Apostles and ride like cowboys, and having food and raiment will thereby be content . . .'

From the point of view of these saintly men and women, the schools could be successful only if they could approximate the values of the Anglican Church – it was these values that were presented to us along with the fairly sparse equipment, the spartan food, the shortage of teachers, and the bush environment we already knew. What could be more appealing to the British character than that call to the most distant borders of undeveloped Queensland to help mold the bodies and souls of her children? Of course, there might have been other satisfactions for the well-off members of distinguished English, Scottish, or Irish families such as Miss Andrews, who, titled or untitled, undoubtedly belonged to the right church and the right establishment. They may have been motivated by something more than noblesse oblige – perhaps even a desire to operate freely, far from the restraints of England, where the full-blooded Empire ways were waning?

But Queenslanders, stimulated by the survival mechanisms of struggling new communities, also had nonreligious aims. They wanted suitable schools, especially schools away from the steaming coast, and discussions about this were common among friends of my father's, and in the small, intensely provincial Cairns *Post*, which was published each week, and which sometimes ran headlines such as 'White Man Proven Equal to Hottest Climate.' There was the hope locally that North Queensland would show herself able to develop and grow rich in spite of lying only fourteen degrees south of the equator; in spite of a heat more fitted to the growth of the mango, the banana, the pineapple, the guava, and the sugarcane than to that of the white man and his family.

Therefore, the debate as to what was suitable and what was not extended far beyond the question of religious affiliation. It concerned itself also with our particular social and environmental circumstances; with what we could adapt to, and what sort of civilized life we would arrange for ourselves in an equatorial belt. We were familiar with the cane gangs – men who traveled in self-reliant groups and were known from the southern borders to the new northern fields of Mossman and the Daintree River. Their skins were burnt to a deep reddish-brown, their shoulders and forearms were well muscled from wielding the deadly cane knife, and they were typical of the heroes of Ray Lawler's popular play, *The Summer of The Seventeenth Doll*. These men carried on the already established tradition of the sheep shearer and the cattle drover – the 'save and splurge' tradition that involved living abstemiously for a season and then 'knocking down their checks,' as it was called, with frantic speed. And they were of many origins – ex-miners from the ranges, perhaps, or new immigrants – often Italians, who flourished in the hot climate and painted their little houses in gay colors. The point is that these strong-bodied men were 'white,' and as such presented different problems than did the bargained-for and half-coerced dark Islanders. It was this blend of good sense, politicization, and natural dislike of labor that was not free which dominated hiring in the canefields as we were growing up.

Our generation saw a decline in the easy entry of Chinese, Japanese, and Malays into Queensland – the result of white men's fear for their jobs, but also more generally encouraged by the mysterious dread of foreigners felt by an insular people. It was whispered about that the Chinese brought with them opium and leprosy, and that the Islanders were the victims of fevers, parasitic diseases, and heathen superstitions! Race, as we came to know, was more complex than it seemed. One day, during lunch hour at school, I pressed my face against the paling fence to see the local constable riding along the main road. Behind him came two policemen, also on horses. In front of him a 'black tracker,' with bare feet and tattered cast-off clothes, was running bent low to the ground like a dog. He was following the trail of some fellow Aboriginal, apparently wanted for breaking the law. Here were elements outside my experience of the Aborigines, whom I thought of in connection with the scrubs, the life of the gunyahs, the occupation of digging for roots, and climbing the jungle trees to find a possum or 'smell' a tree-climbing kangaroo. Here the tracker was using the craft of centuries to read the stony ground, the disturbed pebbles, the drifting sand, and so the secret of a man's flight – how he left, and why, and perhaps even what psychological state he was in. (Later I was to hear such a tracker say, pointing to the circling tracks, 'This feller plurry bad.') Young as I was, I felt the pain of the situation – the sometimes disdained Aborigines, divided one against the other; the victorious well-fed white settlers, with no conscious desire to divide and rule, but automatically doing so, sitting on the horses they had introduced into the country, and following the trail nosed out by indigenous man. This was, after all, the reality of the white occupation.

Other realities seemed far from us as we sat in the schoolrooms of St. Mary's on drowsy mornings, with the teacher demanding in firm but sweet tones: 'Please recite the names and dates of the Tudor monarchs,' or 'Please let me hear the first stanzas of Spenser's *Faerie Queene*.'

We were slowly being conditioned to separate learning from our Australian life, so that we accepted the smothering of the little Princes in the Tower and the burning of Protestants at the stake, but did not think it our business to ponder the racial divisions around us, or to wonder whether the cane gangs or the mining men were closer to us than the traveling Brothers who had been educated in Oxford. I suppose each pupil did absorb knowledge differently, but, in general, the instinctive desire to learn dulled any desire to criticize. Only when some sharp conflict diverted us from our adolescent stupors did we react by considering the lure of English culture as seen against the harsh, materialistic backdrop of a tiny mining community in the ranges behind the Queensland coast. The school – with its core of Sisters and teachers, its small but well-chosen library, and its distant British goals – reflected one side only of our world. Were we British or Australian? If we were true to one ideal, might we not fail the other? Did we believe in the class system of the 'old country'? Or were we with the strikers on the wharves and the gangers on the line? Did we believe in 'good ole George,' as the workers sometimes called the King? Or were we simply egalitarians like William Lane, who, influenced by 'divine discontent,' long ago carried off some of his followers to 'New Australia' in Paraguay.

In some ways we clung to the active life because we were sure of it, just as we were sure of our own large continent with its rich coastlines and its belly of sand and stones. 'Don't let us get soft,' our parents were apt to say, when it was a question of whether to dive or not dive into the water on a coolish day; and our teachers said it, too, even the delectable Miss Andrews, blowing her little whistle to marshal us to the One Mile. I don't think that in my mind I linked this 'not getting soft' with protecting imperialism, for conversations about various aspects of Empire were only just coming into vogue. I knew that my father had said that Cecil Rhodes had urged 'imperialism' on all who desired to avoid civil war, and had asked whether it was not preferable to bring new lands into civilization rather than to leave them pagan and unused. When I asked my father whether he agreed with this, he had laughed and winked, and said that Cecil Rhodes had also said that if it had been possible he would have 'annexed the planets'!

My love of adventure extended to the books of Rider Haggard, though one of my teachers dismissed them as being about 'impossible adventures.' There is a story in my family, remembered by my sister Margot, that Rider Haggard had come to see us during a visit to Queensland, and our father had promised to show him an enormous tree in the jungles.

'Where is this tree?' the then famous writer asked.

'I think it is near Millaa Millaa,' our father said.

'Will it take long to get there?' Rider Haggard asked.

'Only an hour or two,' our confident father answered.

Great preparations were made to see the tree, and Rider Haggard, our father, and several other men set out together, I think in a rail motor. When the rail motor stopped, they plunged into the jungle. Although they saw a number of great trees, they were unable to find *the* tree, the huge, the *enormous* tree.

'The tree has got away,' the great writer of war and hunting stories is said to have remarked, laughing. And this seemed suitable, because the myth and the exaggeration were part of the delight. It was not surprising that we truly believed that men were manly, that war was necessary, that caves held bones and treasures, and that trees were *big*! Nor was such belief separated from the idea that British seamen, through their heroic sacrifice, had found the Great South Land and entrusted it to *us* to guard and develop.

In our years at St. Mary's, the values of peace were blended with the disciplinary tone of the 'Onward, Christian Soldiers' we sang in the chapel; with the solemnity of Kipling's 'Recessional'; and with the fighting stance of the Bush Brothers themselves, whose manners were gracious but who had come out to Queensland in the first place because of a call to struggle.

The reigning Anglican bishop in North Queensland at that time was John Oliver Feetham – known as John of North Queensland, or J.O.N.Q. Tall, thin, ascetic-looking (with a faintly famished expression resulting from hollowed cheeks and large dark eyes surmounted by beetling brows), he came from a family of soldiers, statesmen, and clergy. It was known that he was immensely favorable toward what was called, during the nineteenth century, the Oxford Movement. Because of this movement's concentration upon the earlier Church tradition of dignity and liturgy, vestments and processions, its influence was in dispute in some parts of Australia. J.O.N.Q. had been willing to battle the strong Congregational and Scotch Presbyterian impulse in the country (inherently hostile to the Oxford Movement), and to try to consolidate the Anglican influence, especially in North Queensland. As schoolgirls, we were not disturbed by the details of all this, because it was easy to resolve the whole matter into a question of the natural struggle between High Church and Low Church.

In our school world, the inextricable mingling of the impulse to defend the Empire, and therefore our own country, and to do our duty toward God was so firmly planted that until I went to the university I don't remember it ever being questioned. The occasions that influenced us in this direction came in many guises – on the school grounds, as in the chapel; on nights of Girl Guides camping, as on days of recitation; in teacher commendation, as in family pride:

> *This is the chapel; here, my son,*
> *Your father thought the thoughts of youth,*
> *And heard the words that one by one*
> *The touch of life has turned to truth . . .*

This patriotic and religious concern was also somehow a part of the ritual of the playing fields – when the stick carried in team races was thrust out to the advancing hand, as it had been long ago in Greece; or when, during the relays in the town baths, a swimmer battled up the lane between the tapes with bursting lungs; or when the ball fell into the bucket to the roar of the onlookers: 'Well played! Well played!' But on these occasions what we really learned was to work with the team, to respect with utter faith the decision of the umpire, and what was perhaps most useful, to live up to and even to surpass our capabilities.

It was in such a mood each year that we approached Anzac Day in Herberton, the Australian holiday that is associated with tears, with the sacrifice of World War I and the cataclysmic slaughter at Gallipoli. In the hot morning we gathered eucalyptus boughs, soon to be wilting, and stacked them in piles near the school gate, ready for our departure. A wreath of 'everlastings' – white-and-yellow strawlike daisies from the nearby hills, with their silvery-green foliage as limp as cotton – had been prepared by the Sisters and tied with a bow of purple ribbon.

'Anzac' stood for Australian and New Zealand Army Corps, and the sacred letters had about them the unforgettable aura of the 1914 that we had not experienced. We knew it to be the time when the country's best and bravest marched in dreamlike unison to the boats that took them overseas – their bodies wrapped around in old-fashioned coarse khaki, their puttees spiraling gigantic calves, their enormous boots tramping, and delicate bunches of silvery emu feathers nodding against upturned slouch hats. For some of us, these heroes were conjured up as riders, at one with their horses, whose manes streamed and tails flowed, whose hooves splashed through dunes of sand as they might through water. These dream men, splendid and centaurlike, were reddened by foreign sunsets, a red we knew was the color of blood. Perhaps none of us who were then at school in North Queensland had escaped losing someone in those battles.

Dressed up in our clean uniforms, we emerged at last from the gates, we pupils of St. Mary's – the Sisters with us like winged black birds, someone carrying the wreath, the prefects scooping up the boughs of eucalyptus, all of us going left-right, left-right, down the hard white road to the river, and up the hill to the main street, where the verandas of the wooden hotels were black with people, and others lined the overhangs of Jack and Newell's store and the Mining Assay Office and the butcher's shop and the local café. A brass band was already beginning to play, planted near the tiny triangle of grass at the post office, where the cenotaph stood, the unknown soldier in stained cement, holding his bronze wreath.

In front of us marched the members of the Returned Soldiers League – one-two, one-two – their uniforms old and darned, their medals glinting, their worn faces seamed and serious. Behind them came the invalids still remaining from that faraway time of the Somme and Passchendaele and

94

Vimy Ridge and Gallipoli – one without a leg, one without an arm, and several stooped and hollow-chested. As we lined up at one side of the triangle, the white sea of our panama hats shone under the profound raw blue of the noon sky; across from us, and forming a V, gathered the convent girls with *their* nuns – all of us sitting in a silence broken only by the solemn moaning of the band. None of the old familiar songs – 'Pack Up Your Troubles' or 'Blighty' or 'There's a Long, Long Trail A-winding' – could be sung till later in the day. Now was the time for cemeteries, and invalids, and soldiers in training, and prayers, and addresses, and exhortations. It was a time to screw up our eyes and remember Gallipoli ('Nine times forward . . . and nine times mowed down. Imagine . . . *imagine*'). We sat in the heat, and sweat dampened the linings of our hats and trickled down our faces. We sang 'God Save the King.' The colors were presented, the wreaths were put on the monument, the boughs of eucalyptus were placed against the iron railings and slowly released the perfume of the ranges. We thought of Kipling – 'Lord God of Hosts, be with us yet/Lest we forget – lest we forget!' Everyone bowed their heads. There were tears of pain and patriotism. All around us we felt death, not the death of the dusty old, but the death of the brilliant young, the eternally vigorous.

I don't associate J.O.N.Q. with the prayers on Anzac Day, but he was memorable for his prayers for soldiers in action, and for what he called 'the Nelson attitude.' I think this latter had to do with courage and was typified by the verses we had learned to recite in the old one-room schoolhouse – verses recounting that when Nelson was asked to note the 'progress of the enemy,' he clapped the glass to his sightless eye and then reported, 'I'm damned if I see it!'

J.O.N.Q., in any case, although he gave no sense of strain or effort, had an aura of saintliness about him. I could never quite believe that he was not one of *us* – that at heart he had not needed North Queensland, as North Queensland had needed him. High Church though he was, he was even more informal than we were, and was often to be seen on the little railway sidings, with mud staining his gaiters and habit, his flat silver cross swinging on his purple bib, and all of his belongings in a sugar bag! His air of total delight at having discovered in North Queensland a splendid, if infertile, field for his labors fascinated us; and it was after all J.O.N.Q. who had created our schools. But, schoolgirls as we were, our allegiance was so deeply rooted in our physical selves that we had very little emotion to expend elsewhere.

An enormous amount of our energy was expended upon thinking of food. The school refectory should have pleased us, but proved instead to be a rather bare and unsensuous place, its tables by no means heavily laden, its cooks probably hampered by inadequate supplies. With a country of milk and butter just down the ranges, the butter on our tables was scanty, cream non-existent, and our milk a pale concoction made with water and powder. We sighed and moaned at the meat, so little of it, so stringy, and cooked or overcooked in (for lack of proper utensils) big kerosene tins, with quantities of carrots and turnips. As short of fats as if we were the poor of London, we longed for a certain boiled pudding made with flour, suet, and treacle, and served only on one glorious day a week. To those of us who came from food-conscious homes, where the menus were supplemented by all the produce of farm and property – by unlimited milk and cream and butter, by young calves and piglets fed on mash and separated milk, by mangoes from the coastal trees, and by huge sun-ripened watermelons – this thin school fare had about it a quality associated with the pale and preoccupied faces of the Sisters, so often bent down as if in prayer, yet expressing a cheerfulness that we (little materialists that we were) tended to think artificial.

We managed, however, to create our own compensations. A small group of trustworthy and ingenious souls found a hidden recess in the middle of some underbrush among patches of giant sunflowers that bordered the lower tennis court and were contained by a high wire fence. This green bower was on the legitimate side of the border, yet gave us entire privacy – no one else could tell that it existed, let alone shielded illegal activities. We all made a habit of stealing potatoes and onions from the refectory (easy enough to do, because the pupils took turns clearing the tables between courses, and each of us could dash en route into the storeroom, where the root vegetables were kept in wooden bins, and hide in our uniform pockets whatever we could snatch). Salt and pepper were easy to procure, and butter and fat were obtained in one way or another.

One of our group, having a mechanical turn of mind, had found half a kerosene tin and, turning it upside down, had punched holes in it with a large nail, so that, placed over a small fire, it formed a practical stove, upon which we could cook our sliced potatoes and onions. We did this when the tennis court was not in use, for fear the players might notice the dispersed smoke from the fire. These feasts of greasy half-raw and blackened potatoes and onions, unsatisfying as they were, quieted more than the hunger we felt for suitable food. They were part of the adventurous life we wanted to live, for we mocked at the restraint and obedience forced upon us, and saw ourselves as explorers and pioneers, like our fathers and mothers. Constantly daring each other to go further afield and to further flout the rules, we sometimes went to Joss House, two stony hillsides away, where we could smell strange incenses and buy lichees and ginger and fireworks from the Chinese storekeeper. It was considered especially important to dare to trespass on the forbidden terrain of these alien Chinese, whose English was so bad that they could scarcely interpret our demands. Often we roamed the hillsides without permission – sometimes, on moonlight nights, slipping out of the grounds and scrambling into old mine shafts to pick up pieces of glittering stone. Occasionally we swam in the river, which moved rapidly over its shallow bed of golden stone and was shadowed by the scarlet-flowering bottlebrush. During the wet season, when this river – so casually called the Wild – was swollen to three times its normal size and raged in a small torrent toward the dam in the town, permission to swim would be officially granted, and then we would enjoy the tossing waters that tumbled from the cold, stony hills, and feel a profound satisfaction, a satisfaction made greater by the approval of J.O.N.Q., who preached to us, his eyes alight, quoting Browning, as if aware that only by promising no diminution of our pleasure could he hold our allegiance to the Church:

> *Oh, the wild joys of living! the leaping from rock to rock,*
> *The strong rending of boughs from the fir-tree, the cool*
>   *silver shock*
> *Of the plunge in the pool's living water . . .*

> How good is man's life, the mere living! how fit to employ
> All the heart and the soul and the senses for ever in joy!

But there were other recitations. We used to enjoy declaiming, in voices just too low for the teacher to hear us, something entitled 'The Great Australian Adjective,' one verse of which went like this:

> *He rode up hill, down bloody dale,*
> *The wind it blew a bloody gale . . .*
> *He plunged into the bloody creek,*
> *The bloody horse was bloody weak . . .*

This seemed more in our style at that stage than did Browning, or Shakespeare, or even Henry Lawson. We also delighted in fitting the word 'bloody' neatly into the middle of a word. For instance.

Question: 'Will you please give your essay to Miss Smith today?'

Answer: 'I absobloodylutely will.'

Because J.O.N.Q. came from a civilization more pluralistic than our own, we did not really attend to what was suggested in the complex messages he spelled out for us. Australianization was too rapid in its movement for him to perceive its gains – and in its bush realism, too deeply bound into the colonial life born of transportation and immigration. If on my cubicle ledge I could still withdraw into the world of fictionalized dreams, and if others in that honeycomb of girls also dreamt at night of those impulses which lie deeply buried in the human race, this was not openly admitted. So daylight would find us shrieking and calling to each other like magpies, and loudly professing the crudest materialism.

6

Over the Bump

It was one year in the middle of things – certainly before I myself began to go south to the sister school of St. Margaret's – that my father announced to the family that we were all going down 'over the Bump,' and that soon we would see how it had been done in the past, though we would go by car and not on horseback. Our aim would be to drive from Kureen all the way down to the coast at Port Douglas, to sleep the night there, and, on the following day, to inspect the property he had bought on the Daintree River – that river which lay to the north of us, and was reputed to be 'swarming' with crocodiles. Just as our mother and father had ridden *up* the ranges 'over the Bump,' we would drive *down* them, and so complete the cycle. This impetus to reconstruct the past had been stimulated by the imminent arrival in the north of our two older cousins, Bessie and Isabel Moffat, who had lived in Irvinebank when they were younger, but had then returned to the south to go to school in Sydney. Their father had retired in 1912, and died in 1918, so that our cousins were heirs to whatever remained of Uncle John Moffat's wealth. To make this visit more exciting, they were bringing up on the boat with them their shining new Rolls-Royce, a car that we naturally thought of as being 'fabulous' and that had an engine considered so faultless that it was practically sealed away from human hands. We couldn't imagine how this could be, because we were used to seeing our own old cars in a constant state of being repaired.

'Can *that* car go over the Bump?' we asked of the Rolls. 'Surely it can't do *that* ?'

'Perhaps we can leave it at the Landing?' my mother asked anxiously. (The Landing was a clearing at the top of the range from which travelers could see for miles down the precipitous descent to the Mowbray Valley, and so to the distant coast.)

'We'll get Harry to meet us anyway,' my father said. Harry was the man who owned a little property at the foot of the range, and who rented out a team of horses which, if necessary, could be used to haul a car up over the Bump.

'And how will *we* get down, Daddy?' we asked in chorus.

'Yes, Ted,' our mother demanded, even implored, 'how will *we* get down?'

My father looked rather self-conscious. I suspect that there had been many occasions when his plans had not met with my mother's standards of security.

'Don't worry, Bina.' He looked at her indulgently, but with a hint of a frown. 'We'll cut down a tree and hitch it onto the Dodge to act as a brake. We'll leave the Rolls at the Landing. You will all *walk* down . . . and I will drive the Dodge.'

Although I don't remember all the discussions held and decisions made, I remember vividly the arrival a week later of Bessie and Isabel – both in dark, elegant suits with collars of fur, blouses of georgette, and shoes of lizardskin; Bessie in a little toque, Isabel in a small bonnetlike straw hat with artificial cherries dangling beside her wing of shining hair. True to their reputation, these cousins brought extravagant presents with them – dresses from Paris and stockings from London; perfumes and scented soap and delicious under-wear; books bound in leather and purses with money in them; gadgets from Fortnum and Mason, and chocolates from Belgium – all those things we could not afford ourselves, and couldn't find in Australia even if we could afford them; 'overseas' presents which came at exorbitant prices and in glittering wrappings.

After the excitement of their arrival had died down, the planning began for the great journey to the coast – the collecting of suitable clothes, of sunglasses, face cream, and citronella; the cooking of picnic foods; the packing of towels, bed linen, and fishing gear. My mother got together a few bandages, a bottle of iodine, an antidote for snakebite, and, for bad sunburn, the omnipresent Carron oil. My father and brother conferred about the condition of our Dodge, which only a few years before had been the admiration of the district. Bessie, who was rather tall and plump but singularly dainty-footed, wrapped herself in a smart dustproof cape, and Isabel found a light raincoat, which she buttoned up to her chin, turning the collar up at the neck like a military uniform. The northern tablelands were a far cry from the civilization of Sydney, and our cousins looked upon northern experiences as so attractive and so perilous that they must be dressed accordingly.

On the day we left our old wooden Fleetwood homestead, surrounded by its bright garden and green paddocks, we felt that we were leaving what was tidy and secure – that is, our farming lives – for what was sultry and adventurous. For some reason I was to ride in the Rolls-Royce, and this meant that I would be in the prestigious position of being able to point out to Bessie and Isabel the landmarks they might not have seen yet, or might have forgotten – the hotel at Yungaburra, for example, which the enterprising Williams family had made into a center for local festivities; or the revamped main street of Tolga, which had grown into a township since the days when our father had shared a timber mill there. It was here, on the edge of Atherton's boundary, that the road passed out of the scrub belt nourished by the monsoonal rains and moved north toward forestlike country, with rocky outcrops, gum trees, and occasional anthills. It was at Tolga that my father, newly married to my mother, had first seen the possibilities of commercial milling, and later bought the sawmill plant from its original owner and transported it to Kureen by packhorse and dray, to set up the Tinaroo Timber Company, which was subsequently to ship to the south great quantities of that warm brown walnut wood that lined the walls in our own sitting room and formed the mantelpiece that hung over the red-washed fireplace.

That day, it was at Tolga that we took the road to Mareeba (once called Granite Creek), a stopping place for the teams and the coaches, a place for the horses and mules to rest after their slow and strenuous ascent. It might seem odd that even as late as the 1920s those of us who lived in North Queensland experienced the very edge of the pioneer period. But that was how it was, so it was easy for us to re-create the flavor of what had gone before, and had indeed not quite disappeared. Those who think of pioneering in Australia are apt to forget that, in British terms, the continent wasn't even discovered until Cook sailed up the eastern coast in 1770. The first convicts weren't landed until 1788, and it was thirteen years after the beginning of the nineteenth century before a small party of men had even managed to cross the barrier of the Blue Mountains behind Sydney and look out over the inland plains. It is not surprising, therefore, that in the 1920s the little stores in Mareeba still looked and smelled like pioneer stores, with their hunks of rope, and bags of flour, and tins of bully beef, and American felt hats, and axes, and hurricane lamps.

I know that we had a picnic lunch that day in the 'dry-country' and that we drove nearly all day and that it must have been dusk when we arrived at the Landing, at the top of the ranges, and stood for a while, with the rainy mist swirling about us, looking down at the shrouded fertility of the Mowbray Valley. 'Everybody out but the lady with the baby' was a phrase we had known from our childhood, and although this referred back to coaching days, it applied now, and my father quoted it as we all tumbled out of the cars, and stood around feeling chilly while he cut down a medium-sized tree and attached it to the back of the battered Dodge. This would steady the car and act as a brake for the descent. The grade was about one in three, and the road passed over a great bulge of gray slate, slippery and perilous in the damp weather.

In the fast-fading light we watched the Dodge sliding ahead of us, and I remember saying to Bessie, 'What will happen to Daddy if the tree doesn't hold, and if the car goes too fast?'

And she said, 'I don't think anything like that will happen,' and she tucked my hand over her arm, and we all walked down the road, our shoes sliding on the loose gravel. Someone had a lantern. The calves of my legs trembled, and began to ache from the effort of struggling over the great mass of wet slate – that is, over 'the Bump.'

As night fell, we came to Port Douglas and stood in the vast featureless lounge of the big wooden hotel, where the only concession to decoration was a nugget of gold from the early 'rush' days, reposing in a padlocked glass case, and all at once we were aware of the coastal heat, of the whine of mosquitoes, of the faintly exciting smell of rank mud and salty waters.

In the morning the early sun glittered on the tin roofs and on the dark outline of a fishing boat rocking on the tide. And from the street below there came the faint jangle of bells as someone brought goat's milk to the hotel. It was into this port that boats had sailed hopefully in the early days of the Thornborough rush, long before we were born. Then there had been twenty-five hotels in the town, and two newspapers, and the population had grown to eight thousand in a matter of months. But this excitement had long ago evaporated; in fact, we engaged the full attention of the few people on the jetty as we boarded the launch that morning, situated ourselves under an awning away from the already fierce sun, and watched the captain maneuver slowly upstream between banks dark with mangroves, the chief product of the 'black estuaries' of North Queensland. Here the mangroves, with their shining, almost lacquered leaves, formed a world of their own, into which, moment by moment, there dropped, straight as arrows, the heavy seeds that had already germinated upon the trees, and were ready to grow wherever they fell, or to drift on any tide to any destination.

The journey up the river was long and hot. Crocodiles looked like dark logs in the brown water, until suddenly, at the boat's approach, they would turn and disappear beneath the surface. The captain told how he'd been in the business once of shooting them and selling their hides, and of how at Wyndham, on the west coast, near the meatworks, there'd been what was called the 'blood hole,' fed by thousands of slaughtered cattle. 'The gators,' he said admiringly, 'would swaller up that refuse . . . wise ole men they were, they'd wait to see the tide redden.' He had a quiet voice, and mingled disturbing details with simple science, speaking of the cold dull emerald of the creatures' eyes; and of battles he'd seen 'on the mud flats of this very river, between rival males at mating time. One old chap'd beller half the night, and 'e'd reach around the neck of 'is rival an' try to chew 'is paw off!'

'Yes,' he added, 'they got good eyesight, and they got adjustable filaments in their throat. You see this way they close their throats when they go underwater? And they've got good hearing, I tell you. They can judge when a prey is advancing along the banks, or when humans are swimming in the water.'

The mud flats around us did indeed seem alive, and all through the long hot morning the little Aborigine boy who helped the captain would cry out, 'Crikey . . . crikey, look . . . plenty feller today.'

Late in the afternoon we reached the cottage on the property my father had bought, a low-built place, with a veranda festooned by a giant granadilla vine, its pale lantern-shaped greenish fruit hanging so seductively that my mother and Isabel were soon speaking of granadilla pie, and wondering what sort of stove the cottage had. In a little while we were scrambling out of the boat, and threading our way through the tall rank grass, as high as our heads and negotiable only on a wooden pathway above the slimy mud up which the water climbed when the tide was high. I remember the white china lamp that night, swinging on a metal chain above the table with its white cloth, and the golden crust of the pie made with the seeds and pulp of the granadillas; and later, the buzzing of enormous mosquitoes outside the nets as we lay in bed; and last of all, the hoarse bark of the crocodiles down by the river. These saltwater saurians, living relics of prehistoric times, had been bred in Australia's Center when it was a vast inland sea, fed by numerous rivers. Later, as the waters shrank to lake size, and the inland rivers ceased to run, the crocodiles had retreated to the river estuaries and the sea. These creatures of salt and half-salt water, with tongueless horny palates to absorb their semi-decayed food (long buried in the bottom of the rivers), were easy to imagine as we lay in the dark that night. We knew also that the calves and the ponies and sometimes even the Timor cattle could be dragged down into the water and the smothering mud, and that the great armorplated crocodile could fling itself sideways in a rotating movement called the 'death roll.' I could see the webbed hind feet of these animals gripping the earth, leaving long scars in the banks of the river. With strong, webless, clawed front feet they crawled in my dreams . . .

In the morning all seemed normal again. The sun shone, the granadillas were as delicious as ever, and Bessie told us stories as she sewed on the veranda, every now and then mopping her rosy face with a damp handkerchief. My father cut some wood, and consulted with the man who was managing the property, and they discussed the news that cold-weather cattle were being crossed with Brahmans, which would give the offspring protection against dreaded tropical ticks. Over the rich landscape, with its luxuriant grasses, a veil of silence fell and seemed to merge again with the blue of the coastal range down which we had struggled the day before. Then, again, came that demon of insecurity that lay beneath the challenging surface of the Australian condition. The women began to talk of the last great cyclone, during which the Daintree River had flooded so suddenly that the original house here on the property had been washed away and several of the children of the couple who owned it drowned. The wife and husband managed to reach a big tree, in which they were marooned on the topmost branches – the man with a broken leg, suffered when he tried ineffectually to rescue the children. All night long the woman clung to her youngest child, whom she held in her arms while the water whirled around them. There was nothing to eat, and the only utensil they had for water was a small metal matchbox. When daylight came the man held the child, and the woman climbed down with the matchbox and returned again and again with small portions of water for them to drink. When they were rescued at last, this couple simply wanted to leave the place forever; they sold the property to my parents.

I noticed that my father looked anxiously at us as this story was repeated. He didn't like us to hear too many tales of horror. I think he felt that, as we grew up, we would need all the confidence at our disposal. Sensing this, Bessie began to tell the younger ones an Aboriginal tale about a blue-tongued lizard, whose name was Bungurrah and who kept a source of water hidden under a flat stone. 'Everyone was very thirsty,' said Bessie, 'so the little white rat called Kaaloo was asked to follow him and find out why his tongue was wet. So Kaaloo *pushed* Bungurrah and the water flowed out suddenly with a loud noise, and flooded everywhere, and all the rivers came down from the hills and the water flowed until it reached the sea.'

Bessie had Robin close to her, and Robin's big brown eyes stared ahead and her face wore the abstracted expression children get when they are seeing a world beyond themselves. (I always wanted to protect Robin, because she was the only girl in the family who was younger than I was, and therefore the only one who, whatever the situation, could never attempt to tell me what to do!)

But strange and violent stories were not finished for the day, and when the old man who had been working for our father outside came in to have his afternoon tea, he stood by the stove and began to reminisce about his life in Cooktown, just to the north, and to deplore the fact that the town had no solid trade now and was only a port, a shadow of what it had once been.

'Why, that was a place for real-life stories, that was,' he said. 'Everything happened, I tell you. There was Mrs. Watson. You ever hear about her? She was born in Cornwall, England, and she came here as a governess, so they said, and in the end she married a bêche-de-mer fisherman, Watson, his name was, and the two of them went up to Lizard Island – that's the island where the queer big lizards grow that scientists are so stuck on!'

Bessie, not knowing much about the history of Cooktown, asked questions. The old man went on to tell her how Watson, the fisherman, had left the island on a trip, and how, in his absence, the wild blacks had come in their canoes to the shore, and speared the two Chinamen working for the Watsons, and were advancing toward the hut when Mrs. Watson drove them off with a revolver.

'She took her baby,' the old man said, 'and she put one of the Chinamen (wounded he was, but still alive) into a half-tank, along with some provisions, and water, and an umbrella for shade, and she tried to escape by pushing off the tank onto the reef waters. She managed to pole to another island, but there was blacks there and no water to be found.'

We were all looking at the old man. 'So,' he said, 'they lived for eleven days, and that Mrs. Watson, she wrote it all down. Yes, they found the notes she made in the tank with her body and the baby's. The Chinese man, he was not far off, his head under a tiny bit o' shade. They'd died o' thirst all right . . .'

He was stirring his tea vigorously. 'A brave woman,' he said, but our father came in and cut him short. 'That was a long time ago,' he said briefly. We were all silent, staring out at the tall harsh grass, and at the river glimmering between its banks.

In the evening, as we returned in drowsy silence to Port Douglas, we rubbed our faces and necks with citronella to deter the mosquitoes, watching, from time to time, the pink and crimson blossoms of the marsh flowers fall and float on the water, and waiting for the moon to rise. In a way, I was glad that we would soon leave the river and its humidity and return to the cooler tablelands. I hadn't liked the story about the children and the floods, and even worse had been the hoarse rapacious bark of the crocodiles during the long hours of darkness. Now the story about poor Mrs. Watson haunted us with its terrible undertones of heat and thirst.

'It's hard,' protested Helen, turning her profile, as noble as our grandmother's, as she leaned her head back against the canvas of the boat. 'It's such a hard life up here, in a way . . . even now . . .' Her voice trailed off.

I was thinking of the time of the flood, when the water would have stretched for miles, and the few human beings would have seemed like tiny dark objects in all that glittering expanse. So it was before, and so it would be again. The great land behind would extend inland from the mountains, on and on into the Center, and then on to the western ocean. To think of such distances made my head spin and ache, and, in spite of the slow movement of the boat, the tropical heat that sometimes grows heavier just as night falls sapped the energy out of the air. I wanted to tell Helen that it wasn't only the deaths we had to worry about, but also this strange vague feeling of helplessness – the empty landscape, and the great desire to forget everything, to drift, and to be mesmerized, and so not to think, and to forget . . .

Our mother and father and Isabel were sitting in front of the boat talking quietly. When Helen protested about the struggle of northern life, Bessie nodded wisely, and shut her eyes behind her glasses. Then she expressed herself, with a firm innocent smile: 'In the north here, children, everything is beginning; everything is waiting for you. Everything!'

7

A World of Water

Looking back now, I realize that all this world of water – which stretched through the Timor and Arafura seas and so to the Timor Strait and the Great Barrier Reef – was in reality a world belonging to Southeast Asia. We did not see it then, but it was from the waters south of New Guinea and bounded by the reef, and marked by a thousand islands and atolls, that we derived a great deal of the folklore of our childhood. These were the gateways from the East, the historic pathways traced by the earliest sailors and discoverers, and did not exactly belong to that Australia which Britain had marked for her own. For us, the sea was our second world – we loved it and swam in it; our forefathers and our friends had helped to explore it. All our lives we had heard of its killings and blackbirdings, its cyclones and wrecks, its isolations which led to death by heat or water. There were also all its peoples – its Aborigines, New Guineans, South Sea Islanders, Malayans, and Timorese. In those days our picturesque northern atmosphere was considered no more than part of the indigenous scenery, adding to Australia's beauty and interest, but having nothing to do with the solid Empire value of the colony!

In the northern land where we lived, it was natural for us to love water. Where the eastern plateaus had been thrust up as the coastal troughs subsided in that great shuddering of the Pliocene Epoch, we were left with mysterious, echoing, truncated cones of old volcanoes, and cool, deep, blue crater lakes encircled with ridges of coarse volcanic ash. These satisfied our urge for freshwater swimming.

Water was always prevalent during the wet season when misty rain enfolded us in the clearings and in the rain forest water dripped eternally from the glistening trees and vines, penetrating our clothes and dampening the hides of our horses if we were riding. The deep rich grasses bent under rain so constant that it was easier for children to go barefoot than to be eternally taking off wet shoes and socks. In the Johnstone River the water smelled of the leaf mold of centuries, and a low but thunderous waterfall tempted us to find little rocky caverns where we could hide behind the curtain of spray and feel ourselves in a world of shimmering light.

But, natural as water was to us on the plateau, it was the coast that lured us – with its connotation of sailing and swimming and reef exploring; with its accent upon wharves and ships, and its promises of trade with the outside world. I don't think that it is an exaggeration to say that we longed for the sea. We could not get to this tropical many-islanded watery life as easily as we wanted to. In the beginning, riding had been our mode of transport. We learned to ride early by tumbling on and off the little Shetland pony that cropped the grass outside the garden, and was easily captured with a carrot or a piece of bread. And, in a sense, as for many in Australia, the rhythm of horses came earlier than that of walking. Although cars soon began to appear on the plateau, we still thought of ourselves as horsemen first. (Out of the far, far past, I remember seeing a faded picture of my twin sisters – both of them wearing small straw hats shaped like mushrooms – slung in baskets on either side of a tame old horse. Apparently this was in preparation for a picnic.) And then, of course, there came the train.

It had seemed a miracle when, at last, after much advertisement, the engine steamed around the bend at Kureen on a particularly sunny day, and cut the ribbon held on one side by a local official and on the other by my little brother, who was at the time only two years old, and who wore for the ceremony a cream-colored sailor suit made of tussore and had his fair hair cut in an intriguing Dutch bob, square across his forehead. During the wet season, before we could get onto the train, we would run down the hill with bare feet, perhaps muffled in light coats and with handkerchiefs on our heads, wash our feet under the tap attached to the galvanized iron tank that stood beside the station office; dry our feet with a towel we had carried; put on our shoes and socks in the tiny wooden waiting room; comb out our hair; and emerge, like butterflies from chrysalises, ready to step demurely into one of the carriages.

Not long ago a photograph was unearthed from an attic in Malanda. It showed the Kureen railway siding on that long-ago day when the pioneers gathered to see their railroad opened. It showed women in large hats and long skirts and button boots. It showed men with mustaches, some wearing stiff shirts without collars, held at the neck with studs. The whole group seemed strong and young, but the men looked especially sunburnt, and the very muscles that had cut down the trees strained beneath their coats. Around them the stumps were grouped, as if by their amputation alone this handful of human beings had been allowed to exist. The station building was so tiny that it was almost lost behind the pioneers intent upon using it.

As soon as the railway was built and linked up to our own area, we could get to the coast by making the slow daylong journey to the small but growing port of Cairns, which had once been only a row of tents and wooden huts on a sandy ridge, surrounded by mangroves and almost completely flooded at high tide. But before we could set out, there was the ever-present farm and milk work, the supervision of the dairies and the crops, and the keeping up with orders for the mill – to which the huge logs drawn from the scrubs were pulled, slowly, slowly, on the bullock wagons, and then cut up into timber to be shipped down to the coast. To watch the infinitely dilatory progress of these wagons, to catch on the air the long-drawn echo of the bullocky's litany, and the crack of his greenhide

112

whip, was to be forcibly reminded always of the tedious pioneer lifestyle.

In our time Cairns had a 'real' hotel, which was known as Hides. Its wooden passages were a little uneven, its verandas sloped slightly toward the street. In the dining room the tables were spread with damask cloths, and starched serviettes sprouted like flowers from the glasses. On the walls were photographs of the premiers of Queensland and local celebrities with beards and watchchains draping their shirtfronts. Outside the hotel the streets were sandy and white in the glaring tropical sun, which hurt our eyes after the soft light of the tablelands; this sharp sun contrasted with the gloomy darkness of the huge fig trees under which women, walking slowly in the heat, encountered each other, unfurling their umbrellas for a moment to exchange the latest news. These streets were lined with primitive but spacious wooden buildings – their iron roofs glittering, their long stairways plunging down from latticework verandas to the ground. In the main street a draper's shop predominated, with old-fashioned merchandise in its windows. A machinery shop carried cane knives, and guns and farm implements, cream separators and small water pumps. There was also a teashop, with 'Café' written in gold script across the windows, where dust gathered on tired-looking chocolate boxes.

We loved to visit the tiny shrine of the newsagent, which had blocks of pink and white coconut ice for sale, and sticks of licorice in glass jars, as well as out-of-date weeklies from further south – that is, from Townsville or Bowen or Mackay. Here we would occasionally buy a bag of cherries – a romantic fruit, because cherries were grown only in the cooler uplands of New South Wales and Victoria. The cherries would have been kept on a piece of ice wrapped in sacking, to prevent them from deteriorating during the long trip to the tropical north. When we bought them we would stroll along the streets together popping chilly cherries into our mouths, while my father scanned the weeklies as we walked, making comments about how empty they were of real news, and about how badly propaganda for the north was handled ('Go North, Young Man' and 'Be a Man and Have a Go at the North').

Toward the end of town the buildings grew smaller; their roofs were slanted and made of rusty iron. Some of them were owned by Italians and others by Chinese. The Chinese shops had a certain mystery about them – they were dark and smelled of overripe bananas, and sold tea and scarlet-papered boxes of crackers, and lichee nuts, and, perhaps, opium.

In Cairns, when we didn't stay at the hotel, we sometimes spent a night or two at a certain rambling wooden boardinghouse on the Esplanade, where many beds were placed on the verandas and festooned with snowy-white mosquito nets. We would get up at six in the morning, and if the tide was high, we would join the early risers in the public baths, where we splashed and dived in the warm salty water, were pushed by wavelets against the rough pilings and wire netting, got sand and seaweed in our hair, and finally walked back along the edge of the inlet, past gardens filled with brilliant flowers and speckled crotons, with cascara and jacaranda trees showering petals onto the lawns. After that came the hearty boardinghouse breakfast – porridge and eggs, bacon and sausage, hot strong tea in coarse china cups. My father would deplore the thin powdered milk they served (milk from the tablelands would not keep during the long hot journey to the coast) and he would enlarge upon one of his future projects, which was to institute a freezing plant so that milk could be chilled and sent all the way down to Townsville, where, during those years, the big white P&O liners were beginning to carry travelers around the world.

On those days in Cairns our father would also expatiate about the 'Great White Way' – a dream road he hoped to see descending the gorge of the Barron, winding from the tablelands to the future 'city' of Cairns, and so not only carrying down the produce of the pioneer farmers to market but also bringing up ignorant southerners to show them the beauties of the inland north. Enamored of ancient history as he was, I think that he imagined the 'Great White Way' as the Appian Way – the highway from Rome to Brindisi, the oldest and most famous of Roman roads, built there centuries before the birth of Christ. He continually boosted the idea of such a road, stretching majestically from our own humble muddy red tracks on the tableland to the soon-to-be-enlarged wharves of Cairns, and perhaps far down the eastern coast. He spoke with wonder and awe of what the Romans had done. How could we in the North do less! It was clear that such a road would simplify our lives, although it seemed, at the time, an impossible dream. (The cost of the railway had been bad enough. 'A million and a quarter,' our father said. 'But that was nothing compared to the patient toil, and the great avalanches of earth sliding down during the wet season, and the lives of men lost on those perpendicular cliffs, and the attempt to put up the strong but frail-seeming bridges over the abyss of the Barron!')

Road or no road, the railway provided tablelanders with a very epic descent. The long journey would land us, just at twilight, at a little station called Redlynch, where a buckboard with horses would be waiting to carry us to Trinity Beach, the site of a smallish wooden cottage on top of a cliff, looking over the sea. At this point of the coast, a channel of perhaps ten miles separated us from the Great Barrier Reef, and against the horizon rose the curious shape of what we called Double Island – looking like two hills joined together, or like the two humps on the back of a camel. This island, which had originally formed part of the mainland, owed some of its beauty and its character to that fact – to the long-ago geological uplift and subsidence, some of the land sinking and some uprising, so that the large islands of the immediate coast were simply pieces of the old continent sticking up above the water. Beyond them, in a complex rhythmic pattern, spread the reef proper, two hundred or more cays and atolls formed by coral and detritus anchored by vegetation, and enclosing in smooth crystal-clear lagoons thousands of forms of reef life – anemones, starfish, and tiny darting coral fish of brilliant colors – as a garden might hold flowers. On the seaward side, the delicate many-colored life ceased abruptly; the resistant coral wall sloped quickly to great depths, and was met by the whole force of the ocean, so that it was loud with the roar of leaping surf.

The buckboard, on its way to Double Island, moved slowly along the sandy road, which was white under the moon and bordered on either side by pale, mysterious paperbarks. The horses splashed through little creeks, and we smelled the rank smell of mangroves. At last, we reached the cottage outlined against the sky, where a man holding a lantern waited on the veranda. To visualize those holidays was to obliterate what was more mundane, and to remember only the brilliant shining path of the moon burning its way across the Coral Sea, past the humped shape of Double Island, and straight onto our veranda.

'What are you staring at?' one of my sisters would ask.

'I can't help staring.'

'It's only the *moon*.'

'I know it's only the moon. But look how bright it is! It's like magic . . .'

'It reflects the light of the sea,' suggested Hazel sensibly.

'Besides,' our brother Tracey added, 'the moon is full tonight.' He sat sprawled on the veranda ledge, his legs stretched out in front of him. He had been given the little outside room to sleep in – the room with no proper ceiling, just bare rafters beneath the iron roof. But he didn't complain, only shrugged his shoulders and smiled his kind smile. Something told me that I didn't really know him; in my childish way I thought of him with pain and guilt.

By the time we were all falling asleep, subdued after the long day in the train, the jolting journey in the buckboard, we were already feeling that sensual battering which holidays meant to us then – a rhythm of wild running and leaping and climbing, up and down the rocky face stretching up from

116

the sea to the cottage on its summit; a cycle of sleeping and swimming and eating embellished only by the ritualistic burning of our skins. Soon the coarse wool bathing suits would be perennially damp, would hang – smelling of salt, in scorching sun and pelting downpours – on the little line near the woodpile where Tracey chopped the box trees to burn in the iron stove. Under the smoky walls of the kitchen, her face reflecting the heat, my mother cooked the fresh fish we ate each morning and most nights.

Behind the house there was a path which led to the bay. It was actually called Chinaman's Bay, but I never saw a Chinaman there, only an occasional fisherman who rowed out to the traps, or into reef waters to catch the coral cod, bright red, with markings of electric blue, or the king snapper, with its bands of scarlet upon pinkish silver scales. The fishermen brought their catch up to us early in the morning in a wet salty bag. Sometimes they brought blue crabs – as large as dinner plates, with enormous heavy claws – and these my mother (shutting her eyes in pain) dropped one by one into a kerosene tin of boiling water. I would hear them give one long last sigh as they died, and a string of silvery bubbles would rise to the top of the scalding water. Because it seemed odd to observe my gentle mother taking part in this cruel operation, I held my breath as she did it, trying to pretend that it had not happened. Afterward all dark thoughts were forgotten, for the coral cod had a rich white flesh that tasted wonderful in golden batter, and the crabs were eaten with a thick lemony sauce or failing that, served cold with vinegar and parsley.

As we walked down to the bay we smelled the rank rotting smell of the inlet and felt under our feet the white sand of the track, over which hung huge tamarind trees, heavy with furred brown pods that could be boiled or crushed to make a pleasant acid drink. Long before the British reached the northern shores, these trees had been planted, probably by the Macassarmen, who arrived every year with the trade winds, looking for dugong or trepang (sea cucumbers, as they were called), swept along in their raftlike boats, mounted with one small cabin in which men, women, children, and perhaps dogs all huddled together. These early traders made their seasonal camps on Australian shores. They built fires to dry their trepang, mingled and traded with the Aborigines, and along with their Eastern features, they left tiny tamarind trees to mark their passage. We didn't care much about the tamarind but thought, instead, of the big old crocodile who lived in the mangroves, where a tiny salt stream trickled out into bay waters. It was a huge estuarine crocodile, like those we had seen and heard on the Daintree River, and I hated it when my older and bolder sisters beat with a stick on one of the paperbark trees, and called out loudly, 'Come out . . . Come out there . . . Let's have a *look* at you!'

Even the placid shut-in bay had its dangers. One day when our grandmother was at Double Island with us, she sat beside a gum tree, and I remember the white splash of her button-up blouse under the speckled shade, and a long hatpin with a shiny bead at the end, which held the hat she wore perched over her forehead. Suddenly she said that she would give a prize of five shillings to whoever floated on their back for the longest time. We at once took up the challenge, and I was determined to win. I remember that I almost fell into a dream of floating in the warm still water, until I was lonely enough to open my eyes, and saw my grandmother on the shore, waving her hat wildly in the air. Everyone else was out of the water, so I ran out too, and asked, 'Granny, did I win the five shillings?' They looked at me with a kind of horror.

'You won all right!' Hazel said. 'There was a shark circling round and round you.'

'I *saw* its fin going *round* and *round*,' one of the twins added solemnly.

'We *did* shout, darling,' our grandmother said in a faint voice.

'I would have gone in,' Hazel said, smiling with relief, 'but it wasn't *necessary*.'

Even Hazel, the tallest and the best swimmer, might have been vulnerable in this tropical water, where there were, after all, many hazards besides sharks – barracuda, stonefish, gropers, and rays of various kinds with trailing tentacles so fine it was hard to see them in stormy weather. One day I came sliding and slipping down the steep face of the rocky cliff to see Hazel running in circles on the beach, and everyone else coming out of the water to find out what was the matter with her. She was tearing at her bathing suit and screaming, and I saw my mother throw a big towel over her and help her to roll naked on the sand so that she could scrape off what was causing so much agony. We had been told that rough sand was the best thing to rub off the delicate hairlike barbs which clung to the appendages of the poisonous jellyfish which at certain times of the year rocked here in the tide. I remember only Hazel's screams and the red weals on her flesh, and later her slow sobbing as my mother rubbed her with oil of some kind. It was always said that Queensland not only had more poisonous snakes (six hundred different varieties) than any other part of Australia but had perhaps more than any other part of the world; and that it also had in the waters around it the most poisonous jellyfish on the globe – especially here, where the islands and the intricacies of the reef acted as a conduit for them during the wet season. Most poisonous of all, and the most immediate in its effect (more so than the evil-looking grayish-brown stonefish which clung to the shallow waters), was what was called sea wasp or box jelly. This creature was squarish and white, and dangled its long, delicate, almost transparent tentacles like one of those box kites that trail long strings behind them. In rough waters this box jelly is not easily seen, but in the dark mangrove-fringed inlets of the northern estuaries, it stands out in the black water like some pallid and beautiful angel of death. I was to see many of them in later years on the western shore of the Gulf of Carpentaria, where, on hot days, the Aboriginal children don't hesitate to jump off the old wooden jetties as if no such danger existed.

119

(In the 1960s when I was visiting the bauxite mine at Weipa on the Gulf coast, such a little boy from Mapoon village, about seven years old, jumped in and almost immediately rose again screaming with pain. He was dragged out and died within five minutes, his body striped with the terrible scars which come from the whiplike cords of the creature's tentacles, his lungs paralyzed by the poison.)

During the days we spent at the beach, my father, who had written away to India for some mango seeds, planted fourteen varieties on a hillside he had bought some years before. It was a great pleasure to us when we returned, year after year, to pick the young green coconuts on the beach so that we could drink their milk, and then to leave the hot sand and the crackling groves and walk slowly up the hill to where the mango trees stretched like umbrellas, their branches mingling in deepest shade. The ripe mangoes – the big green turpentines, the flat-sided Manilas, and the small rosy strawberry mangoes – fell easily to the ground and it seemed that we could eat them forever in this air heavy with their perfume, the yellow juice staining our faces and our fingers. This dreamlike state was renewed at dusk if we had our supper by the sea, sitting between two small fires as the Aborigines did, roasting fish and tearing it apart, listening to the tide lisping on the sand, and waiting for the billy to boil.

On other days we would go to the islands of the reef, to visit the atolls at the time when the birds were nesting, when the sandy surfaces were so honeycombed that we could scarcely walk without crunching eggs under our feet. Occasionally we would cross to one of the mainland islands with hunters of the Torres Strait pigeons; just at dusk the flocks came homing to the nutmeg trees. Professionals would smear the branches with a sort of glue they called lime, and the birds' feet would become so entangled that they couldn't fly. I hated to see this, because the laden sacks of captive birds heaved before my eyes on the ground and because the idea of captivity is alien to the free child.

'It is cruel, cruel,' I would say to my father, and he would tell me not to watch it, and my mother would say, 'So it is, so it is,' and when I was little I would hide my face against her skirt.

Even the big game fish had more chance than these birds had, for when the men went trolling with a hard cord line to catch the huge Spanish mackerel, the fish leapt and shimmered in the sun and, unless they were carefully played until they were tired enough to be dragged aboard, sometimes escaped. Yet I knew that the hunters and fishermen were heroes, too, who fought for their lives, and were sometimes lost in storms and accidents.

One evening as we came home from the reef in someone else's boat, a terrible storm arose and an ominous black cloud, edged with a strange electric green, bore down upon us and seemed to pursue us like a fury as we made across the channel for the mainland. We children were sitting near the rail of the boat in our bathing suits, and the coming storm whipped our wet hair back and stung our sunburned faces.

'You all go down,' ordered my father. 'Get down in that cabin with your mother and shut the door. Quickly now!'

'Oh, Daddy, oh no, it's fun here, we want to stay here!'

The boat was plunging like a terrified horse, and we clung like demons to the railings, raising our faces to drink the rain, feeling joy at the pelting water that beat on our eyelids.

'Go *down!*' he shouted to us as he struggled to help the man who owned the boat and the black boy who steered it. 'It's a bad storm . . . It's easy to slip . . . Now go down below!'

We all began to sing, and pretended not to hear him in the tumult of the wind and the rain and our voices. In the end he let us stay – proud, I think, that while two other children on the boat were safely in the cabin with their mother, and *our* mother, *his* children were braving it out on deck. Although my mother was more timid than my father, she did her best to be a true Australian woman and to pretend on such occasions that nothing at all was happening. I think she sometimes wondered how it was that she had brought such active, obstreperous, and daring children into the world.

We didn't get back to the bay that night until it was nearly dark. Because of the high tides, we had to berth at a different jetty, an old stone one covered with oyster shells. In the screaming wind, I was glad to be treated like a little girl again, letting my father carry me and plant me safely beyond the slippery rocks overgrown with razor-sharp shells and onto the bay sand. The wind shrieked. The boat plunged at its anchor. The black boy held up an acetylene lantern to guide my father's passage to the shore.

There was talk next day of the tail end of a cyclone, and when we went outside after breakfast we found the ground swept clean as if a great broom had brushed the sand and left it shining and clear of pebbles and grass. Around the coconut trees on the headlands we found sheets of galvanized iron wrapped as if they had been as pliable as paper.

The area in which we lived was famous for its cyclones, especially in those key months of February and March, when the big winds came sweeping into Cyclone Alley and headed south. The classic Coral Sea cyclone is a parabola, curving to the coast, swinging south as it nears land, and turning away again to the southeast. But it is always hard to predict what will happen, for great whirlpools of air spring up from isolated low-pressure areas, and into these the surrounding air spirals turn in a clockwise direction, creating unpredictable patterns of movement. People and animals are killed by these dreadful storms – by shipwreck and floods, by what are called storm surges, and by sweeping tidal waves.

Surviving legends among the Aborigines tell of rivers bursting their banks, of 'big-feller waters' spreading across broad valleys, of the tribes being driven up into the hills, of Aboriginal camps being inundated when the surge tides ran head-on into swollen rivers boiling with mud and trees. At first the settlers smiled at these tribal tales, some of them so old that it was impossible to tell how long they had been told. But soon the newcomers found out for themselves that, especially in this northern corner, legend was less than reality.

When big blows came, people could be thrown off their feet, or bowled along the streets; whole buildings would be lifted from their blocks; herds of cattle swept away; ships driven onto beaches; people killed inside their houses as the beams collapsed; or else carried off and drowned by twenty-five-foot walls of water. In the few days of cyclone intensity, fifty to one hundred inches of rain would fall, and so much fresh water would pour into the ocean that rolling rivers of it floated on top of the sea – killing the marine life for miles around.

Although the tablelands seldom suffered as much as the coast did, we were respectful enough at the approach of any storm.

'Look,' my father would say, pointing out a dark cloud, edged with that familiar black-green, on the horizon. We would rein in our horses to feel the wind freshening; then we would turn them and give them their heads – better to be caught at home than out in the open where the trees might crash around us.

We never underestimated what wind could do up on this ledge above the Pacific – although here the rain forests sheltered us, and behind us stood the barrier of the Great Divide. There were no scientific forecasts in those days and we had nothing but the sky to warn us, or the odd rumor from the coast, or the old stories which stretched back in time. We had heard of the great disaster of Princess Charlotte Bay – that lonely open bay on the eastern shore of the Cape York Peninsula – where, one Saturday evening in 1899, before our parents had come north, the pearling fleets had gathered for a night of drumming and singing after the week's taking of shell. Then, almost without preparation, as that calm sweltering day came to an end, a strangely shaped cloud threw an odd shadow over the glistening water.

123

'The Islanders and the Aborigines knew that it was Kooinar,' our mother said, 'the great flattener of trees, as they called it.'

'If they knew, couldn't they prepare for it?' one of us asked.

'I don't think they could; all the boats were exposed . . . There was a white constable named Kenny who was in charge of the Eight Mile police station and he was about to spend the night above the shore at Barrow Point with his troopers, but they were awakened by the screaming of the wind and their tents were blown away and they had to crouch in the open away from the crashing trees . . . They said that about five in the morning a great white ghostly wave came sweeping from the sea and seemed to rear up in the air and then to roll over the landscape. They said that trees, branches, and large live fish swirled about them. It was a forty-eight-foot storm surge that reached three miles inland, killing game and horses, leaving sharks, dugong, sea snakes, and seabirds in its wake.'

'How terrible to see that wave,' Hazel said.

We all agreed to this, not only because most Australian swimmers had a healthy respect for the power of the sea but because we had been taught the necessity of swimming directly toward the oncoming wave, so as not to be caught in its curve and dumped onto the beach. But such a wave as this – how cope with it at all?

The coastal activities which formed so important a part of our lives and which drew us, as children, further and further afield to more and more islands on the reef, to further exploration of the coast to the north and the coast to the south, drew us also into more and more consciousness of the adult world. At first we took only short trips by motorized boats, or a passage on some coastal steamer, and it was common to see in the reef channel the great spouts of water sent into the air by the blowing of the blue whales, and the agitation of the water surface by the thrashing of these creatures' tails. All around the larger boats, shoals of dolphins would play and leap, their shining curvaceous bodies so full of energy that they seemed unable to contain their muscular joy. Once on a deck, when I was small enough to see through the railings, I stared at the horizon and watched some sort of contest played out between a giant swordfish and what looked like a great shark – their silhouettes dark on the sky as they leapt into the air in what was probably a duel to the death. The great serrated cartilaginous projection of the swordfish was clearly seen and was itself about six feet long; and the broad powerful shape of its antagonist twisted in the air as if to escape any possible thrust. I remember also being lifted from my bunk at night and carried on deck to watch the waters at the boat's stern, brilliant from phosphorescence, glittering as the waves broke, like diamonds poured from a giant's hand . . .

These water images were, of course, strictly northern, and at first, because I had not traveled far, I half believed that the whole world was like this untamed area – that is, either full of blazing tropical sunshine or else in the process of being drowned in floods and storms. For it was only here that we faced the strange somewhat cruel north, the multitude of unknown islands, the two-hundred-mile-wide finger of Cape York pointing up from Princess Charlotte Bay on the east, and the embroidery of the reef spreading to the very shores of New Guinea . . .

One day news arrived that a great scientific expedition was to come to Australia from Cambridge University with the aim of studying the natural life of the Great Barrier Reef. A camp was to be set up on Low Woodie Island (about forty-five miles north of Cairns) and a team of scientists led by a certain Dr. David Yonge and his wife would live and work for six months registering the tides and climatic conditions; observing the habits and conditions of fish, mollusks, corals, etc.; collecting specimens from the reef itself; and, in general, carrying back, as Darwin had done long ago, information to European scientific circles. I don't know how my mother and father were involved in the local arrangements for this expedition, but my father was among those who greeted Dr. Yonge in Cairns, and it was afterward decided that the family should all visit the island and see the scientists at work.

The Great Barrier Reef lies like a protective shield along the coast of Queensland, stretching for more than a thousand miles from New Guinea to the Tropic of Capricorn in the south. It is the largest feature of its kind in the world, and its beauties are completely visible only to the underwater explorer. I thought of this reef with childish wonder and delight, and on the intricate, extended stony rampart between the ocean and the tropical lagoons – in a fierce light that pierced the water like golden daggers – it was possible to feel divorced from the ordinary earth and completely native to a mysterious watery kingdom.

On this particular day at Low Woodie Island, where the expedition had set up its laboratory, we sat with the scientists under the speckled gray-boled pisonia trees to have morning tea. David Yonge and his assistant workers, growing beards in the island isolation, wore baggy English shorts and usually went around barefoot. Mrs. Yonge, a charming woman with dark bobbed hair and an attractive profile, was also barefoot and dressed in the same practical manner as the men. She had that confident air women possess when their professional interests put them on the same level as their husbands, and there was something else about her as well – something offhand and boyish, suggesting an intellectual liberation that Australian women had still not attained.

'Yes, she's doing very well,' her husband said with a smile, in answer to a question from our father. 'She's a scientist, too, you know.' He addressed her. 'You find it jolly, don't you, dear?'

'Quite jolly,' admitted his wife.

'She does all the housekeeping as well,' Dr. Yonge said.

'Well, housekeeping ...' Mrs. Yonge made a grimace, and swept the view with her hand – the top of the small cay only about six feet above the water, the camp behind us, the bathroom hut, a lizard on a sheet of iron in the sun, the expanse of sand with its tiny biting sand flies, and the lighthouse in the distance. Beyond that, nothing but Pacific water. She bent her neat bobbed head toward my mother.

'I order the groceries from Cairns, Mrs. Heale, and we get all the bread and the meat from Port Douglas ... But Gracie cooks.' (Gracie was a half-Aboriginal woman who had just brought the tea out on an improvised tray.)

Accompanied by the youngest and blondest assistant – whose face, arms, and legs were of a deep strawberry pink from the tropical sun – Dr. Yonge took us down to inspect the dinghy, which was fitted with an air pump and held a large diving helmet.

'This is how we collect our specimens. Someone dives with the helmet on, and someone else works the machine in the boat and keeps him supplied with air.'

'Unless the chap in the boat goes to sleep.' This was obviously an 'in' joke, and there was a good-natured roar of laughter.

Later, at low tide, I caught up with Mrs. Yonge on the reef and showed her the collection of creatures I had sloshing about in my bucket – a hairy-looking hermit crab, a starfish of a brilliant blue, tiny coral fish caught as the tide ebbed, and a baby swordfish, about four inches long, sword and all, which I had picked out from under a coral knob. It seemed impossible to believe that this tiny creature could ever grow into a great game fish such as the one I had seen long ago leaping above the channel waters.

'It *is* a swordfish,' Mrs. Yonge affirmed kindly. 'Here on the reef small fish have perfect growing conditions. In fact, the reef is like a nursery for the fish of the Pacific.'

We wandered for a while, staring into the pools where anemones put out their fine poisonous hairlike tentacles to paralyze small marine creatures for future devouring. Mrs. Yonge pointed out the minute, brightly colored fish that

127

were darting unafraid in and out of the dangerous petal-like tentacles of the anemones.

'They have become immune to the effect of the poison, and so can shelter close to their anemone host. It's all a matter of development.' She indicated another, larger fish with a dark eye mark on its tail. 'That's the beaked coral fish. The idea of the mark is to confuse predators about the direction in which the fish is traveling.'

'Look,' she insisted again, 'adaptation goes on everywhere . . . See how bright this fish is? Color frightens off intruders; but still it's got a venomous spine for good measure.'

As she spoke, it seemed that big and little fish, odd colors and shapes, the sea anemones, the very gardens of coral themselves, took their correct place in the universe. She reminded me that nothing had happened in a haphazard manner. The water had grown shallower in the Pleistocene Epoch, to the exact depth necessary for the growth of coral, and after that had come a spurt in the building of the reef. 'That was half a million years ago . . . Although this reef is one of the finest in the world, it is not the only place where coral is found in large amounts. You can find coral in deep valleys and at the tops of mountains. You can find it where there is not a drop of water. You can walk on your own Australian mainland and see stones with the same structure as the coral has right here . . . So,' she said with a little laugh, 'human beings are not so important, are they?'

On the way home on the boat late that afternoon, I tried to tell my father, who was sitting beside me, how Mrs. Yonge had made me feel.

'It's only the scientific way,' my father said. 'Did you see all the specimens in bottles? Well – in a way – science puts us all in bottles.'

'Dr. Yonge was surprised,' I said, 'by what he called a giant clam, but the clam was only *four* feet long!'

'Yes,' my father said, 'they should have been here in the early days.'

Years before, we had all been at Double Island and had gone at dawn to the reef – the boat cutting through the calm water, landing us at the end of one of the atolls. The sun hadn't quite risen, and we ate breakfast there on the rocks while the water receded, leaving the reef rich and bare to our gaze. I remembered seeing the giant clams – how they stood there at intervals, like primitive monuments – most of them as tall as a man, some taller – huge bivalves with coarse, convoluted, ripple-edged shells. I remember my father saying, 'They are the biggest mollusks in the world!' An Aboriginal had helped run the boat, and he invited me to come close to one of the shells, which was lying open to reveal the great mantle of gelatinous light brown flesh, quivering like lace and spotted with brilliant emerald.

'Big-feller fish,' the Aboriginal said to me, while holding me back with one hand. 'Alla time jump, jump, jump.'

Then he indicated the hinge at the back of the shell, and prodded the creature with his stick so that the great lid crashed shut with tremendous force and the stick broke in two. I jumped back, frightened. At times fishermen had been caught when these shells closed, and were held there until the tide came in and they were drowned. On that faraway morning the reef had seemed a place of ominous sacrifice, a temple of the past, pagan in its rich and strange variety. 'A pair of these shells were taken to St. Sulpice in Paris,' my father said, 'to hold holy water for the cathedral!'

Now my father and I sat alone at the end of the boat, with the red sun sinking to stain the water, and we seemed like two members of a dying tribe.

'The boats began to come from Southeast Asia,' he said, 'all along through the Torres Strait, and into reef waters, looking for trochus shell, and bêche-de-mer, and clam meat. They broke up the big clams and carried away the flesh. Few people have seen them as we have seen them.'

8

Doomed to Happiness

Perhaps it has not yet been decided whether boarding schools are really advantageous to small children. At any event, however much we might have felt at home in the hills of Herberton, at this now established school, and however much we might have taken over that mantle of behavior expected of us at a church institution, we often felt lonely there. Emotion, while not frowned upon, was not exactly encouraged. To add to the spartan school atmosphere, there was something forbidding about those resolute ranges, against which the primitive wooden buildings thrust into the sky; and the skies themselves, behind the dark hills, although stained with bright colors at sunset, imposed their own somber, slightly savage accent. When the sad pealing of the church bell called us to evensong, we walked under the shadow of the harsh turpentine trees to the chapel, our white veils fluttering, our faces decorous; while the dignified figure of the Bush Brother awaited us in his robes at the altar. Then we heard the solemn words of the Lord's Prayer ascend toward the roof, followed by the *Gloria in excelsis* ('O Lord, open thou our lips, and our mouths shall show forth thy praise'), the *Magnificat*, the psalm, and, last of all, the *Nunc dimittis* ('Now lettest thou thy servant depart in peace, according to thy word') – noble admonitions that sent us away with the seal of approval set upon the day.

For a short time there had been five children from our family of six at St. Mary's. The youngest, Robin, was still at home, and Tracey, the only boy at the school, was rapidly withdrawn. I think my father, in an excess of enthusiasm for private schools in the north, had sent him as a gesture only.

130

Certainly the remaining four of us added up to a healthy percentage of the first school population, and only later were we able to merge gracefully into the ever-growing ranks of pupils, who looked somewhat alike in their navy-blue cambric uniforms laced up with tan cords and panama hats bearing bands embroidered with the school shield. Because going away to school when we were so young (six or seven) had separated us early from our parents, it also made clear – in that objective state that boarding school encourages – that we were little people on our own, responsible for our own good behavior, and required to be 'affable' to those around us.

I remember the effect of this official, if gentle coercion – it is comparatively easy to make children sober. But while it suppressed us, it also helped us to enjoy what the outer world had to offer. 'We must *look* all right,' our eldest sister, Hazel, said on Sundays as she lined the three of us up outside the school gate to inspect our collars, our faces, and the shininess of our shoes. Before us stretched the gravelly white road that wandered down the hill to the town. To the right another road turned off to ascend another hill, at the top of which our Uncle John Newell had built the house he called Elderslie. It was this John Newell, an uncle by marriage only (his wife was the sister of Auntie Bea, Uncle Tony's wife), who had long ago swum the Wild River at midnight and hastened through the bush to register the claim to the Great Northern tin mine.

To reach his road we passed the buildings of the Roman Catholic convent, where numerous paths spread out, and various colored replicas of saints were scattered, in what we might have been encouraged to feel was an 'overindulgent' way. Our sense of superiority (which told us that we were after all members of the 'in' religion) meant that we did not dwell on the fact that the girls on the convent side had been coached likewise, not to admire *us*. Later, one girl who went to the Roman Catholic convent told me that she had felt that to enter our gates (not to speak of the doorway of our chapel) might, unless accompanied by special permission, be considered a mortal sin.

The little gate at the bottom of the Elderslie garden was unlatched. We entered, I always felt, to a green peace, diametrically opposed to the atmosphere in the school grounds, where grass scarcely grew and where our feet pounded wildly over the gravel – especially when the bell clanged for meals, or between classes when a prefect holding a great basin of bread slices, sparsely spread with jam, would advance toward the shouting pupils.

But these harsh voices were left behind when at Elderslie we walked under the great boughs of the jacaranda tree – at blooming time spreading a carpet of lavender under our feet – and mounted the stone steps near the tennis court, past wooden tubs of hydrangeas and a fence overgrown with blossoms of cup of gold. We were given tea in the living room, and saw again familiar items of furniture – a shining piano, bent-cane chairs with satin cushions, portraits of various members of the family in round gold frames. We explored the back part of the house, where the kitchen and laundry lay in the drowsy afternoon sunshine, with a cat asleep by the stove and the white wooden tables worn thin by scrubbing, rooms more tranquil and lavish than our own kitchen and laundry at home. The Elderslie house was well built and appeared prosperous, besides having a commanding outlook over the town. The veranda had pleasant white lattice railings through which one could see the flowers in the garden, the bedrooms had brass beds with shiny knobs and soft satin eiderdowns in pastel colors – and always the scent of eau de cologne and talcum powder and bay rum.

Uncle John Newell, with his Vandyke beard and small bright eyes, sometimes wearing a soft gray English cardigan, would greet us kindly. His wife, whom we called Auntie Gen, was handsome and bosomy, with a wholesome head of hair pinned up on her head with celluloid pins and combs. She was so like Auntie Bea (whom we saw more frequently because she lived closer to us) that I might have mixed them up. They both tended to wear cameo brooches, lace at their necks, and watches on chains suspended from their button-holes. Generous to us when we came hungry from school, Auntie Gen gave us Sunday suppers of cold meat, pan-fried potatoes, salads, and homemade chutneys; the desserts were quite unlike the pallid blancmanges served at school. There was an air of restraint in their household, which, young as I was, sometimes struck me as unexciting; but to sit in the garden under the jacaranda tree, to be wrapped for a while in a sense of lavish comfort after the bare clamorous tumult of the dormitories and schoolrooms, was like a warm rest from what sometimes seemed to us a life of struggle.

Behind these visits with my sisters to Elderslie, and separate from them, are memories associated with my real cousin, Maidie Linedale, the daughter of Uncle Tony. At some point in my childhood, Maidie had adopted me.

She must have been at least fifteen years older than I was and I was first conscious of her devotion one afternoon when she sat stitching at a gray linen bag, with pockets all around it, upon which she was embroidering my initials in white thread. When it was finished I was faintly disappointed, because I learned that it was to be my 'sewing' bag, and was to hold reels of cotton, hanks of wool, ordinary needles and darning needles, pieces of elastic, a measuring tape, and a pair of scissors. It was the first attempt on anyone's part to turn me into a tidy and competent little female, someone who was not reduced to putting up a plunging hem with safety pins or wearing socks that had holes in the heels. Perhaps the attempt reminded me that my mother had a lot of children and couldn't be expected to do everything for them; so that immediately I had a clear memory of my mother – as we said good night to her after a long day – sitting half asleep, the lids drooping over her deep-cut eyes, and her worn hands lying in her lap on top of a pile of unfinished mending.

Maidie, who was round-faced with pink cheeks, brown hair, and sympathetic brown eyes, had no sisters, and I

133

remember now how she exuded a femininity more potent and more ready for motherhood than either of Auntie Gen's daughters or, indeed, than most of her younger cousins, including ourselves. Perhaps I knew that she was drawn to mother me, less because she thought that I needed it – coming as I did in the middle of the family and having my share of shy reserve – than because she herself needed to mother someone.

We were all sitting under the jacaranda tree one afternoon at Elderslie, with the late sunshine piercing the green shadows of the garden and catching the glitter of teaspoons on the afternoon tea tray. The older generation was not there, but all of the younger Newells were present – Isabel and Peggy, and Bun and William – along with Maidie (up from Atherton) with her brown hair straying from the knot on her neck, and dimples showing in her cheeks. I was there as a little offsider, visiting Maidie, I suppose, and there was a tall, lanky, muscled young man called Maurice, whose Irish and Catholic parents owned the property next door to Beecroft, Uncle Tony and Aunt Bea's house on the outskirts of Atherton. Everyone had been playing tennis and the racquets were strewn about on the grass, but for a long time now there had been nothing but tea and conversation, and I remember wondering why Maurice was sitting so close to Maidie, and hoping that he would soon go away. At the same time I knew that Maurice was handsome, with his dark curly hair and white teeth and his beautiful long-lashed blue eyes.

'The child has so many mosquito bites,' Isabel said, frowning and running her hand down my bare legs.

'I know,' Maidie said, glancing toward her cousin over my head. 'We've had so many mosquitoes lately, it's been like a plague; perhaps I should put her in long trousers for a while ... I was even afraid she'd get blood poisoning, she had so many bites ... I bought some cod-liver oil and malt at the chemist's in Atherton. Dr. Nye recommended it.'

'How *is* that charming Dr. Nye?' Isabel asked, laughing a little.

Maidie blushed. 'He's very busy,' she said simply. Dr. Nye was the new bachelor doctor in Atherton, and a friend of my father and mother. I remembered his coming to Maidie's house in Atherton, a tall hawk-nosed man with keen black eyes and black hair slicked straight back from his forehead. Maidie had been at the piano, on the top of which a great bowl of roses tumbled their colors together, singing one of those songs popular at the time – perhaps it was 'On the road to Mandalay, / Where the flyin' fishes play' – and she had blushed the color of the roses themselves as the doctor turned the pages for her.

Another memory seems to be confused with this one. Maidie was taking me and some of my sisters to the dentist in Atherton – an itinerant dentist who had come to the town and rented an office, which was continually filled with all the people of the district, who had necessarily neglected their teeth for too long. I had never been to a dentist before and I was afraid, but Maidie, in her gentle skillful way, had promised me five shillings to spend if I gave in and didn't cry. In the end, rather than remembering the pain of the drill or the extractions, I remembered the cheap tin bracelets with which I had been able to festoon my thin little arms, and the jujubes I'd been able to buy, and the copies of *The Schoolgirl's Own*, which was the right thing to read at St. Mary's. The five shillings had gone long before it was time to climb onto the dreaded dentist's padded chair.

It was not only jealousy that made me so conscious that afternoon at Elderslie that Maurice somehow threatened the way I was looked after by Maidie (rather as if she were my mother, and not my cousin). It was more that I sensed a material world advancing toward me, a world I could not slow up or hinder, the world of the future, whose advent I was not sure that I liked. Although no one put it into words, because we did not think of ourselves in this way, members of our family were a little like poor relations, living there in the

135

scrub, on the edge of barbarity, instead of in the settlements. Uncle Tony had made his money through mining, Uncle John Newell had made his not only through his shares in the Great Northern (the sound of whose stampers penetrated even to our school grounds on the hill) but also through his all-purpose stores, branches of which were set up in several towns. But our father – never quite satisfied with farming *per se*, or even with the timber mill that sometimes paid and sometimes did not – had precariously little to show for his efforts but beautiful pieces of land; mountaintops with views, the borders of attractive rivers, and what he called 'splendid sites' (which later were to be sold to strangers who were psychologically fitted to make money out of them). My father was sometimes dismissed as a dreamer, and it is true that he was an 'odd man out' in a stable farming community, and that, although he engaged in status occupations, he did not value these for the status they might have given him, but rather for other and more communal reasons.

The atmosphere in our house was quite different from that in either Elderslie or Beecroft. Ours was a pioneer's house, charming but added onto piece by piece; bearing the marks of taste without money, of skillful camouflage and make-do. The blankets were old and worn and showed signs of having been washed in the big copper at the back of the house, sometimes with a wild-looking Aboriginal woman tending the fire. In our house the kitchen was dark and narrow, and the bathroom lacked the shiny details we were beginning to see in *The Ladies' Home Journal*, which voyaged across the seas from America to end up, its edges battered, in the mailbags at the Kureen station. Our house was not a house of peace, but rather a house of struggle: we held it as our right, and as a bulwark against the enemy of loss and deprivation. This kind of thinking at Fleetwood did not exist at the more secure Beecroft or Elderslie, and it had something to do, I think, with my father's tendency toward argument, with his particular kind of ambition, and with the passion we all had for the challenges of justice.

For me, of course, such distinctions were not yet clarified. But as I sat under the big tree at Elderslie, feeling a little reserved, I perhaps hoped for some explanation as to why this world was not like mine. I loved Maidie, and enjoyed playing with Bun, who was a sturdy masculine-seeming man, whose face was rough and bristly when he kissed me. He would get me to comb his unruly hair with the little tortoiseshell comb he kept in his pocket, and then he would lift me up and hold me out at arm's length until I screamed to come down. Bun, however, was not beautiful in the graceful way that Maurice was, nor would he ever have left his shirt unbuttoned to the waist as Maurice sometimes did.

'Stop fussing with the sewing for that child,' Maurice said to Maidie. His voice was both playful and authoritative, and I stared at him – this was *my* sewing! Maidie blushed and let the sewing sink into her lap, as Maurice moved closer and touched her arm with his hand. 'Would you like to walk up to the falls?' he asked. What he meant was quite evident: 'Would you like to get away from all these people?'

Later the other relatives talked about Maurice and Maidie, who, it now seemed, were going to get married. I remember someone's protest: 'But he's such a *farmer*.' (This didn't mean that there was something undignified about being a farmer, but rather that Maurice was sunk deep into the earth, and that Maidie would soon also be like that, and perhaps neither of them would ever escape from that deep, rich tableland soil.)

I myself forgave Maidie for marrying him, because I knew somehow that she was unable to resist. But my Aunt Kate, our father's sister, who had recently arrived with her family from India to live with our grandmother, said that it was a great mistake for Maidie to marry a 'Mick.' This was the disrespectful term by which Catholics were called in Australia, and I saw at once that Aunt Kate – leaning against the kitchen wall in my grandmother's house, carefully testing the hot spirit iron she held up before lowering it down onto one of her husband's shirts – really *believed* that Maidie was doing something foolish. 'We all know that we should marry our own kind,' she stated in a reasonable way. 'If poor dear Maidie is tied up to a Catholic, this means that when the children come ... and I wouldn't be surprised if there were many of them ... then they'll have to be Catholic, too.' I did not quite understand that Aunt Kate, who had preserved her middle-class English standards all through her time in beautiful and multifaceted India, found some relief in gossiping about Maidie – that it eased her spirit, because she was, after all, living without the benefit of Indian servants, in the house of her voluble and independent mother, in a tiny muddy settlement far away from everything, and surrounded by noncommunicative rain forest. Although I shrank a little when I heard her use the term 'Mick' instead of 'Catholic' I was sorry for her as I watched her engaged in this interminable task of ironing, surrounded by shirts and petticoats and men's white jackets, and holding up the spirit iron to the down-streaming veranda light. Just as I was sorry for Maidie several years later when I returned from school again and came into the pleasant Beecroft kitchen, where the red coals shone through the gratings of the old black polished stove (fed endlessly by the corncobs from the barn), and found her with her once smooth hair untidy, and her stockings tied beneath her knees, because, pregnant with her second child, she could not bear anything around her waist.

It was in that period of incomplete realization of the sexual structure that stands behind the lives of men and women, in that period when young girls seem to walk in their sleep along corridors and through doors so easily opened to them, that many of us at school saw the shadows of our teachers fall upon the brilliant bare walls of the dormitory. We saw them as puppets, nodding and dipping against the light. There were short verandas linking the staff rooms in the front of the building, and these served as stages upon which could be acted out small dramas, with few words but much animation. As we passed on our way upstairs or downstairs, on the worn wooden steps hollowed by restless feet, we could pause for a moment and see the heads of the two women who lived in the front rooms – Miss Mavis Lahey and Miss Mirabel Parker – as they visited each other, or as they spoke to those who visited *them*, or as they went down to collect the mail, or called sometimes over the veranda railing.

One day I heard Miss Parker (Mirabel, as we called her among ourselves), who had washed her abundant brown hair and was hanging it in a curtain over the railing, calling down to one of the Sisters. 'Why, Sister . . . I'll come as soon as I get my hair under control.' Mirabel was not pretty – in fact her skin was poor and her eyes strained-looking – but she had a good figure with a pronounced waist, and she had also a certain slightly wild quality which added up to what was called 'it' – sex appeal. More alluring than her looks was her wonderful soprano voice, which at its best rose into the air with that soul-arresting quality that certain feminine voices have. Sometimes she sang to us at picnics, which in that savage terrain started in the afternoon and lasted until the campfire died down and the moon rose over the craggy ranges, leaving us all in a state of pleasant fatigue and lassitude. And on these occasions, her rising voice, filled with pathos and longing, seemed to beg us to forgive her and, indeed, have pity upon her! Caught by that voice, I went to the railing of the inner staircase one day, and saw Mirabel push quickly out of her room – her face flushed, her hair half down around her shoulders, her breast heaving. She had been talking to the Bush Brother Robin Moline, and he was there, too, somewhere, his voice quieter than hers, and with a strangled quality. She herself spoke urgently: 'Go away now. I don't want to *think* of it anymore. *Please go!*' A minute later I saw her back turned to me as she pressed against the veranda rails, with her head bent, and her hands gripping the bars. Obviously there had been some kind of crisis. Nor was this all, because the room to the left belonged to Miss Mavis Lahey. She taught science, I think, and was petite, with clear golden skin, a full, slightly protruding mouth, and dark wavy hair modeled neatly to her head.

Among ourselves we had sometimes had arguments about whether Mavis Lahey had more 'it' than Mirabel Parker had; the general consensus was: 'No – she hadn't,' although we thought perhaps that Mavis might make the better wife for one of those idealistic Bush Brothers – especially for Robin Moline, whose clear English skin turned red so easily and who was apparently attracted to both women. I think I guessed – especially on this afternoon when I witnessed what I thought might have been a 'scene of passion' – that Mirabel would win out in the end, which, indeed, turned out to be the case. Long afterward, when I met Mavis Lahey in what might be called 'civilian life,' she suggested that Robin Moline had been *hers*, and that during a short period when she was away in the south, he had somehow or other been tempted away from her.

I am not sure, in any case, that I myself was objective about Robin Moline, because we were already accustomed to gather on Sunday afternoons in the house of the Bush Brothers, and to listen to him read to us out of Kipling's *Just So Stories*; then my large adolescent eyes would fasten upon him with deep interest. He would entertain us afterward by making tea and passing around Iced Vo-Vos, a sweet biscuit of which we were inordinately fond, and at that time he would also talk to us personally, as one adult to others. It seemed as if in this atmosphere of literature and ease, he was offering to us something especially desirable – offering it as a gift, and as part of the knowledge we did not yet have.

Robin Moline appeared to us less the disciple of Christ than a male of a new kind. His long thin fingers gripped the red cover of the Kipling edition with a fascinating vigor, and his habit was thrown back to show the sleeves of his white shirt rolled up on arms not yet sunburnt, and never to be hairy, as were those of the traditional pioneer. He seemed like some formal and holy plant bred for something other than this alien soil – something very old and strong and delicate; only long afterward did I realize that his aura was the product of centuries of gentlemanly Christianity.

I wanted him to notice me, and I remember that I tried very hard to smile at him whenever there seemed to be an opportunity. One Saturday evening he sat not far from me when Mirabel was singing at the battered piano in the school hall, her voice lifting up above the ink-stained tables and forms (the song being, perhaps, 'Robin Adair' – and perhaps appropriate since one line said, 'What's this dull town to me?/Robin's not here'). I know that I heard him exclaim afterward, in a tone close to despair: 'What a *voice!*' – words that pierced my child's heart.

And I experienced surprise as well as sorrow, for it was now possible to see the school as a stage for passions I had not suspected; simple words as a cover for wild anguish and desire. In my love for Maidie I had been able to forgive her for deserting me, her pseudo-child, because I saw that she was actually soon to make real children for herself. But now, in half-blind, half-adolescent fashion, and perhaps because the pioneer environment had fostered a sense of nature's rapacious quality, I was taken aback by the rapidity with which such changes could happen, and worried about their outcome.

Long afterward, when I myself had married and was living in London, I visited Mirabel and Robin Moline. I remembered the almost artless grace with which he had once said in Herberton, 'My ambition is to return to London and serve in the poorest parish there.' And here they were in a large brick house that stood in a vast, dark, slaty yard in the city slums, and Mirabel had at last had a child, which had died only a few months before. She had been ill, and after supper, when she stood beside me in the church, she was silent. I waited for the voice that had thrilled us in the past. At last she opened her mouth and I heard one or two perfect notes; then she dropped her head and was silent again.

9

Born to Fly Upwards

As we got a little older, and as we began, one by one, to go south for those last few years of schooling at St. Margaret's, the influence of our early years became more obvious. It was possible to see not only that we were 'northerners' but that we were 'northerners' of a special kind – that upon our innocent and instinct-prone condition, British, especially Anglican, influences had been imposed.

Most of our friends at St. Mary's were not as much influenced as we were. The frontier does not tend to produce conformists. Some of the girls were not from the coast or the tablelands, but came from 'beyond the beyond,' or 'beyond the black stump' – that is, from the 'real' outback – and might therefore not have wanted to make themselves available to 'foreign' philosophies. One of these girls (whom I easily outstripped in the simple scholarship expected of us, but whom I felt to be my superior in boldness) came from a cattle station as large as the whole British Isles, where she saw little more of the world than the double strand of wire that wandered off, mile after mile, to the nearest town.

'I've run away from every school I've been to,' she boasted.

'*Every* school . . .?'

'Yes. I've run from St. Anne's and St. Margaret's and St. Gabriel's' – the dimples appeared in her cheeks – 'and I'm going to run from here.'

'How will you get away? They'll stop you at the station.'

'I'll go down the ranges with the mules,' she mocked. 'They go at night . . . I hear their bells.'

She was drawing the heads of horses all over the badly prepared homework she was doing, and her dark curly head lifted now and then as if to show her birdlike profile, and to drink the wind.

'What will your *father* say?'

'He'll get tired of sending me away to school eventually.'

'And your mother?'

'She's dead.'

'Oh.' I felt a faint pity, but I knew that the pity wouldn't be well received. In a little while she announced that when she grew older she would help run the cattle station, and that she had already 'winged' (shot in the arm) a duffer who had tried to escape with stock taken from her father's property, and that no one would get away with *that* while *she* was around!

This girl, who remained untamable all through her short stay at St. Mary's, finally managed to ostracize herself by getting out of bed at midnight and swinging on the rope of the chapel bell. She had little remorse, because she did not think of the church as the sole house of God.

'God is in the rocks,' she announced.

I myself was not as sure as this girl was of where God lived. One morning I saw a small procession marching up the hill from the town to the wooden chapel that stood under the turpentine trees – a procession made up, not of visitors, but of respectable-looking local women, their clothes freshly ironed, their faces a little red from the heat. One of the Bush Brothers – I think it was Brother Belcher – had held prayers in the chapel that morning, and as we walked down the steps and stood to one side, with our white veils over our heads and our hymnbooks in our hands, I saw, to my surprise, that my Aunt Kate (who, having left her mother's house in Kureen, was now living in Herberton) seemed to be the leader of the delegation. She tried not to look nervous as she clutched a handkerchief in her hand and mopped at her face, flushed under her straw hat. We could not hear all that was said, but the discussion (of more interest to me now than it was on that long-ago hot morning) made clear that the women's delegation came to protest the trend toward High Church ritual – the use of incense at services, the prevalence of robes and embroidery, and the encouragement of what was called 'voluntary confession.'

When I asked my sister Hazel about this, she dismissed it as a matter of intellectual taste. Aunt Kate, she said, was more interested in doctrine than our grandmother, who loved religion for itself and did not question the details. Aunt Kate, on the other hand, felt it a point of honor to resist, in her own town and in her own church, the advance of what might be called 'popery'; she was convinced that the Irish Catholic tendency in Australia was, or might be, 'infectious' and that it veered toward saying the rosary and lighting candles, rather than toward seeking salvation.

Yet the Anglican religious field was broad and fertile. The missions sent to New Guinea and the islands, and to parts of our more familiar watery world, were always kept before our view (at a minimum via the collection boxes into which we put some of our pocket money!), and the hope of conversion went as far afield as the countries of Southeast Asia – not to mention India and Africa.

There was, of course, a streak of real romanticism in the religion offered to us in these northern Church of England schools, and I think that it made many of us want to be noble and heroic. Bishop John of North Queensland (J.O.N.Q.), on those occasions when he visited the school, showed that he had become noticeably more propagandistic toward the New Guinea cause, although he had always tended to identify most with what was called the El Dorado period – that is, the time before *our* time, when towns were built and ports made, shipping firms developed and the interior penetrated. He had sympathized with the very earliest Brothers, who had moved serenely through camps and settlements aswim with grog and given over to the 'devil,' and through cyclones which seemed determined to rip the roofs off churches. Now he felt that the church militant must 'smite paganism' further north, in New Guinea, where he had seen and approved of the ardor of the new black Christians.

To our parents, at various school festivals, in sober speeches which were part of a campaign to raise money, he explained seriously that to 'go to New Guinea was to be taken back to the time of the New Testament.' And we ourselves, getting older, and given to long discussions in the dormitories, would sometimes discuss J.O.N.Q. himself – this strange, holy, eccentric man, enamored of the lonely outback towns of wood and iron; this man who loved 'the bravely dumb who did their deed/Men of the plain heroic breed.' He even tried, it seemed, to act out the discipline of heroism – sleeping on the floor of his little cottage on the school grounds, to give the newest Brother a bed; spending the night in a strange town, praying and fasting in a church tower; bedding down on the lawn when he visited an outback station, so as not to indulge himself; or meditating at midnight under a tamarind tree in the garden.

It seemed that no one of great purpose had been able to resist New Guinea, with its tender chants and frenzied blood songs, and we wondered whether J.O.N.Q., on his visit there, had found it all too much for him – its joyous dances of welcome, with the young, smooth-muscled acolytes in red robes, red hibiscus in their hair, their eyes full of faith. ('This sight will make your heart sore,' begged the tribal leader who sent a smoked human arm to a French missionary as proof of cannibalism. 'You will go to live among them . . . and bring them the peace of Jesus.') It was no wonder that the Bishop was fascinated with the idea of taking up 'the white man's burden' in those broken mountains. Like the government servants on the island during this high-minded and high-handed time, who were permitted to fire their guns *only* when their lives were in danger (and who joked among themselves: 'We get killed, and *then* we open fire!'), J.O.N.Q. might, had he not been bound to North Queensland, have gone willingly into New Guinea, to face death in the Highlands, as so many in the Church had done before him.

This sort of danger and sacrifice began to impress us greatly. When asked to pray for the Bush Brothers, and for what was called the 'Apostolic succession,' we would consider making some kind of religious commitment. But at the same time, most of us were aware that we wanted to preserve ourselves for some other, more worldly future.

The world, it is said, is always with us, and during our long vacations it was easy to forget the disciplines and conflicts of education, and to try to act out on the veranda of the old Fleetwood house polite performances that would link us up to the wider social experience. We had, after all, to pass through the rites of admission before we could enjoy adult life, and this, I suppose we thought secretly, took precedence over everything else.

To the home veranda the train carried many visitors of a more worldly nature than the Bush Brothers – mining men and mining magnates, investors, writers, government officials, scientists, Members of Parliament, and odd friends and relations. Some of these visitors were from England, and had titles; and many others were important in one way or another. (It was because of their importance and their interest in colonial law, education, politics, and presumably trade or other rewards, that they had come to the tableland in the first place, and so had been directed to our father's house.)

It was the second half of the 1920s, a time when the British were 'inspecting' Australia – not only because most of the country's trade was with the United Kingdom but also because, by the Balfour Declaration of 1926, the colonies were to be considered autonomous communities within the British Empire, equal in status, and having their own separate responsibility in foreign affairs. The period of British patronage was giving way, then, to a cheerful understanding of Australia's 'special needs,' and here, far away from the more pluralistic south, it was recognized that there must also be a philosophical acceptance of the 'irreverence' of North Queenslanders.

It was not because our father was so knowledgeable that he was picked out as a guide, informant, and host for these members of the British Establishment, but rather because he spoke the same language to some extent and understood the *noblesse oblige* of development. And also, of course, because he was always so enthusiastic!

On a less worthy level, his children operated as the moment required, and since the whole social tenor of col onial life revolved, or seemed still to revolve, around the distant British court, and in a de facto sense around the neo-grandeurs of the local Government House (Hazel had already 'come out' at Government House), it was not strange that we were slightly pleased, and slightly amused, by the fantasy of nobility.

On one occasion, an English parliamentary delegation came to the north and it was arranged for Lady Alicia Cecil and her daughter to stay in our house, while her husband, Sir Evelyn Cecil (who was to be raised to the peerage as the first Baron Rockley of Lytchett Heath some years later), continued on with the delegation. With him was the fourth Marquess of Salisbury, his cousin and at the time Lord Privy Seal and the Leader of the House of Lords – a figure who, because of his tall, bony, and somehow elegant frame, and his manner of charming yet aloof affability, appealed more to our curiosity than did Sir Evelyn himself. It was certainly not because of our house's splendors that it was chosen for these distinguished visitors; the truth is that, in those days, there was very little choice. In any case, our pliable parents, isolated in what was essentially a farming community, enjoyed having educated English visitors, as they had often enjoyed having important Australian personages like Sir Mathew Nathan, the governor of the state.

For the special long-awaited visit of the Cecils to the tablelands, my mother made delicious food, with the help of several hot-and-bothered local women and the famous Mrs. Beeton's cookbook. And I remember her kneeling earnestly on the sitting-room floor, holding pins in her mouth, while she re-covered a chair with dark blue cloth. The results of these preparations had their reward in the intimacy of an evening when Lady Cecil's daughter played the piano in the firelight, and Brother Belcher, invited down from Herberton, stood by, turning the pages and singing suitable English songs. I was amazed to hear our piano player confess, when complimented on the pale green georgette dress she wore, 'I was so pleased with it that I had three more made exactly like it!' And Lady Cecil, a larger and more verbal woman, seemed appealing when we found out that she was a professional watercolorist in the best British tradition, and had arrived with a great wooden box filled with colors. Later, in something like a white linen safari suit, her head tied up in a rosy veil, she would venture boldly into the nearby scrub to paint flowers – many of which she said were not yet classified and would delight the knowledgeable at Kew Gardens. When she emerged each day from the scrub, flushed and with her veil torn by the branches, and showed us her delicate paintings on fine white paper – the scarlet and gold of the bean-tree flower, the flat radiating blossoms of the fire wheel – I remember that I felt for the first time not so much that the flowers were paintable as that they had a special value to others as well as to ourselves, and that the British felt an exalted sense of duty about depicting and recording them.

I don't think we were especially alert to the importance of these visitors. We may have realized that some of them had roles in deciding the fate of English policy toward the Dominions, but we looked upon them superficially, as members of a species new to us, and attempted to incorporate them into our lives. Perhaps there was a certain recognition that they were allied to us by political structure rather than consanguinity; and even – in a complex way – that we were justified in putting up a certain resistance to what was so politely proprietary toward us. We were, after all, tough colonial products.

Our bush entertainments were also colonial products. At night, in an immensity without theaters, by candlelight (after the generator had been turned off), we would act out scraps

148

of Shakespeare and Wilde and Shaw, as well as certain plays of more dubious merit, like one about Henry VIII and his wives, which was written in verse and which we knew by heart, and which began as Henry blundered into his wife's room:

> *I heard her snore*
> *As I stood at the door,*
> *Oh, Catherine Parr-r-r-r,*
> *What a plague you are! . . .*
> *Cannot bear a light forsooth,*
> *Says it wakes her up . . .*

It was here on the veranda, as I watched Hazel improvising the part of Hamlet, in a half-crazed, half-proud manner, that I not only first appreciated the profound appeal of drama but also realized how much talent my sister had. It seemed natural to us then that she should play this part so well on a half-dark pioneer veranda, with no applause other than her family's, accompanied by the croak of frogs in the pawpaw trees.

As we grew older, Hazel, as the eldest, became the social arbiter of the family, and naturally took first place as entertainer, planner, and, after our parents, director. She was very good at this, and cared a great deal about it. 'We won't wear long dresses on Saturday,' she would announce. (Long dresses only meant simple cotton frocks of greater length than those worn in the afternoon, but still longer than the fuller, twirling-skirted affairs that, as we approached the dancing age, were just coming into fashion.) These narrow questions – to wear or not to wear long dresses, to use or not to use a little rouge on our cheeks, to persuade or not to persuade our father to buy us liquor (he didn't drink himself and did not think it appropriate that we should offer liquor to our friends), to invite or not to invite some young man whom we all thought attractive – became more onerous than necessary, because in this northern outback the rules had not yet been clearly laid down, so that we were a little unsure of our place as women, not only in the world at large but in the simpler world around us.

It is true that in Australia there had never existed that prison of femininity which Octavio Paz describes in his *Labyrinth of Solitude* – that situation in which women lived only under the patronage of men and there was one set of rules for the *señor* and another for the women and children. In Australia, for all its heritage of masculinity and patriarchy and authority, women were still regarded as members of the human race. The shortage of women in colonial society gave them greater value, and the familiarity with nature and the challenge to the false reserve of the English gave them a special confidence. Australian girls did not trip daintily but were allowed to stride along – to swing their arms to and fro, to be handsome rather than pretty, robust rather than elegant. They were mothers of large families, good swimmers, competent tennis players, fearless riders, and excellent substitutes for men in difficult situations.

But they were still not seen as equal to men. Shoulder to shoulder with their males (but in actuality one step behind them), they learned to set unnatural limits upon their own social suitability. It was customary for the women to separate themselves from the men at all sorts of local gatherings – to cluster around the stove or teapot, to busy themselves with the nourishment factor, to guard the children, to be mothers, nursemaids, and providers. Our own family did not accept this limited standard; we were encouraged in fact to join in on all occasions, and to take part in all conversations. Yet the technical feminine skills were also expected of us, and this meant, in fact, that our primary role was to see that everything possible had been done for the comfort of the opposite sex before we felt free to converse. We scarcely knew who we were – young women of the British provinces or young women of the great open spaces? In this dilemma, we turned to what has been the solace through the years of so many isolated women. As we had when we were younger, we read novels.

It might be said that one reads from interest and curiosity. But it might also be said that one reads to restrain longings, to relieve oneself of emotion, to pass from one temperamental precipice to another – in other words, to deaden pain. ('My head is humming,' wrote Malinowski years earlier, on the shores of New Guinea, 'and my eyes and brain . . . yet I read, read, and keep on reading without letup as though I were reading myself to death . . .') Although it all seemed rather far away and unreal, I could identify with the scenes described by Somerset Maugham and Joseph Conrad – Englishmen proving their mettle on desolate tropical riverbanks, women turning to adultery on Malayan rubber plantations or timber-cutting stations in Burma, little village girls who waited weeping under coconut trees for the sahib who had abandoned them – and of course that perennial Sadie Thompson, whose torrid effect upon the fundamentalist missionary had multiplied itself all through the East Samoan deluge. It is in this manner that those who are literate but disadvantaged define the limits of their world, and go on to find their way toward a larger one.

But the interesting thing was that these novels that we found so readable and those characters which engaged our sympathies so thoroughly did not exactly entertain us when translated into real life. A man who had been stationed in India in some minor military capacity (he had the title of captain) inhabited, with his wife and sister-in-law, a little wooden cottage that was on our property, but some distance away from the house – across the paddocks and close to the road which led to Atherton. I don't think they were there for very long, but one day my sisters and I walked over the green, uneven pastures and crawled through several wire fences to the little bare wooden cottage to play bridge with them. We sat erect in straight chairs, surrounded by the lares and penates – the bamboo screens, the embroidered linen cloths, the tinkling temple bells, the paper reproductions of

151

Hindu gods, the brass bowls and candlesticks and Buddhas – that had somehow come safely all the way from New Delhi to be displayed in a room redolent with incense and draped with rugs and hangings, while outside the bare bright green paddocks rolled against the sunlit Australian sky. It wasn't because the captain concerned was not, as my father said, 'a quite decent chap,' or his wife and sister-in-law not similarly cheerful and kind, that our contacts were unfruitful, but rather that these wanderers had escaped from some big Midlands city in England, and now were even more out of place here than they had been in India, for all the tinkling chimes in the cottage doorway and the strange mixtures of cultures inside it. Their kindness to us, and even the peanuts and chocolates we munched at the bridge table, seemed unsuitable, because we were all of us like castaways in the middle of the half-cleared land. And when the kind captain said to me, in relation to the halfhearted bridge I was playing, 'Ef ye'd only *concentrate*,' I knew that our minds would never meet. Like the attempt to find some link between the healthy-looking but inarticulate young farmers with whom we danced at the local gatherings and the heroes of Maugham and Kipling and Conrad, it was a lost cause from the beginning.

The home space was invaded now and shrank all the time – the world passed by and sometimes lingered there. One afternoon my father came out onto the veranda to introduce us to a young man known as Robbie McClaren, and we all looked up with the mixed emotions of the lonely and the young. He was a thin man with a reddish, bony face and a ginger-colored mustache who seemed very conscious of his spotless whipcord riding trousers and who talked a lot about Malaysia, where he'd been for 'quite a wee while,' until he had become 'bloody well fed up with it' and wanted to 'get to a white man's country' again (so badly, in fact, that one day he'd simply gone down and booked his passage to Australia on the very first boat heading south from the Singapore wharves).

152

In those days we were vaguely ashamed of our father's abstemious habits and would protest laughingly that '*everybody* drank,' meanwhile smuggling bottles of hard liquor into the house and holding them in readiness for any attractive male visitor who might appear on the scene. So it was that, as this particular afternoon wore on and our guest indicated that 'tea was all very well' but a spot of that rich North Queensland rum might be a great thing with which to toast the sunset, Hazel was able to produce a bottle of gin from some hidden place, and before long was being guided around the veranda to learn the latest variation on the fox-trot, as it was danced at this very moment at Raffles. Naturally then, as the evening wore on, it became obvious that Robbie McClaren could not be trusted to drive safely to the local hotel. My mother, conferring quietly with my father in the dining room, agreed that, short of space though we were, he must be offered hospitality, and that two of the children must be put into one bed.

A day or two later, when our guest had managed to reach the hotel and then had returned – not with gifts for my mother, or even with the loaf of fresh bread we had asked him to buy, but with a number of splendid bottles of whiskey and rum – he delighted my sister yet again by introducing jazz onto our rural veranda, and worried my mother by passing out in the late afternoon, only to revive and want to begin all over again just as we were ready for bed. By this time my father's tolerance had worn thin, and he was soon denouncing McClaren as a worthless alcoholic, while my mother, in the discussion that followed, pursed up her mouth in the wry way she had, and said with a sad shake of her head that young men went out to those lonely jobs in the East and were corrupted by the heat and the drinking and the luxury. Here her voice dropped a little, and she remarked that such men even tended to have children by the native women without taking any responsibility, and then when they finally decided to marry some British girl, the poor native woman would be packed off to a suitable distant village.

She wondered aloud that people could so easily shelve their old British values! ... Afterward I realized that I had not forgotten poor Robbie McClaren because of this perhaps apocryphal story about the half-caste children – and also because he himself had looked so pathetic and unattractive as he lay passed out on the veranda sofa, with his pale mustache decorating his wide-open mouth.

Was it on such occasions that we became aware of the great difference in behavior between our father and such tropical drifters as the feckless Robbie McClaren? Or had this difference been experienced long ago and become incorporated into the tapestry of life itself? There were, for instance, certain friends from the hotter and more casual coast whose attitude toward life was not like that of our father or our uncles – perhaps because down there in the heat a certain self-indulgence, a certain vanity and frivolity, seemed more natural than it did on the cooler and more earnest tablelands.

What geography had to do with it, I don't know, but we felt it to be true all the same. Different as our parents were from those people from the coast, and perhaps because we found money and success less interesting than they did, there always seemed to be a separation between us. Visitors like the Cecils, on the other hand, whose slightly haughty but thoroughly objective view of reality – whose 'world view,' one might say – shone with an unfamiliar but haunting light, did not seem bound by the provinciality of even the kindest and most considerate of our Australian guests.

I think it was partly the very originality of such men and women as the Cecils, and their unpretentious touch of moral seriousness, that attracted us to them. Yet, perversely, this also helped us to feel that we must separate ourselves from a certain colonial dependence, and even from the trivial obligations of tribal groups. Undoubtedly this influenced me, because I was at that time considering the whole question of writing talent, and how I could develop it. Should I try,

154

perhaps, to pick up the old battered typewriter Hazel had passed on to me, and set out somewhere to turn myself into a writer living, as I had heard writers did, in some obscure room in Bloomsbury? Should I forget about the university, and pack up my belongings, and go to London as Dick Whittington had done?

The whole question of talent, of course, directed us toward solving our future problems. Most of the girls at St. Mary's knew that, should they go to the university at all, they would eventually spend those pre-university days at the sister school of St. Margaret's in Brisbane – and it was one of those unchanging facts that everyone who *could* went away to school. There was also a tradition that, after *some* schooling at least, young women did not need a college education. Hazel, for instance, was already living in Townsville and was uncertain of how she should earn her living, and only one of the twins (Helen) seemed to want to go to the university. In any case, it would have been difficult for my parents to send us all south on that long, expensive journey in the rattling little train.

In those days during the wet season, there existed the daily expectation of being cut off from the south because of flooded railway lines. If the train *was* running, the journey took three or four days to Brisbane, the capital of the state of Queensland, and was somewhat of a hazard itself, for part of the journey lay through the low-lying coastal area just south of Townsville – a country of sodden wastes and depressed hollows. I remember times at Townsville, just north of the area where the Burdekin River gathers together its many tributaries, when news would come of high water on the bay and of buildings near the sea battered by forty-mile winds. When the train started, and moved through heavy downpours, we would expect to hear that the Burdekin had 'come down' and that there lay before us long hours of delay. Once that particular part of the line had been safely passed, the train was generally successful in reaching the New South Wales border, where in true parochial fashion the passengers had to get out and change to the Sydney train, and so onto a line of wider gauge.

We did not complain about any of these difficulties; we could only be glad that any train existed at all, and that the trip – composed as it was of the luxury of long hours for reading and dreaming and conversation, happily punctuated by a wild rush at the railway stations when a cow bell summoned us to meals at the station restaurant – should also take us on and on, past new towns and unknown rivers, through mysterious pearly mornings and shadowy nights, and should open up for us a whole southern world.

To start the journey in the early morning from the Cairns railway station, which was aswing with baskets of tropical ferns, had its own excitements – sitting stiffly as we did in our crackling-new navy-blue uniforms, with the books we hoped to read and the boxes of food we were always given to supplement the station meals. And at that hour, before the pearly morning mist had quite lifted from the green canefields past which the train steamed, we could see the engine's plume of smoke mingling with the miasmas of the jungle-clad cliffs and the clouds of tropical flowers. On one such morning, the pyramidal mountain at Hambledon seemed to shift on its base, to reveal an especially beautiful cane plantation and its house – a house that had long ago set up in me a pattern of envy and desire which I could later transform into the more basic pattern of ordinary approval.

The houses of the sugar growers tended to be attractive, and this particular house had a broad latticed veranda and a lofty lower story, and when we visited it occasionally, as we had in the past, we sat on exquisitely woven antique cane chairs from Southeast Asia, looking through a screen of vines and orchids to the garden ablaze with flowers. We were served drinks by soft-footed dark servants in spotless white jackets and trousers, but it was not the fact that there were servants that made such an impression – since servants of some kind or other were still common enough in pioneer households – it was rather the grace and good looks of

156

the servants themselves, and the fact that one of them wore a scarlet hibiscus in his halo of black hair, as he might have done on his native island. These servants were the descendants of those who, in the preceding century, had been brought from the South Seas to work in the Queensland sugar fields.

I think that we were all attracted by the ease with which the plantation people cultivated the graces of life, and aware that we, the pioneers on the tablelands, had to contend too bitterly with the land for the small amount of leisure obtained from it. I think that there had been implanted in our natures, like a small sturdy tree growing in the soil of genuine hardship, some taste for, and a harsh knowledge of, essential work. In this isolated world we could not count upon a social structure, or imported produce, or special stores – we had to grow, and sometimes process, most of what we ate; see that our meat was killed and hung; our chickens killed and cleaned and plucked; and sometimes we had to make our own bread and butter. These old necessities were embedded in our sense of security. But with our mother's need to help our father, the rest of us were often left to our own devices, and became tired and quarrelsome as we coped with cooking and housework. I was hoping that this would soon be behind me, and was projecting myself toward a life of writing and reading and scholarship – fantasizing that someday, in the house of which I would be the 'mistress,' I could manage to have the work done by smiling servants, so that I could escape the exacting standards of family life.

If, when we were on our way south, the Burdekin River had 'come down,' we would continue to travel beyond Townsville, and would be gazing out onto a sodden plain. As night approached, the train might come to a stop in endlessly stretching wastes of water, and once the porter had made up the berths in the evening – with their stiff sheets and coarse gray blankets – there would be no space in the compartment to do more than lie down, so that, as the ordinary train lights

H.O.T.—8

157

failed, the world was left illuminated only by mysterious reaches of pearly water, and by the faraway haze of the Milky Way. Staring out at this desolate liquid landscape, one could see on the vague horizon the heads of half-drowned trees.

If I remember those nights, I also remember the mornings, when the mind would seem empty, only to be filled again with brilliant impressions from the little coastal sugar ports – women standing at the stations in voile or cotton dresses, men sunburnt to mahogany in white shirts and loose trousers, thin-legged dark Aborigines in brilliant colors, workers from the Islands with haloes of fuzzy hair, passengers dragging suitcases tied up with rope, and wan local beauties, pale from the tropics, with old-fashioned hats wreathed around with artificial daisies. Beyond the stations, where the canefields rippled in the heat, as if bevies of birds with beating wings were hiding among their stalks, the air was filled with the sickly-sweet scent of sugar. Loving to read the stories of the pioneers, I knew that the train moved through some of our own history, and that even while the rain fell, here in this feast-or-famine country, not very far away in the west cattle might be dying and hawks gathering above their blackened carcasses. At such times in the past, squatters had abandoned their homesteads to trek with their families to the nearest water hole. It was the country to the west which had provided some of the best cattle pasture in the state. Its outlet was Rockhampton, almost directly on the Tropic of Capricorn, where the slow brown Fitzroy River might also be swollen with rain, and where the houses were set up high on stilts above the ground. The main street, with its ornamental hotels – iron-rich, painted and gilded – reminded everyone of gold-crazed southerners, who trooped hopefully to the newly discovered fields of the 1870s and 1880s. I remember that it was said in Cairns that Rockhampton – Rocky, as they called it – used to be a symbol of division between the solid and conservative south and the wild and godless north, and that in many of our northern towns, minerals came before trade, and that

158

afterward, and in this order, came houses, respectability, and religion.

And so the journey continued until at last the train drew into the main Brisbane station. There we were, with our luggage and our boxes, tired and a little grimy, but with our faces washed and our hair brushed, and our school hats – the bands that encircled them embroidered with the school motto, *Per Volar Su Nata* (that is, 'Born to Fly Upwards') – placed very firmly on our heads.

10

Thoughtless Heaven

Memory is selective. I don't know what my sisters felt about leaving one school and going to another; I don't think we discussed it very much because it was simply part of what was. But each moment of my years at St Mary's seemed imprinted on my mind – the seats I sat in at class, the routes through the sketchy barrackslike buildings, the lemony scent of the eucalyptus in the ranges, and the barriers of golden stone across which ran the Wild River.

My memories of St Margaret's seemed to lack that sharp physical immediacy. The wide elevated frontage of the school looked over an urban landscape, past one or two spreading trees to the gridiron of an overgrown country town which pretended to be a city. We saw, in a dim blue distance of glinting galvanized roofs and brick towers, a winding central street called after the Queen which had once been a track for bullock teams. We knew how many comfortable houses there were in these suburbs, shaded by palms and mango trees and brightened by beds of tropical flowers. But, although Brisbane was Queensland's capital and therefore good enough for us, we guessed also that strangers might find its center mediocre. For us Queen Street was important for our happiness. We warmed to its sprawling stores and emporiums, to the bridge in the distance, to the post office of golden stone, to the darkly discreet Lennon's Hotel lounge, to which we were sometimes summoned when our families were in town. We were familiar with George Street, which had bookstores, and occasional cafés, where tea with cakes or sandwiches could be had. And, as a family, we especially identified with the Hotel Cecil, also darkish – its wooden floors sloping, its rickety stairs leading up to verandas where old-time businessmen, and figures in the mining world, and solid gentlemen from Sydney and Melbourne sat smoking quietly.

Uncle Tony, who sometimes went on little trips to the southern cities, partly to keep in touch with mining, now made his home more or less in Brisbane, and had settled in at the Hotel Cecil, where I would make my way to lunch on Saturdays, and sit before the white starched tablecloth, and smile into his kind dark eyes, and listen to his stories, and acknowledge that yes, I would love some ice cream and fruit salad for dessert. The web of streets beyond and behind this hotel had their own tarnished romance, a romance of storehouses built by the convicts, of shipping companies running boats up and down the coast, of shady hotels supposed to house prostitutes, and hot city apartments for those who could not afford to rent in the suburbs. On the way back to school I liked to leave respectable George Street, and walk down past these less defined buildings, making a zigzag toward the wharves, where a street which had once been a creek marked a key corner and a huge fig tree stood black against the dazzling tropical light.

In despair I yearned for private adventures, for vaguely glimpsed love, for exotic experience. Most of all I suffered hunger for what I did not know existed, for a muse I had not discovered, for something to assuage indescribable longings. Thwarted by colossal ignorance, I might buy a magazine not obtainable at school, or chocolates which in the heat would melt into a sticky mess in my uniform pocket. Something close to melancholy would oppress me. 'O World! O Life! O Time! . . .'

But almost invisible as the signals were, and almost unappreciated by us, the hours at St Margaret's were slowly yielding up the outline of life's secrets. I might have been a pretty enough child, but I think that I was a plain adolescent, thin and a little sticklike, straight-haired and shy; nor at first could I believe it if I saw in myself some beauty – a rounding

161

of the body, an eloquence of the eye, and an upwelling of teenage vivacity which strangers might value.

We were urged to display our talents, to run and jump or play tennis 'for the school,' to write or draw for the school magazine, to act in the school plays, to contribute some of our precious free time to cleaning and decorating the chapel. We went, suitably chaperoned, to dances celebrating various events at the boys' schools; in halls where the tunes we had come to know best beat out their seductive rhythms ('It's three o'clock in the morning, I've danced the whole night through,' etc.) and the doors opened between dances onto shadowy suburban yards with one streetlight over the gates and a moon and stars hanging in the sky. It was the time when the girls of the older forms began to approach the stature of their teachers, and when most of the older boys were bogged down in coming manhood. I was considered very lucky by the sports-conscious at St Margaret's because a well-built stocky boy, apparently a hero on the football field, had chosen me to circle the floor with him (although, as far as I remember, we did this in absolute silence). As we parted, our hands clinging for a moment, he said, 'D'you want to come with me to the Churchy dance before the Christmas hols?' To which I replied doubtfully that I'd like to, 'but I'll have to *ask*.' Weeks later I was fetched from class to the Sisters' sitting room, and confronted by my sports hero, who asked if I *really* wanted to come to the 'Churchy' dance; it was promised in the presence of the Sister that 'suitable transport would be arranged.'

Again we circled the floor, again and again in the same profound silence, and I retain to this day some memory of his arm which pumped up and down, the blond slightly wooden face above his massive shoulders, and the vulnerable look about his mouth. On that same evening I also danced with the man who taught mathematics to the Churchy boys, and who seemed to be courting the tall untidy Burne-Jones beauty who was my history teacher at St Margaret's. This man was adequately tall, somewhat tweedy, smoked a pipe, and was a joyous, if clumsy, dancer. I think that I considered him far

162

above me, but after the dance, seated on some big roots under a banyan tree, I suddenly found myself able to chatter, which I did so willingly that when he released me in the hall again, he gave me the small affectionate squeeze one might give a child. That night I stared into the discolored glass in the school bathroom, to find only that I was a bit pinker than usual, and that my immature shoulders curved under the stretchy lavender dress clinging to my self-conscious body.

'Will I do?' I asked the glass, knowing that, in any case, this face, this body, was all I had. But I was happy beyond reason, and it was as if the mathematics teacher had spoken to me in poetry: 'Think, would it not be sweet to live with me, All alone, my child, my love?'

Imperceptibly the time passed. There were the gaunt eyes of one of the Sisters, demanding gently that I write stories for the school paper. There were the shadowy eyes of another, to whom I was sent because I had a headache, and who said to me, as a serious Christian might, 'When I have a bad headache, I simply do the accounts, or set myself the task of writing a hundred letters to ask for contributions to our school.'

'I am sorry, Sister,' I said, bowing my head before her wrinkled forehead, enfolded by bands of starched white.

And there was the round face of a young postulant who was about to take her final vows, and whose Christian name was the same as mine. I hung over the railing, looking up at her as if she had been some strange creature from a still undiscovered planet.

'How *can* you?' I begged her. 'How *can* you give it all up?'

She reprimanded me stiffly: 'Please be quiet! You just don't understand!'

There was a blond girl from the middle school who begged me to go home with her for one of the holidays, and explained that to get there we would have to take the train to Windorah, where we would be met by men with horses and would ride for five days to her father's station, camping out on the way

163

– an expedition which sounded ambitious even by ordinary Australian standards. The blond and beautiful girl, whose name I have forgotten, was new to the school, and why she had chosen to admire me I couldn't guess, because it wasn't considered suitable in this hierarchichal world to go home for the holidays with girls younger than oneself. This was a question of status, and when one day on the staircase she fell to her knees and clasped mine, I was acutely embarrassed in case one of my friends should see us in this strange situation. 'Please change your mind,' the girl begged, her face pressed against my cambric skirt. 'Please, please . . .' And she began to talk of her mother and her brother, of riding and picnics, of an especially beautiful horse for me, of secret caves, and billabongs, and chasms in nearby rocky hills, so that although I said no, partly because of the logistics of time, in dreams afterward I took that outback train, and descended with her at the station, and met the handsome silent outback men, and set off into the hazy distance, riding and riding, penetrating into the red-and-black desert, going as far as the horizon, as far as we could travel . . .

There was also an evening when we dressed up as 'historical characters' or 'famous pictures,' making our own costumes out of colored sateen and buckram and straw, and sewing late into the night. A girl called Olga became the Laughing Cavalier, complete with a dagger made of wood and ostrich plumes borrowed from a dressmaker in the town. And I dressed up as the Laughing Cavalier's lady, making a tight rose-colored bodice and a full skirt and a brilliant blue hat with feathers. We painted our faces, and the girl who had asked me to go home for the holidays whispered, 'Oh, you're *beautiful . . . beautiful*,' and someone else looked puzzled and said rather tactlessly, 'I didn't think that dressing up could make so much difference!'

How many times in those days did we change our characters, our faces; how often did we vow to change ourselves? How many times did we deny the vanity, the sloth and laziness, the greed and scorn which we were possessed by, and promise virtues we had read of, or heard about? And, indeed, how many times did we sulk or cry in private, or imagine that some knowledge could save us? There were things we did not know, and these might have helped us. We could not guess that, in spite of the links with our families and the kinship of scattered communities, we operated in a near-vacuum; that the veneer of houses and roads and the web of burgeoning industries and farms, linked by delicate strands of human effort, did not yet add up to taking over a continent.

In those days it took more than six weeks for a letter to reach Australia from England by boat. The new books which we could buy were almost forgotten in London when they were being read in Sydney for the first time. The tendrils of our desire reached out to that old core of belonging, but they could not touch the banks of the Thames, and when they did had little to cling to, and often shriveled unwanted in the cooler air of the Northern Hemisphere. 'Do you *like* Australia?' we would ask with puzzled wonder of the robust travelers from the United Kingdom who came, not for formal reasons, but intent upon finding out what we were *really* like.

Between the world wars, modern Australia was not much more than a hundred and fifty years old and presented a brash and innocent face to the rest of the world. But it was not true that international concerns did not penetrate our environment, or that newspapers were not read, or current affairs discussed – it was rather that information was as thin and scattered as grass during a drought. Sometimes at school there were discussions about the meaning of history, but this history had its compartments, and those that were not boring had little relationship to our lives, because history was not there, it was elsewhere. It was not the old bullock-wagon track in Brisbane which had been turned into a street. Or the rounded mill made of stone with the tread worked by the convicts. Or the broken spars of the old sailing boats rotting by the riverbank. Or even the remnants of the boardinghouse in which Joseph Conrad was supposed to have lived for a month or two between voyages. History was far away and ineffectual, and separated from us by the glass of distance against which vague fluttering ideas broke their wings like tired butterflies. I did hear that when I went to the university I might meet some 'Bolsheviks,' and that these generally wore red ties and refused to 'serve their country.' I had the idea that the Russian Revolution had produced bloodshed and carnage, but when I tried to read about it I found only lurid novels in which the Cossacks came riding out of the taiga and whipped half-dressed village girls; or treatises which bored me because they talked of the 'tradition of the rebellious working class' and claimed as sympathizers Theodore Dreiser, and Gorky and Whitman, whom I had not yet read.

Strangely enough, what we knew most about was that for which we took least credit. It was that point of view which came with the convicts and was able to take root and spread beneficently, although with endless effort, across an empty landscape – the idea that everyone should have a 'second chance,' that Old World reforms, long delayed, could in Australia be put into action almost overnight. Yet because we had, so to speak, been born to it, this concept was too familiar to be appreciated.

'Do you believe in strikes?' I asked one girl.

'Of course I do,' the girl whipped back.

'But *everyone* doesn't believe in them.'

'*My* father's a navvy on the line!'

The girl had a wiry body and tousled hair, and a direct gaze which intrigued me. I think that I wanted to discover her secret soul.

'But is a strike *always* right?'

'Of course not. A strike's a "con," that's what it is. It's solidarity.'

I smiled at her because I liked her, and she looked at me confidingly. 'I'm here on a scholarship,' she said. 'The Sisters took me because my mum had to leave my dad, because he was knocking her about.'

166

It was at moments like this that I felt myself transported back to the family circle at Fleetwood, where life moved at a slower pace, where human relationships had been dictated by the realities of the pioneer-settler situation. Then (feeling the world communal), I had been able to identify with the people in the cottages we had, cottages which my father had built for the dairy workers and the families whose men worked in the mill.

I remembered running barefoot down the hill to the cottage of Peter and Ana (Peter had once been a forester in Lithuania), and feeling as though I had come into a woodsy bower because it was, they said, a Lithuanian feast day, and they had decorated the rooms with green boughs from the scrubs, and also the little cradle which Peter had made for the baby. Peter and Ana, with their broad, flat impassive faces, and dark eyes set a little aslant, had seemed of a different tribe than the rest of us, as they were, of course – quiet and long-suffering and not aware of exactly what Australia had to offer them or how they had had the courage to come from the dark forests of Lithuania to the dark jungles of North Queensland. It was hard to talk to them, because Peter's English wasn't good, and Ana's scarcely existed. One of their children had died, and Ana folded her hands and placed her cheek against them to show me how it had been, and big tears rolled down her unlined face.

Now that I was at the southern school, my mother telephoned one day to tell me that Ana and Peter were travelling the thousand miles from our railway siding at Kureen to Brisbane because another of their children had an obstruction in its throat which the northern doctors had not been able to remove. I met them at the station in Brisbane to show them where the hospital was – both of them big and bulky and foreign-looking, both of them with that same grave, slightly hopeless expression – and I saw the sick child wrapped in a blanket nearly as white as its little face. This child died, too, because it was so weak when they finally got it to the hospital that it could not recover after the doctors operated upon it. I felt guilty, as if, younger and stronger and native to the country, I should have been able to help them more than I did – but also because I had not even, through this barrier of silence, known how to express my feelings to them. The image of something like this remains in our minds because through it one comes to understand the meaning of the sufferings of others.

Somehow it was easier to understand the inarticulate distress of the Lithuanians than it was to sympathize with the struggle for the egalitarian condition which was so much talked about. From childhood we had heard of the need for unions, and had seen them in action, just as we had heard of the 'Wobblies' – the militant radical international trade union organization which had been so important in America and had had an inspirational effect in Australia, bringing with it a dramatic identification with the themes of the Russian Revolution and with the idea of 'direct action' to spur on the worldwide revolutionary movement. This organization was also called the Industrial Workers of the World, or the I.W.W. for short (the initials translating for some hostile Queensland souls as 'I won't Work'). We also knew about the 'Sons of Toil,' a union which had had its origin on the very railway that pushed its way up from Cairns to our own tablelands. And there was considerable pride in the first great workers' union in Australia, the Amalgamated Workers' Union, or the A.W.U., which played a vital role in the growth of government by labor, especially in North Queensland. These associations and unions, and their slogans and songs, and their meetings under the shadow of the great fig tree in Townsville known as the 'Tree of Knowledge,' had been taken for granted all through our youth, but for me there had been more stable memories which challenged the narrowness of the purely political view – standing beside my father in the jungle, for instance, when he talked to the Aborigines, or at the camp for gangers on the railway line when the men gathered in their gray flannel singlets and coarse baggy trousers, looking at him from attentive eyes in their dark sunburnt faces. I had seen through an open door the desolate interior of the tin shed where the men slept – ten disordered canvas stretchers were crowded onto the floor of bare earth, a few gray blankets flung here and there, and work clothes stiff with red dust hung from the tent pole along with two blackened kerosene lanterns; all was permeated with a smell of jungle-damp sourness. I felt pity for these narrow primitive lives, for this male society which had nothing at night for diversion after the long hours under a tropical sun – that is, nothing beyond the beef and damper cooked under the lean-to outside, and the trip to the earth closet hidden behind three saplings. To glimpse the way in which Queensland's traveling proletariat lived (seldom were there women among them) was to know that it was not the material element of which they were deprived so much as that elusive combination of cleanliness, color, and light which my mother had somehow arranged that we should never be without.

The ballads the workmen sang so rarely seemed to dwell upon endurance rather than upon enjoyment. A wailing voice – accompanied by an old banjo, played, perhaps, in the hot golden noon at 'smoko' time, under the bluish shade of trees that had not yet been cut down – would tell of the long stretches of road, of endless dust, of the 'mates' they had left behind them, and always of the charms of whiskey.

> *If water was scarce . . .*
> *And the whiskey was there . . .*
> *Then what they didn't* swalle-er
> *They rubbed in their . . .* ha-air . . .

I don't know where this old song came from, because such folk ballads were carried along over the great distances of Australia by the nomad workers – the shearers and the cane cutters and the drovers, who made their way from town to town or station to station or field to field or bush track to bush track, by whatever means were available to them. The words of the songs were often changed, or swallowed up or modified by the condition of the men who sang them – men

169

who had been for too long without a home or a woman and who needed that oblivion of drink as much as they needed food or sleep. Yet behind this instinctive searching, this chaos of human movement, this continual reaching for 'places further out,' the situation in Australia had hope in it, and the sad songs meant nothing in a way. They were the songs of those who needed to show that they had souls.

It had once been said on the Continent that it was better 'to have a full belly in the colonies than to starve in London town'; but it was clear that when this primary need had been fulfilled, and men ceased to starve, they then tended to yearn for some greater good. If we were all part of the better life (for Australia was boosted throughout the world as Shangri-la for labor, and as superior to the hierarchical English world which we had rejected), then we had little to worry about. But I could not think that this delicate question of happiness had been decided by such simple means, and it was clear to me that urban life in a small city like Brisbane was by no means superior to our own battling existence on the frontiers of the north. In the south our mode of life hovered between English puritanism and colonial *laissez-faire*, so that there, an important yet imperceptible change took place in our lifestyle. The cultural vacuum in the south, for instance, was filled up with sport – not as it had been in the north by wild picnics in rugged country or walks at night along moonlit roads. At home we had all learned to swim as soon as we had learned to walk, and to ride horses by climbing on and falling off while the horses themselves contentedly cropped the grass. We were accustomed to physical activity, but this did not mean that we were especially good at organized school sport. From this school sport emanated a rather stern tyranny, which could not be avoided without some misery. Sport, it seemed, was involved with social respectability. Charm and intelligence were helpless against the tennis courts and the cricket grounds. And citizens wore sports garb as they wore armor. I think that my sisters were less resentful of this sports mania than I was.

170

But by a strange anomaly, and as a by-product of the 'sports-conscious' life, the girls in the upper forms at St Margaret's were sometimes allowed to go to the races on Saturdays; and perversely, and because of my love for horses, this delighted me. We generally managed to get permission by inducing one of the day girls to invite us to her house for the weekend, and I would arrange to be invited by a tall handsome blond girl called Betty Anning, whose parents knew *my* parents (and were relatives of those Annings who had long ago gone north in a covered van with 'Melbourne Ice Company' painted on the sides). At school we sometimes called Betty Blue-eyed Bet, because the social life of her mother and father tended to be reported on the women's page in the local newspaper, accounts which would include comments such as: 'Mrs Anning's eldest daughter, Blue-eyed Bet, was also present.' On race days I never failed to be filled with joy as, from the enclosure dappled with shade, the crowds came pressing forward to the cry of 'They're off!' and the horses came up the straight gleaming in the sun. Nor did I mind the betting itself, which necessitated an interest and knowledge I didn't possess, but which I felt I wanted to cultivate, in a way I had never wanted to cultivate the disciplines of other organized sports.

Going to the races on sunny Saturday afternoons, however, held a slight social hazard because I had difficulty in collecting the right clothes, and generally felt inadequately dressed, or at least not as glamorous and as sophisticated-looking as Betty, or as another girl also called Betty, who for cooler afternoons possessed a fur coat!

How could I regard their statuesque figures and the dresses they wore other than with acute jealousy, even while they both registered a certain mournful despair?

'I have *nothing* to wear,' Betty would say wearily.

'My *earrings* are broken,' the other Betty would reply, nervously fingering her ears, and patting at the waves in her hair, and swaying a little in high-heeled shoes.

Our bets were generally small. Blue-eyed Bet would make hers boldly, laughing and curving her red lips as she passed over the money; the other Betty would somewhat reluctantly fish up notes and silver from a little satin purse, and cast her eyelashes down into cheeks which I suspected were colored and powered at her mother's dressing table.

'I think I'll bet something on Bonzer,' I announced one day. (The horse called Bonzer reminded me of my father, who, when he was feeling enthusiastic, often used this strange Australian adjective which means 'good' or 'excellent.') At the same time I tried to hide from the others how little money I was actually betting, and felt guilty to be spending money at all, because I knew that my parents in these years were finding it harder and harder to obtain it. I don't know whether Blue-eyed Bet and the other Betty understood these mixed motives and sensitivities, but they teased me for my strange method of choosing a horse, when the favorite, Gentleman's Choice, or perhaps the runner-up, The Prince of Wales, would have been more rewarding.

'Oh, look at that horse on the far left – is that *Bonzer?*' cried Blue-eyed Bet in fake excitement. And at the end of the race, the other Betty pretended to wipe her eyes with a pretty lace handkerchief, because Bonzer came in last.

But although these two girls were my companions-in-arms on the adult terrain we were beginning to invade, and although I respected them for their beauty and bravado, and could see how easily they would fit into the social world celebrated each week in the columns of the Brisbane *Courier-Mail* – a world where aristocratic forebears were not absolutely necessary, but where it was considered an advantage to be well groomed, and to excel at sports, and to be good to look at, and in some way also to tune in with the limited but cheerful and generous standards thought desirable in provincial Australia – I knew at least that this world was not mine. The trouble was that I did not know where my world was ... Nor did I know whether, if I found my world, I could fit into it.

***

And what was this medley of instruction where life was lived by rote and timetable, this jangle of bells and whistles for change of class or appearance on the hockey field? Where were the moments of time as we had known them in the past? Where was the real world, I wondered, which promising to be more a question of spirit than of matter, had beckoned me long ago? Perhaps it is true that, in our first separation from the far north, both for myself and for my sisters, a certain schizophrenia presented itself, an uncertainty as to what our personal values were, and a doubt as to whether to identify with the north or the south. To record these shifts between old and new loyalties, to try to test the world with the family thermometer, was only part of an effort to set up a satisfactory continuum of living. We were being introduced to alien values and seeing around us girls whose material advantages were superior to our own, and I think that we didn't know what our reaction to this was. I don't think we knew whether we cared or not.

I thought of my mother trying with the help of an itinerant dressmaker (who would come for two weeks at a time to stay in our guest room at Fleetwood) to work out some affordable allotment of the materials available and the respective clothes needed for five clamorous daughters. I remember being fitted for a simple longish dress, made of fine muslin with a pattern of cherries on it – one of those dresses that turn out to be so satisfactory that the very sight of them afterward (cast in a heap on a chair, or worn-out but still kept in a drawer) brings up memories of a female satisfaction which haunts warm evenings, as the sun sinks lower in the sky through gold to red to vague pink, until at last night falls.

My restlessness at standing so long while the pins were set in place and the hem adjusted was a signal for my grandmother to soothe my mother, whose brow wrinkled in anxiety as she knelt at my feet ('Poor dear Bina, it's never for herself that these dresses are made'), and to chide me a little ('As for you, child: *Il faut souffrir pour être belle!*').

I could never remember without anguish and regret any indifference shown to my mother's feelings. Afterward, I could also associate this scene with dissonances in the family harmony, and with my father turning to my mother for her usual devotion and service – not for ordinary advice, or for approval of a *fait accompli*, but for comfort against the financial pressure which was beginning to dominate his existence, and to force him to face unpleasant facts about the land, the loan from the bank, the falling returns from the property, and, perhaps, about himself. I seemed then to hear in my memory the words 'every last penny' and to see against the light my parents bending together over a great sheet of figures, and at the same time bending nearer and nearer toward the earth.

11

Veil of Unconsciousness

As the year 1929 ended and 1930 began, I left school and found myself as if by magic studying at the university – not, of course, without the usual formalities, not without satisfying certain scholastic requirements, not without saying long farewells to school friends and promising not to forget them, and yet without expecting the many startling changes that would now take place in everyday life. This particular kind of unawareness was probably partly due to the optimism which, again and again, served our generation as a barrier against disillusionment.

I left St. Margaret's and took up residence at the Women's College on the other side of the city – that is, at Kangaroo Point, which was linked directly by a ferryboat with the city proper. Brisbane remained the same, a slightly sprawling, slightly ordinary provincial city; our sleeping quarters, though more individualized than the dormitories of St. Margaret's, were not much more commodious; we were still all 'girls together' in another long wooden building, and with another set of rules; and we studied much the same subjects, though without the same supervision.

Yet the differences in autonomy and privacy were there; the shedding of uniforms for an informality of clothing, the inestimable privilege of choosing how to spend one's time and in what way to create one's successes, or make one's mistakes.

On our way from the Women's College to the university, we crossed the river on the little ferryboat, which was crowded each day not only with the men and women who went to the university but also with numerous regular commuters, who set out each morning to their jobs in the streets around the city center. In crossing the sparkling river, shadowed on either side by tropical trees, these diverse groups of travelers also crossed a Rubicon which divided their nine-to-five duties in offices, stores, classrooms, banks, from their private lives – lives which might remind them obscurely of a past when the future of the river had only to do with convicts, and when, except for those of the big gum trees and hoop pines, few reflections fell into the slow-moving water.

The jacaranda bloomed in Brisbane in November, and when the fallen flowers covered the pavements of Edward Street it was as if the sky had descended, but a sky more delicate than the one above our heads. We walked to the university, which was then housed in the dignified Government House buildings. Our feet moved through the pale blossoms on Edward Street and we would notice that while ragged tufts of lavender still hung to the almost bare blackish branches above us, the classically even poinciana trees (as uniform as umbrellas) were beginning to be covered with scarlet golden-tongued flowers. This double blooming of jacaranda and poinciana – a counterpoint of softest purple and tigerish red – was a brilliant *coup de force* of nature, often presented along whole broad city avenues.

It was nearly Christmastime and for us the time of heat – that is, it was summer. The university, which shared a border with the Botanical Gardens, seemed also to share its giant palms, and massive figs, and pagodas, and grandstands, and to remain a haven of quiet in the glaring humid mornings. Its entrance was on George Street, a street of printers and bookshops, civil servants' offices and hotels. Facing the gardens was the House of Parliament, where I had sometimes been with my father when he came from the north to present his views on the development of North Queensland. It was in that building, feeling a little bored and listening only briefly to the debates which eddied around such questions as strikes, droughts, and the prices of primary products, that I found myself revising whatever childish view of government I had already formed. For it appeared that these debaters were amateurs, men who, by personal force only, were trying, here in sunny Queensland, to create an 'original Australian ethos,' even while they engaged in attempts to cut laws and procedures into suitable shapes for a pioneers' state. The old humor of long ago seemed more understandable now, and it was easier to laugh at the story of the obstreperous member who had appeared in the House in a pair of striped pajamas and announced that he was descended from convicts and proud of it! It was interesting to look back with humor and affection upon our own local scene, and to question what politics meant and where reality lay. Affected, though only mildly, by the need for status, I began to copy the popular radical wisdom, so that I sometimes posed as rebel rather than student, as actor rather than observer. For instance, I pretended to be against the monarchy, although my skeptical nature drew me to wonder whether, after all, the monarchy did any harm. Even then I think it was in history that I found my corrective, and the surprises of history were more attractive to me than the satisfaction of being part of the group.

It had seemed that in our growing up none of us had thought much about the convicts, not even during those first exciting visits to Sydney, when we passed each day, without remark, landmarks such as Mattenwaya – a mere rock jutting out of the harbor, which had been built up as a place for refractory prisoners and nicknamed Pinchgut. Yet in actuality (in some emotional way not then clear to me) I had considered that long-ago convict period with mingled horror and sympathy.

I realize now that to all Australians, not only in our adolescence but in the adolescence of Australia itself, the convicts were important. To that small percentage of 'guests of the Crown' had been added a great flood of immigrants, but we still thought of the convicts. We thought of them as human beings, becoming indignant with the authorities when we learned that they could be flogged for what seemed to us quite minor indiscretions – 'being found rambling in the bush' or 'being absent without leave' or 'going to bed in the middle of the day.' And in a sense we respected them for their catalytic role in Australian history. I remember that when I read *For the Term of His Natural Life* by Marcus Clarke (or relived its gruesome scenes in nightmares), I brooded about the escaped prisoners, about the ax which had drunk 'so much human blood,' and about the cannibalism in the gray hostile Sydney bush as, one by one, the escapees were killed to provide the others with food. It may have been this horror – repeating that old horror of the northern past – which had driven me to want to know more of the convicts. Once when I was in Brisbane with my father, he indicated a big stone building on the left side of George Street, near Parliament House.

'That's where they keep the convict records for Queensland,' he said. 'In the basement of that building.'

'Do you think I could *see* them?'

My father smiled; it amused and perhaps pleased him that anything to do with history seemed romantic to me.

'I don't see why not. I think anyone can see them. You go in there and find out. You can meet me over at Parliament House.'

I did go and I did find out. An old man, guardian of the records, seemed surprised at my age and inexperience, but he showed me dusty shelves holding stacks of equally dusty ledgers with tartan covers and oilcloth bindings, and shuffled off to other duties. The ceiling was high in that old building – the light came in through windows near the street level. The smell of old papers hung in the undisturbed air. But what was so surprising was that these ledgers with the ruled lines had nothing in them but long lists of convict names, and opposite these, scanty addresses, and beside these, a very brief account of the crime concerned, and an even briefer note of the sentence. With a scratchy nib and pale blue ink, someone had entered notes rather like this: '*Mary Bailey*. Bockhampton, Dorset. *Crime*: Stealing a bundle of washing. *Sentence*: 7 years.'

I stood there, my fingers dark with dust, and turned the pages slowly. They seemed inadequate and bare of life. After a while I closed the books and thanked the old man and went to look for my father. I don't know why I did not remember anything more about that impulse on a hot summer's afternoon, but I decided long afterward that I had wanted something and had not found it. Quite apart from the convicts, it was in this way that I began to dramatize the country's condition of isolation and intellectual loneliness.

The discoveries made in that first year at the university, unimportant as they seemed, tended to satisfy a growing need to accept and explore the extended world. When I went to a dance in the town of Gympie, some miles northeast of Brisbane, with my friends Eunice and Mostyn Hanger, I found myself in a mining district rather different from those I had known before. But it spoke to me of those smaller towns around Herberton and Atherton, 'lost towns' as I thought of them, but saturated with the history of past endeavors. Gympie also represented something else. Thomas Hanger, the father of these two friends, was at that time headmaster of the Gympie high school, where the dance was to be held, and he told me later that he had started as a pupil-teacher at the age of thirteen, and that there had been times then when he felt that the occasional public thrashings at the school were lingeringly reminiscent of convict times. This fascinated me. It was as if a curtain had suddenly risen upon a not so distant past. The town, somewhat chillier than the coast, and set among green hills – with the school itself, like most Queensland buildings, high on stilts and standing in the midst of a great expanse of golden gravel – gave the impression of the primacy of bare nature. Here 'education' certainly continued the stand it had begun long ago; but the building, stark and abrupt and jutting up from its foundation posts made of small trees, seemed to say, 'Do your best to create a civilization – reality will defeat you.'

The atmosphere in this town and the bare aspect of the school were equally impressive. Thomas Hanger, very serious and dignified, standing in the doorway of the school to greet many of his students and their friends, told us something about the pioneering times in Central Queensland, and of how rough and spontaneous they had been. He had lived first in Rockhampton in the tent town near the railway line, and his first memories were of the glow of the red-hot iron in the forges, the flicker of campfires, and the points of light made by the hurricane lanterns hanging beneath the wagons. Otherwise his recollections were dominated by noisy bars and billiard rooms, by drunken men and women who were 'going on the booze,' as it was called, by the spectacle of frequent fistfights, and by medical problems such as the scarred sore eyes caused by an almost universal 'sandy blight.'

'We thought it a privilege to be a teacher . . . and I was grateful for it, you can be sure . . . there was no idea that the state would look after you if you had no job.'

On that night – as we all began to dance between the walls decorated with green boughs from the surrounding hills (sometimes to form squares and circles, and sometimes to 'sashay' from one end of the hall to the other), and as the moon rose to turn the bare roads of this chilly little mining town to silver – I would desert the dancing for a while to talk to my old host, and to listen to his stories of the outback schools like the one at Jericho, 360 miles out to the west, which had had no doctor, no chemist, no dentist, and no resident clergyman; where, as he said, the high school was to the township what the monastery had been to the village in medieval England. It was clear that it was not only the lives of successful explorers and adventurers, of squatters and pioneers, which had determined Australia's considerable progress in those years, but also that firm puritanical belief in self-control and discipline brought by churchmen, educators, and schoolteachers – that inheritance which had somehow conquered the diverse strains of inertia in the country.

'I'll never forget your father,' I said to Eunice that night. Eunice was the 'bright' girl in a 'bright' family, and was later to become a lecturer at the university.

'My father?'

'Yes ... he's so much more important than we are,' I said. 'Like *my* father is. We will never be as important as our fathers were!'

But insights like this did little to help me be more serious at the university. Here, in this place of new opportunities and countless books, I remembered those monsoon evenings at Kureen when we would come running into the house with damp clothes and misted hair, to change into warm clothes for the evening, to eat dinner, to light a fire of crackling wood in the red-washed fireplace, and, then, to pick up books for a night of reading. But a few miles from our own house it was not considered the thing to be a reader. 'You don't want her to be a bluestocking,' a friend of my father's had replied in horror when my father said that he hoped I could go to the university. 'I wouldn't want that for *my* daughter.' To be a bluestocking in the Australia of that time meant that a girl had an inordinate interest in learning, a strange disregard of masculine attraction, and risked most foolishly the fate of not being attractive to men.

Fortunately my feelings had not been hurt by this conversation, for although I did not fear being thought a bluestocking, I did fear that my father might decide *not* to send me to the university, since in any case it cost money to do so. The compelling motivation, however, and this in spite of those laden library shelves, and in spite of the deep inner yearning to make them mine, revealed itself to me as I went to and fro on the ferry across the river – for clearly the university was not only a place of books but also a place where men abounded. In fact, the mere act of traveling from Kangaroo Point on the small chugging ferryboat was instrumental in putting me in touch with a certain man, who a year later was writing to me at a box at the central post office, and calling me 'The Queen of the Ferries.' It was soothing to remember later those emotions which had had about them something desperately primitive – emotions which he seemed to have set in motion by merely sitting at the other end of the ferryboat (students tended to stay in the back), lost in thought, and holding a little book tucked under his arm. In youth what is physically pleasing to us takes on a sacred character, so that minor associations – color, scent, shape, style – become allied to the central theme, and cannot be separated from it. Because this man pleased me I fantasized for a long time that I had already met him, although I knew nothing about him except that his name was John Evelyn and that he worked somewhere up in Queen Street – 'in a bank,' it was said.

John's well-cut suits and soft felt hats, the straight mobile profile I would glimpse beneath a slightly rakish pulled-down hat brim as he turned to step off the ferry (bearing to the right toward town while I went straight ahead up Edward Street toward the university), were so attractive to my eyes that I decided at once that I knew all the secrets of his personality. So complete was this revelation that my only anxiety then became the need to know what book he carried under his arm. Even from a distance the book appeared to be one I might have carried myself, but like some fortune-teller who hopes that the right card will come up, I was convinced that if I knew the book's name, this alone would tell me whether I was or was not on the right course! I was so intent upon discovery that I found myself pressing forward a little – to almost brush his elbow, to see the slight pink in his tanned cheek, and even to catch a glance from his intelligent brown eyes, which seemed at first to seek me out and then to turn away in polite nonrecognition – and was able to read, not the title of the book, but the name of its author – Siegfried Sassoon.

At that time I was emotional, and doggedly tenacious – in fact, this complete stranger was to be important to me as much because I had decided that he was to be so as because of any innate suitability. I went up Edward Street under the jacaranda trees, my feet in the blossoms, my head in the clouds, like some mysteriously appointed bride among her careless contemporaries. A tall, dark, long-faced graduate in entomology walked at my side, a young man called Norman, with a soft voice and an erect bearing, who was by way of being my 'beau.' (My sister Helen was the companion of one of his friends, and my best friend, Joan Cue – we were known as 'the two Joans' – was friendly with another. Joan Cue was extremely pretty, a dark-haired beauty of the roguish kind, and we shared somewhat the same sense of humor. The six of us gathered at the dances, and at midnight, under a nearly always steadily luminous moon, climbed the fence of the Botanical Gardens and wandered among masses of perfumed roses and over damp grasses.)

'Oh, hullo,' I said.

'Hullo.' Norman touched my elbow respectfully. 'I was *hoping* you would catch the ten-of-nine.'

My smile was affectionate, but tinged with haste. 'I have to go to the library, so I came early.'

'Not too much work, I hope,' he said ironically.

'*The Yellow Book,* as usual,' I admitted. *The Yellow Book,* the famous London journal of the late nineties, was a modernist experiment of a kind, featuring stories by Arnold Bennett, H.G. Wells, Henry James, and poems such as I had found long ago in the Georgian Poetry series and which I had read curled up in the big red leather chair in our sitting room at Fleetwood. Out of date as it might appear, *The Yellow Book* was still the first journal I had ever seen which was devoted to sophisticated modern literature, so that it was as attractive to me as honey is to the bee, and I was reading my way through it, volume by volume.

'It's all that I can understand,' I said to Norman, with coquettish emphasis upon my intellectual frailty.

'No,' he replied with a severe smile, 'you can understand more than that.'

'Well . . . it's all I care about.'

'Could you be lazy?' he asked, with a little squeeze of my arm.

'Nowhere here in Australia, can I find what I find in *The Yellow Book* . . .'

'Aren't you supposed to be getting a degree?'

'Yes . . . but there will be time . . .'

Truly alarmed for my future, he protested at once: 'There *won't* be much time . . .'

I had not considered, and certainly not yet dared to admit, that I wanted to do nothing but read and write, so that now I could not explain myself to him, nor could I defend my instinct toward apprenticeship. From the point of view of apprenticeship, *The Yellow Book*, with its distinguished writers and its recognition of modern social problems such as divorce, infidelity, and the emancipation of women, was the perfect reading material for me, and it was not surprising that I acted rather as if I had become addicted to some terrible drug, and so followed the same monotonous course each day. Starved for good books and unused to the self-imposed disciplines of college life – accustomed to the informalities of the northern school – I would find my way to the stacks in the library, and sink down into a crouching position upon the floor near some large window. Deep in whatever interested me, oblivious of the sun moving far overhead, drowsy from the sheltered warmth of these avenues empty of people but filled with volumes, I would miss lectures and forget lunch, as I read my way through some English novel of middle-class life; or pondered over the lines of a poet new to me; or started yet again on the third volume of *The Yellow Book*, with its weary but urbane illustrations by Aubrey Beardsley. I didn't altogether understand, as I read *The Yellow Book*, that I used it as a vehicle of migration, which transformed Kangaroo Point into London's bohemia, and switched my psychological allegiance from Australia to England.

The education we get is very often a continuation of the education we have already had: when I entered the big gates leading from George Street into the university grounds, flushed and hot from traveling all the way from Kangaroo Point, and paused at the library door with the best intentions to study, but with my emotions leading me elsewhere (to the particular shelves given over to literature and poetry), I was only repeating what I had done all of my life. Had I not often in the years of my childhood saved some end of a candle to light after the rest of the family were in bed so that I could read a little bit more of a fairy tale I had been told to put away? Had I not sometimes skimped the housework I was supposed to do in order to skim across the back paddock to the barn to unearth some interesting volume from under the hay? Then I had had no guilt, but now something told me that this could not go on forever.

Old Government House was an impressive sandstone building with imposing columns and graceful arches; a giant hoop pine shaded its front, and all day long students passed by its circular entrance, where once a helmeted soldier on a white horse had guarded the door. When I got as far as the library I had the same sense of sovereignty that I had had as a child. The library, like the barn, had all the measurements of a world, and here I felt equality – at least as far as my imaginary life was concerned. In the end I had only been able to attend the university because of the generosity of my Uncle Tony, and perhaps I might have thought of this as I squandered hour after hour on literature when I should have been learning irregular French verbs or attempting to make headway with what was called Logic I. But thoughts of my uncle, loving as they were, were also naïvely dissociated from any possible examination at the end of the year; I thought that my father and mother, as well as my uncle, would like me to belong to the literary world, and I even had illusions that they recognized me as a worthy entrant, and indeed trusted me not only to pass exams but to do much more. What that 'more' was, I did not yet try to imagine, because to analyze it would have given it too much reality.

It is true that our equanimity was often disturbed in those days because of the depression said to be coming.

The confidence with which we had been brought up, and the gusto with which we had depended upon the earth and the fruits of the earth to govern and sustain our lives, were faltering. Now it was said that there had been a great failure on the New York Stock Exchange, and that, as a result, banks were failing in England and Australia as well.

I was reminded of an incident that had occurred in Kureen several years before when Margot and I, out in the paddocks one day, saw a swarthy bearded man building a fire dangerously close to a fence. We drew nearer to see what he was doing, and I remember that I felt timid at the full view of his face, red and glistening with its stubby beard. He had roasted a slab of meat over the fire and was cutting it into hunks with a clasp knife. We warned him about the fence, at which he grunted, and then we stood watching him silently – half repelled, half fascinated by his sweat-stained singlet and filthy boots, by his eyes, which, like an animal's, lifted to look at us from the meat he was stuffing into his mouth. We were 'little women' wishing to put the world to rights, filled with pity and officious concern. Finally one of us said gently, 'Do you find it hard to get work?'

He looked at us with his mouth full, chewing noisily; his chin shone with grease, a merry yet scornful smile appeared on his face.

'Carn't yer see me jaws are workin'?' he asked belligerently; and then he let forth a bellow of raucous laughter which sent us hurrying from the spot.

This may have been the time when the depression was just beginning, a time when – even more than usual – men were ranging through the north, living off the land, and camping out of doors.

Now in Brisbane I said to Helen, who was studying science and went to different classes in different buildings, 'It can't go on like this, can it? What will Daddy do? *Everyone* will owe money to the banks, and *then* what will the banks do?'

Helen was the sober member of the family, who could always be trusted to think before she spoke. In spite of

186

being an almost exact physical copy of her identical twin, she seemed less emotional than Margot, and had a gentle, rather mature manner suggesting a certain wisdom (conventional as it may have been). 'When we get our degrees,' she said, as if she had already thought it over, 'we will just have to get jobs and look after ourselves.'

'Yes, of course,' I said.

But I worked no harder because of it. Instead, I walked into an ugly little building on George Street which housed a secretarial school and put my name down for a typing course. I spent one evening a week sitting in a classroom surrounded by strangers from the town, trying to type out, correctly and rapidly, the lines read to us by a gimlet-eyed little woman, who paced restlessly up and down the aisles of typewriters – chanting aloud and sometimes beating the desks with a long ruler.

My typing was inferior, and on such evenings, sitting on the late ferry, my hands purple from the cheap typewriter ribbons, I was particularly dissatisfied with my image. In spite of this, however, and in spite of my weary eyes and aching fingers, it did not occur to me that failure was possible, either in typing classes or elsewhere. Nor was I deterred by the fact that the stories I hoped to type out with my new skills had not yet been written!

On the ferry I was content to watch for the broad shoulders and the crushed hat brim of this man I had chosen to dream about. I liked to see what sort of tie he had on, what his mood seemed to be, how many times his gaze wandered to the end of the ferry where I sat, preoccupied and tense. I saw him take off his hat in the sunshine and let the wind blow his hair across his forehead. I saw him greet some stranger, generally a man, and spend a few minutes talking to him. 'It was a good party,' I heard him say once, and then my equanimity deserted me as I imagined him living a sophisticated life far away from me, a life of parties with attractive people, especially attractive women. Immediately

I thought that I might not have any charms for him at all, and became acutely conscious of the body with which I sat on the ferry, of my somewhat limited wardrobe, and of ways in which I might improve them both so as to make them more desirable. 'Look,' I would think, straightening up and elevating my small shoulders, 'look here ... this way ... please look at me,' and once I did think that he looked at me, and that some gleam of recognition and reassurance sped from his eyes to mine.

Where the glinting tide swelled from the distant sea, and rolled slowly by toward the up-country, all motion seemed marvelous – small craft of various kinds beat up with the wind, heavy vines aswing on the cliffs, and branches half drowned in the waters beneath. Sometimes I watched John's back receding from the ferry, and dreamt that as I followed far behind he suddenly turned, took my hand, and drew me after him, on some unknown journey. Even as my feet moved resolutely up Edward Street, I told myself that he was the father of children (he was sometimes seen with a little blond boy, tightly buttoned into a well-cut linen coat, with a high waist *à l'anglaise*), but this made no difference to my urgent fantasies. I was more impressed by the fact that during one certain week he carried, not the familiar Sassoon, or the volume of Galsworthy, but something called *Isles of Illusion*, which I afterward found out was the story of a man who lived alone on a tropical island and suffered the disillusionments of someone who had once believed in Paradise. I deduced from this another strand of the mutuality by which I could draw him closer to me, and in fact imagined myself living with him in a thatched gunyah such as the Aborigines built, only larger and furnished with rugs and cushions. I saw the dark serrated palms swaying against the endless open vistas of the sea – our food set out on green leaves, our drink in shells of coconut. I felt that all my life had been a preface to this – South Sea maid and gunyah builder, mistress and companion traveler. I heard him tell someone on the ferry that he had 'run off' that weekend to 'Tambourine,' and immediately I was ready to transfer my longings to the mountains – to the valleys of ancient cycads, to the purple evenings perfumed by wild myrtle and lit only by the stars. I was not to be cured of my obsession, because such are the extremes to which our senses carry us, and when I did go up to that mountain with a group of university friends, I found his name written in the guest book of an old cottage called the Cedars and accordingly spent the whole night in wakefulness, the name written on my flesh. Ignorant as I was of sexual embraces, my imagination prophesied one final embrace from which to expect delirious pleasure.

In the end I was of course introduced to him, and then in a most normal way – that is, through the president of the Women's College, a Miss Freda Bage, who happened to be traveling with us on the ferry that day to attend a meeting at the university, and to whom John lifted his hat, whereupon she greeted him ('Oh, Mr Evelyn . . .') and then introduced two of us to him as 'her charges for this first year,' and went on talking in a breathless way about such subjects as the League of Nations, and the future of Kangaroo Point, and even about the 'kind of gardens which might be encouraged' in the street upon which both his house and the Women's College bordered. John seemed to be saying that he thought better of '*in*formal' gardens, at which Miss Bage, almost standing on tiptoe, short as she was, and shaking her head adorned with an exceptionally plain brown hat, shouted into his ear that he should 'think it over' and give her regards to Mrs Evelyn, and not forget to come soon to visit the college, while I looked on as indifferently as I could, only knowing that should I meet John again face to face, I would at least be permitted to smile at him.

It was not very long after this that we began to exchange letters. The golden sandstone columns of the old central post office – often a cool refuge from the burning heat outside, and, besides, the central focus in Queen Street for all the uses which post offices fill – became invested for me with a glamour far beyond usefulness or good sense. As

I turned from the street and walked up the steps and into the privacy of the pillars where the letter boxes were, I experienced a tumult of feelings, richer and more powerful than those I experienced on the ferry when I actually saw John in the flesh.

I think this was because, childish and rural as I possibly was, I was not without an objective recognition of the need for social ties and social responsibilities, and to encounter John socially, to see him approach me in the street and lift his hat and murmur about some plan to meet me, had stirred a feeling of unsuitability. I even felt that I was doing harm to my brave faraway enduring parents by sending and receiving this torrent of clandestine letters, and hoping for whatever more could be managed. It was by this route that pain and some embarrassment entered the relationship, even while it made it more important – something sad, joyful and frenetic, a sense of the richness but also of the impermanence of life itself.

In these letters John was able to tell me facts about himself for which there was no time in our brief encounters: that, for instance, he had had to leave school at fifteen because his father had had a nervous breakdown; that his mother, fearing that John might get into trouble in a less respectable job, managed to get him into a bank as a messenger boy; that he had advanced rapidly, and had been a banker ever since (not because he liked it, but because he had gradually managed to work efficiently, so that he was able in his leisure to indulge in his great passion for books, and for gardening).

The letters, written in haste and deposited in secret, were messages sent across that sprawling, tin-roofed, not very beautiful city – letters searching for kinship and fulfillment in the desert of provincial living. Like bread cast upon the waters, like songs which any romantic singer could pick up and finish, they were letters to establish trust. 'England is my spiritual home,' wrote John. 'I don't like places where there is no older civilization.'

'I know what you mean,' I wrote back. 'I want to see the house where Tennyson lived, and the forest gate where Tess of the d'Urbervilles met Angel.'

John wrote: 'I listened to the lyrebirds up at Mount Tambourine . . .' and a little further on: 'Why do Australians have such a passion for cutting down trees?'

And I wrote back: 'Will you take me up to Mount Tambourine some day?. . . It is so long since I heard a lyrebird singing,' and 'Yes, the life of a tree is almost more important than the life of a man!'

'But if I belong to this century,' he admitted in a letter, 'I love the nineties more. I love hansom cabs and women in voluminous skirts, and artists like Whistler and Sickert . . . and here I am in a bank, and you, my precious, with long legs and short skirts – my Queen of the Ferries.'

These letters made me more sympathetic not only toward John but toward myself as well. I saw that he had been forced to go to work before he was ready for it. I saw that he would have liked to go to a university, and that in spite of his bookish nature he had actually been deprived of the opportunity to find a more interesting way of making his living. I realized that he was a wage slave, and that I myself was at least enjoying that little respite from wage earning which so few people in the world are allowed. I felt a surge of feeling for him, more realistic than any I had felt before.

Now I was conscious that his letters were more to me than the letters of a lover. They represented the urge to the larger life, the pushing forward of a door already half open; and in this epistolary exercise, even as we were so obviously homeless, we looked despairingly for our spiritual home. Eventually, although conscious of unseemliness, we made use of a shadowy lounge in the Carlton Hotel – a hotel without any particular reputation but definitely a place where we were unlikely to run into friends; a place of deep gloomy carpets, pale blond chairs padded with crimson, a clock which ticked away the minutes and reverberated in our time-conscious hearts; a long room with (far away at

191

the other end) a little bar, sporadically attended by a sharp-featured woman with hair that was flat and shiny like patent leather, who grew used to us eventually and, having brought us automatically the two drinks we allowed ourselves, would then disappear from view.

I was sometimes conscious of my clothes, as I had been at school when we were allowed to go to the races, for John's friends were among the better-dressed and the more worldly in the town. But crushed into these cavernous chairs, and under these dim lights, my clothes would cease to seem important, and his smart tropical suits would wilt down to my own practical university level, until eventually we became unaware of our public image altogether, and would continue to sip at our drinks and to look slowly across the glasses in which the ice melted as easily as did our apprehension. In that long-ago time of numerous restraints and conventions, it did not seem safe to meet in public places, so John devised a method whereby, during the lunch hour, we could drive together to a certain lonely road in the bush not far from One-Tree Hill, and park the car and walk up an even lonelier tract to a sheltered spot which was hidden by the arrangements of the eucalypts and screened from the road by the overhang of the earthen banks. Here, in a little enclosure which might have been arranged for us, we had an even greater time problem than we had had in the city; but we had the real advantage of being at least able to stand in each other's arms, trying to forget ourselves in an uncomfortable swoon of heat and passion – our feet on the stony dry soil among the crackling eucalyptus leaves, our faces and arms and sometimes even our lips stung by mosquitoes (if, as sometimes happened, it was in the late afternoon), and always conscious of the steady march of the minutes, which John had to obey in a mechanical and faithful way (because he was the superintendent of the department in which he worked, and therefore responsible each afternoon for the safe passage of money to the vaults).

Long afterward, in a letter, John talked about a play he had seen 'in the days of our first love,' and after all those years it stirred me again, because, for me, it had indeed been a first love, and based as much upon what seemed an absolute physical necessity as upon my approval of his smooth healthy features, and warm broad fingers, and a certain air of reassuring confidence, or as upon whatever it was we had in common. If it is true that nothing happens to us without a due process of barter going on, then John and I were paying in full each time we met, for when we put our arms around each other, it was clear that later we must be brusquely torn apart, although with flushed faces and haggard eyes.

By the time I actually slept with John – meeting him at an easily accessible and rather disreputable hotel in a side street, its dark entrance covered with tangled tropical vines – it was hard for me to realize that sex could be an abandoned and lively crescendo, rather than a physical straining in situations and positions where it was impossible to move naturally. I was at last allowed to know how right my original instincts had been in choosing this man for a partner, and how all the fears I had had of going to what the novels called 'a house of assignation' were quickly eliminated by his mere presence, and by a strong sense of the renewal of love. Not that we were to be rid in the future of the nagging fear of being 'seen,' or of the knowledge of limited time, but for half an hour the world could be well lost . . .

My unsuitable addiction to this man, who was almost old enough to be my father, set some tone to my life – something which, like a river running underground through dark caverns before it comes out into the light again, made it impossible for me to retain for very much longer the indiscriminate contentment of youth.

12

When Trouble Came

I don't know when it was that I began to think of trouble not only as something which might come to others but as something which might come to me. My sense of what trouble was seemed to have shifted, so that quite suddenly my love for John had become a source of self-doubt. Occasionally I would leave the library and walk outside along the gravel driveways and into the Botanical Gardens, where the trees had that brooding quality only possible where water flows and warmth encourages growth, and on such occasions, leaning against the broad damp trunk of an enormous tree, I would be aware what I feared most was to be in a position of helpless subjection. I felt that I must always have the power to save myself, that I could not bear to submit any control over my life to others whose values might not be mine.

It is easier for me to analyze this complex of feelings now than it was in those days when I was subject to many different influences, all of them competing for my attention. It is true that I had been trained for freedom, and that images of captivity roused my fighting spirit – the example presented to us as children had always been that of 'the aggressive stance,' the concept of struggling against heavy odds, against passivity, against danger and disaster. On one occasion at Fleetwood, when Helen was confronted by something she thought unfair, she quoted a verse of William Ernest Henley's, even while her eyes were full of tears; I don't think it occurred to us that she was being overdramatic. The title of the poem was 'Unconquerable' and the line was 'My head is bloody, but unbowed.' We thought it natural that she should express herself that way; but it seemed to me that I had little reason to be distressed, and that I was not forced into any irreconcilable position. Perhaps considering the restrictive conditions of the times, and the pattern of a colonial society which strove to rise above its origins by repressing unconventional sexuality, it was a little surprising that I had been bold enough simply to take what I thought I needed.

All the same, when I put my books and notes rapidly into my locker, changed into a clean blouse, brushed my hair, and set off up George Street, hastening rapidly toward Queen Street and the lounge of the Carlton (where as if by accident, and outwardly indifferent, but with a beating heart, I would encounter John), some feeling of dismay would overcome me. Across the glitter of the glasses which provided our excuse, and allowed us to make smiling remarks about the good luck of so unforeseen an encounter, I could smile in the old way; but I could not quite escape a sense of irony, for had I not foreseen the constant imposition of what was clandestine, and was I ever now to escape it?

What John thought of, I didn't know, but years later he wrote me of his sense of confusion, and even despair: 'I can't tell you how it was in those days. I loved you, but I felt bad about it. I think that I treated you badly . . . I think that I should never have taken you to lounges like the Carlton Hotel, or to that other place where we were at least at ease for a while . . . At first it was only that "great excitement," and then I was deep into it . . . After you left I never climbed the hill which led up from the ferry without thinking of you, but when I got closer to my own house I would experience the dead horrible feeling of a fruitless marriage . . . smothered . . . mired down. I knew how much I loved you, but I loved you in a fog.'

Eventually, when I found in myself a restlessness which went beyond the frustrations of the relationship with John, and beyond the dichotomy of my personal struggle between scholarship and creativity, I began to wander from group to group on the university campus, seemingly looking for an avenue for my talents. I wondered whether this mild recurrence of malaise was mine only, or whether it extended to others, and I tried to believe that my discontent had something to do with the economic depression. If, as some said, the economic depression was a reality, then the very core of Australian life was threatened (for the national philosophy claimed that each family had a right to a house, to a decent standard of living, and to a primary education for its children). But not yet having such responsibilities myself, I could scarcely claim them as reason for dissatisfaction. As soon as I got to the university I think I realized that writing was one of my main compulsions and perhaps my only real gift. But with great stubbornness I had refused to develop this talent seriously because I was suffering from delusions about 'creativity,' and thought that inspiration was something that descended upon the would-be writer like a gift from on high – a beneficent clarification, for which I waited in vain. Miracles are not, as a rule, for the young, but for those who have suffered for a long time in silence.

In the meantime, at the university it was impossible not to become more aware of the scene around me, so that I could observe that many students were interested in politics as I was interested in writing, and that they brought to politics the same banked-up energy which I had experienced in myself. I found that I had picked up from the more articulate students phrases such as '*laissez-faire* capitalism,' 'contradictions of society,' and 'libertarian socialism,' and had even ventured to try to separate what was said glibly by these students from what seemed to be objectively true. With my new acquisition of rhetoric I recognized early that the battle cries of one group ('rampant colonialism' and 'diverting egalitarianism' and 'upper-class patronage,' for instance) could 'momentarily' be shouted down by the counter-cries of another group (such as 'betraying the interests of the cocky farmers and the migrant workers'). The 'cocky' farmers were the small unorganized farmers who pecked a living from the soil, almost as birds did, and like the migrant workers, they often did not feel comfortable identifying with unions.

I think that I was trying to learn about politics in a way satisfactory to myself; and perhaps also in a way which recognized my father's needs and interests. I knew that in Queensland the work force, if inarticulate culturally, was vociferous politically, and could not be said to be without influence; and I wondered whether the enemy could *always* be the old 'class' enemy which public rhetoric was attacking and deriding. Surely it could not be because some Australians owned land that the prices of primary produce, copper, wool, hides, tin, etc., were plunging?

When I put these questions to others, I could see that many were uninterested, and that many more were confused. Yet one small group – those who claimed great sympathy with the Russian Revolution – appeared sure of some infallible logic in their position. And it was this group which roused my interest and distrust. I was also half envious of their rhetoric, and liked or was developing a liking for their verbal sparring.

Yet one afternoon – when I happened to tell Norman that I was reading Mayakovsky, the great poet of the Russian Revolution, and Norman was quiet, as he always was when I told him about my hopes for broadening the world I lived in, and my determination to leave Australia as soon as I could – I felt ashamed, because my rhetoric was as bad as anyone else's, and it disgusted me to think that I should pretend that I was familiar with Mayakovsky when I had only heard about him a few days before! I knew also that Norman didn't feel as I felt – that he was more realistic than I was and didn't let Australian deficiencies bother him. I think that the fate he most truly desired was to live and work in Australia. But in his gentle way he wooed me, and his kindness to me was unfailing, so that there were times when I thought of him gratefully, as if, in the end, he and no one else might help me if 'trouble came.'

One day I went to see Uncle Tony at the Hotel Cecil and sat in the dining room, with its spotless napery, and its stiff aged off-white blinds at the windows, and its 'permanent' guests scattered around the room at the tables where they had always sat, and sat now, with the same air of habitual satisfaction. I knew that the proletariat were on the move in Queensland, looking for work and unable to believe they couldn't get it – camping in the bush, living under lean-tos or bridges, wearing out the soles of their shoes. I had seen them in the Brisbane streets, gathering wherever there was a tree to shelter them or a wall to lean against. It made me uncomfortable to look at them, as if ordinary men had suddenly become invalids who must be humored, or cheered up, or apologized to.

'It's happening everywhere,' my uncle explained. 'In New York people who are bankrupt are jumping out of buildings . . . Two whole years ago, when Joe Shelley was in Townsville, I walked down from the Queens Hotel to listen to him "bring his message to the masses," and his message was that there had to be a socialist government in Queensland.' (Joe Shelley was a radical seaman who had deserted the Wobblies for the Communist Party, and he was famous in labor circles for preferring to go to prison rather than 'move on,' as the police had asked him to do.)

Uncle Tony was slowly eating his ice cream, and he called to the elderly waitress, teasing her, 'By crikey, you *promised* me strawberry!'

The waitress blushed and protested, 'Oh, Mr. Linedale . . . there *wasn't* no strawberry!'

'Uncle,' I said, 'will the workers go over to the Communists because of the depression?'

'A lot of people don't like to fight,' he answered sadly. 'With the Communists it's always a case of fight 'em or give in.' He added with an ironic inflection: 'You see, now they've got Moscow to help them. This new idea has a base. They can go to Moscow and be with their mates; then they can come back here as *bosses*!'

My uncle's picture of Russia as a base for radical action in Australia was new to me, and I let it pass without comment. I

198

did not know then that I was actually contemporaneous with many of the political personages who would later fascinate me (some of whom I would get to know) – Orwell and Muggeridge, Auden and Spender, the spies-to-be of the great English public schools (not to mention John Desmond Bernal, one of their gurus), as well as others of the politically conscious at that time in the United States, like Max Eastman and Carlo Tresca, and Bert and Ella Wolfe, and Herbert Solow and Malcolm Cowley, and James T. Farrell. Nor, of course, did I realize what riches in human development and political interest waited for me right there in my own native land, in that lonely vacuum, far away (as I thought) from all that was interesting in the world!

Because one is not completely aware of a situation does not mean that one is not aware at all. The fact that at the university I had not been able to regulate my studies did not mean that I was not naturally studious; nor did my vagueness about the main intellectual and political currents of my time mean that I was completely frivolous.

In those days politics were mysterious to me because it seemed impossible to unravel the origins of political acts; I felt more at ease with literary personages, who were as close as next-door neighbors and who urged me by their literary confidences to take pad and pencil and write down whatever came into my head. I did not admire myself for this – it seemed unnatural and even a little frightening, as if I were a medium through which other voices spoke.

But at a much earlier time, at home in Kureen, against the almost unbroken silence of unobtrusive nature, unrealized ambitions had appeared natural enough. My siblings had spent time in drawing and sewing, in collecting orchids, in photography with Brownie cameras, in pressing flowers and grasses, in poring over cookbooks; I alone dared to talk of being a 'real' writer, and to fill marbled exercise books with unfinished stories. I alone joined the Junior Literary Society, where I sometimes won innocuous prizes, and eventually corresponded with a young writer pen friend from Fiji, who sent me a sepia studio photograph of himself seated in a cane chair, with palm leaves in the background and an animal skin over his bare and beautiful shoulder. For some reason I had expected this pen friend to be white, but after gazing at his dignified warm brown face, I fantasized about whether we might not fall in love, and about how – should this eventuate – I would manage the introduction to my parents!

Later, of course, thought processes were less romantic. At the Herberton school I had been momentarily under the influence of Edgar Allan Poe and had wandered over the stony hillsides with his *Tales of Mystery and Imagination* clutched in my hand, my head whirling with impossible and turgid plots. Sometimes at night, Poe's fevered images broke into my sleep, and always for background there were the massive cliffs and tors of outback places, writhed over by the grappling roots of water-hungry trees, and haunted by strange animals as recognizable in the Australian pantheon as were the griffins and unicorns in medieval tapestries.

At one point I had written, or rather tried to write, a story for the St. Margaret's school magazine which began:

I was alone, alone, alone – never in my life had I dreamed of such vast loneliness. It sounded in my ears, it crowded upon my vision, it threatened the very peace of my soul.

Black awful rocks loomed beside me and above me – and in fear I moved forward to stand upon the brink of the sullen sea . . .

I remember that I could not finish the piece, that it seemed like an inconclusive dream, to which there was no ending. The landscapes of Australia, those places I was seeing in the south – the odd dark red plateaus which extended beyond Charters Towers, the smooth strange stones strewn from early volcanoes, the country of the outback which had stirred poets to explain their suffering – were devastatingly prevalent.

Where brown summer and death have mated –
That's where the dead men lie!
Loving with fiery lust unsated –
That's where the dead men lie!
Out where the grinning skulls bleach whitely
Under the salt bush sparkling brightly;
Out where the wild dogs chorus nightly –
That's where the dead men lie!

These scenes, described by Barcroft Boake, could be easily translated into an Edgar Allan Poe idiom, but what did they mean, why did the words and the rhythm flow so easily, and yet seem to disappear into some deep underground cavern? I was haunted by the impulse to imitate. I read, from one end to the other, the little volume of Poe my mother had bought me (picking her way slowly through a Sydney bookstore on one of our earlier visits to that city, her small serious face absorbed, her eyes large and glowing with love, her fingers encased in the city gloves she had darned so painstakingly before we left Kureen); but I was no better off than before. Where were the cadaverous raven-dark women of Poe's world, the men with their sick fancies about cats, and extracting teeth from corpses, and walling up enemies, and burying mistresses before they were dead? How could I compete with these images which, although I couldn't fathom them, were undoubtedly powerful? Because the stories did not seem 'true' to me, and because I did not yet know that in cases like this truth was irrelevant, I was uncertain of their value. I read the word 'Gothic' in the introduction to the book, and I dimly understood that Australia itself was Gothic, and that the melancholia which it fostered was somehow akin to my own adolescent loneliness, to my own acknowledgment of difference, my own instinct for internal travel. On those journeys of dislocation ('where the traveler meets aghast/Sheeted memories of the past') I tried to dissociate myself from one world in order to identify with another . . .

13

A Pair of Cotton Pajamas

Helen and I were returning to the tablelands for the long vacation after nine months in the south. The little train swung around the corner, and the late sunshine illuminated the scene, as if to warn onlookers that soon shadow would flood the valley and that after that – with one swift stride – the dark would come.

I got up on my knees on the carriage seat, and leaned far out so that the wind blew the hair from my face. We had always done this in the past when the train took that corner into the valley and we yearned to see again the green arc of the paddocks and the familiar red roads, the roof of our grandmother's house crowned by umbrella trees, and, there on the other hill, Fleetwood's roof, with the bulk of the barn behind it.

'It's still the same,' Helen said.

'How can it be so much the same when we are away from it? Doesn't our presence mean *anything* ?'

'That's a philosophical question,' Helen said.

We laughed and climbed down from the carriage to stare around us, to see the tiny group of onlookers, the welcoming smile of the postmistress, one of her children beside her grown so big now that we didn't know him.

'Tracey's coming,' she said. 'He's at the mill, and your dad's in Atherton.'

And soon Tracey was there, grinning at us in the familiar way, apologizing for his old work clothes, heaving our suitcases into the car, telling us briefly about some emergency at the mill, about anxieties caused by the depression – looking wryly at us sideways, not wanting to worry us at that precious moment of arrival.

And somehow the moment of arrival did maintain its old clear quality of charm and novelty, in spite of our mother's looking more tired than we had remembered her, her hair a little thinner over her brow as she stood there among the tall shaggy tree ferns at the side door, waiting for us with her tender timid smile. It even seemed, perhaps, that the house looked a little worn and bare. But there was always something new or bright to see, a cushion, a coat of paint on a floor, a yellow table carrying a jug of blue plumbago, or whatever flower was blooming at that time – something we did not expect to see and which caught us at that moment with a sense of rapture.

But during this holiday the depression tended to dominate. We could see the trail of it everywhere, as if it had been a fire that one could follow where it had burnt here, and not burnt there. At one place it had eaten up a whole family, and at another a whole herd of precious dairy cows, and at another a prosperous store. We remembered how, long ago at St. Mary's, when some of the girls had had to leave school because their parents could not pay the bills, the girls had suddenly disappeared, leaving empty spaces behind them. Now there were tales of formerly prosperous station owners from the western cattle areas who lived only by the tolerance of their mortgage holders. One such friend had to present his shopping list to the bank each week. When the list noted 'a pair of silk pajamas,' it had been revised by the bank manager to read 'a pair of cotton pajamas.'

Even to our untutored eyes, the changes in our own way of life were obvious, and our mother looked perpetually anxious, while our father tended toward moodiness and irritability. 'I turn somebody away every day,' he complained as he asked us to 'give a bit of tucker to that man at the back door.' When I asked my mother about something I needed, she looked at me blankly, and then said, 'I'm not sure . . . I'm not sure, dear.'

Because the old spirit of success had always hovered

over the tableland pioneers, our father simply could not believe that serious reversals were possible. In any case, his way had always been to shift his concerns to a wider scene – in this case to the tobacco farms around Mareeba, where less rain fell than in those areas which lay directly in the path of the monsoons. Tobacco farming had been one of those innovations which he himself had helped to instigate; and in that drier belt not far away the settlers were engaged in the backbreaking task of grubbing out the old boxwood and bloodwood trees and, at night, burning the roots, which were consumed infinitely slowly, making brilliant scarlet and purple caverns in the inferno of the earth. My father feared for these settlers. 'They might go under,' he said. 'They're new chums . . . They say this will be a black year.'

I think my father was prescient about the future, and this prescience included the fact that the Japanese were encroaching upon the Australian coasts. My father saw the Japanese only from the standpoint of the reef, and from the hilltop he had bought on the coast at Trinity Bay, he would stare out at the Coral Sea and say, 'I wonder how many maps they are making? They're out there fishing for trochus for three-quarters of the year . . . There's something wrong with *us* if the Japanese know that reef better than we know it!'

Another unfamiliar aspect of our home environment was that our strong and indomitable grandmother had been ill – first with influenza, then with a damaged hip bone. She had been in bed now for a long period. Aunt Kate had to come down from Herberton at intervals, and lately our parents had had to get a young girl from Kulara to live in the house.

'Poor Gran . . . she doesn't like to lie in bed,' our mother said.

'She has a lot of stamina,' our father added proudly.

I remembered being in my grandmother's house in the past, sitting in the big living room where she always had church services, and where I could see in memory the rich folded sleeve of the Bush Brother as he held the Eucharist up to the light. In this room there was a couch covered with brown hessian-like material and velveteen cushions, and there were watercolors on the wall, and a bookcase with books (through which I would search hopefully, trying to find something I had not read, but which wasn't written by Hall Caine or Marie Corelli). Here one could always see the trees outside, remnants of the ancient rain forest, where on one hot summer's day long ago I had glimpsed an azure snake lifting its bright greenish head in delicate question as it investigated the eggs in the nest of a black-and-white peewit. Like the serpent of Eve, this glorious blue tree snake had taken part in the last stand of the pagan garden which the timber cutters had abolished, and on this day, seeming to be ashamed of itself, had suddenly uncoiled and retreated from my gaze.

During this vacation Helen and I went to see our grandmother several times, finding her in bed, but talking of getting up soon, talking of having her usual cold bath, talking of walking over the paddocks to see us. Her commanding noble-featured face was wrinkled and fallen, her white hair disordered, her complaints numerous – especially her complaints about the soulless cooking of the little girl from Kulara. On the rickety table near her bed lay the Holy Bible and *The Pilgrim's Progress*, along with several half-finished letters written with a scratchy steel-nibbed pen in pale blue ink. Seeing her like this, I tried to imagine her erect again, and found myself preferring to remember that when I was very tiny she had come sweeping into the Fleetwood house on one occasion after returning from a trip to Rockhampton. She wore skirts of rich black silk, but when she saw me she sank down onto the floor to embrace me, telling me in a joyous voice, 'I've just been to see the biggest mine in the *world*!' Now the sense of a mine's glamour was the last thing she thought of.

As long as we had lived, night after night, the light from our grandmother's house had been seen far away across the paddocks. It had appeared then, in the ragged shadows of Australia's wilderness, that only light could dispel fear. In the rain forest the eyes of the Aborigines would glimmer in the dusk which hung above the tiny fires in front of their gunyahs. A small settler's hut would hold the glow of light as if it were a transparent shell. The wavering lights of a buggy would sway along a rough bush track, as if it were traveling far into the night, and would be traveling so forever.

Every morning our grandmother carried her oil lamps from the inside rooms to a bench on the back veranda. Here she refilled them, washed the smoke-blackened globes, and left them to be lit again when night came. If some of us came to see her after dark, she would stand upright at the door, holding a lamp above her head, her eyes peering out, her voice startled. 'Who is there? Who *is* it? . . . Oh, it's *you* girls . . . Come in, come in.'

On the long vacation when Helen and I walked across the paddocks to see her, neither of us knew that we would never see our grandmother again. She was to die soon after our return to the south.

During that vacation at Kureen we sometimes didn't know what to do with ourselves, because old pleasures were curtailed, and because our parents were continually preoccupied.

Since we were emancipated now, and knew that there was a wider world around us, the idea struck us to travel down to the coast and visit a friend called Derwent, who was studying with Helen at the university. We found him in a big wooden house on the usual high stilts, the underhang fenced in with vine-covered latticework that enclosed a dark and rather primitive kitchen, where Derwent's mother, her face flushed from the heat of the wood stove, baked numerous incredibly light sponge cakes. The street outside was sandy and white in the moonlight, and I couldn't sleep at first because of the barking of the stray dogs and the unaccustomed town noises, including the incessant playing of a piano next door. In the daytime we sailed in a small boat Derwent had borrowed, and stood upright clinging to the rigging while quick fierce tropical storms poured down upon us, wetting us from head to foot. A few minutes later, under brilliant sun, we would be completely dry again. Once we landed on a small green island, beached the boat, raced up a hill to a natural waterfall, and washed ourselves clean of salt. Dry again in a couple of minutes, we made a fire on the beach, and had our breakfast of smoky bacon and bread and billy tea. When we returned to the tableland again, Helen and I were still dissatisfied, so we took to organizing parties with a few friends from the coast and a young farmer from Atherton and his brother. My father tried to dissuade us, on the grounds that there was too much to do, and too much to worry about.

But his children danced. We danced to the old gramophone which had to be wound up for every record, and which years before had made the veranda echo to inadequate recordings of Galli-Curci's piercing notes and the deep rolling bass of Paul Robeson, singing in his youth of Ol' Man River, which 'jus' keep rollin' along,' and also of Jack o' Diamonds, who 'robba da pocket, robba da pocket . . . o' da silva and da go-oold.'

And over the horizon the moon rose in all its tropical glory.

In that year, to return to the university was to return to a certain sobriety. Without admitting it to myself I was attempting to look for other men to take the place of my profound addiction to John, and viewed all those who entered the graduate program with a half-serious air of consideration. When one night a broad-shouldered Englishman in a heavy jacket appeared at the university dance hall, parking his motorbike among the bushes near the door, I looked at his eager face and dark upstanding hair and rather narrow merry eyes with interest; and I could not help hoping (when he told us that his name was Francis Ratcliffe, that he was doing flying fox research and had been born in India and studied biology at Oxford under Sir Julian Huxley) that he would be as sophisticated and ambitious as his personality suggested. 'Call me Freddy,' he said as we circled the hall.

207

There was also a rather languid young man, who had beautiful heavy-lidded, long-lashed eyes and who tried to indoctrinate me into 'art for art's sake,' showing me portraits of colonial personages and reproductions of Norman Lindsay's drawings, and talking to me about the Vitalists, and taking me one Saturday afternoon to the dusty ill-kept art gallery. But although he danced well, and although his almost feminine eyes were attractive, he seemed far away from life, and innocently I worried about him as if he had some fatal disease.

Freddy, however, had a robust character, and explained to me about his research, and how he camped alone – penetrating into mangrove swamps and jungles, reaching the sites of the big fruit-bearing trees where the foxes made their camps. These foxes, taking a lesson from the birds, that of seasonal migration, had adapted themselves to feeding at blooming time on the honey-rich flowers of the eucalypts. I was attracted by Freddy's conversation. I could see him clad in oilskins and boots, finding his way through pockets of scrub, through groves of wild fig trees, through steaming swamps and river estuaries where mosquitoes hummed around his ears, and the minute lice from handling the foxes crept into his clothes. I knew that he was devoted to the cause of science, and I liked to listen to his poetic descriptions of the bush – the din the crickets made, the cough of a possum in the silent night, the howl of a dog from a mountain farm.

After a long conversation about flying foxes, he asked if he was boring me, and I said no and he held my hands and said, 'Oh ... women ... women.' He also wrote me letters from his camp under the stars, and talked about my eyes and called me 'the kitten from Kureen,' and sent me poems, which I kept for a long time in the drawer of my dressing table among my socks and handkerchiefs, and I thought that he was in love with me ...

I was flattered by Freddy's minor attentions, thinking of him as a 'graduate' and a 'scientist,' while I myself was unformed, waiting for some intellectual inspiration on which to center my attention. But when I heard that he had developed a serious interest in an older girl from some big New South Wales station, and that he would soon return to Oxford, I had no choice but to be reconciled to his disappearance. How was it then that although I felt that I was too young for him, I felt at the same time as old as the world?

I thought afterward that Freddy was a little like my father in his love of the rain forest, or like one of the explorers I had always admired; in a sense he became an intellectual model for me, so that suddenly I wanted to imitate him, to find out Australia's secrets, and to see my country as separate from myself. As I had once wandered the stony hillsides of the Herberton ranges, with Edgar Allan Poe's *Tales of Mystery and Imagination* in my pocket, I found myself exploring the ranked thickets of thin-stemmed gums which lay no more than a mile away from the Women's College, discovering nothing there but the edges of an old road and a broken-down piece of rusting machinery. It was as if I were trying to find my way out of a forest, looking, like Hansel and Gretel, for signs on the path marked earlier in the day. It was no longer enough for me to talk with grandiose confidence of 'going overseas'; it was first necessary to find out where I lived now, and this desire drove straight as an arrow through all my emotional defenses.

I began to reread Henry Lawson, the Australian poet and short story writer, who had written of the general Australian fate, of the grinding labor in the bush, and of the 'bushies' themselves – station hands, drovers, shearers, cocky farmers, diggers. He wrote of out-of-the-way places, of hidden pockets in the ranges, of families at the end of long dark gullies, and away out on godforsaken native-apple or stringy-bark flats, where they had lived for generations in inconceivable darkness. 'Some,' he wrote, 'are descended from a convict of the worst type on one side or the other, perhaps on both; and if not born criminal are trained in shady ways from childhood. Conceived and bred under the shadow

209

of exile, hardship or trouble, the sullen brooding spirit which enwraps their . . . homes will carry further their degradation . . . we want light in those places.'

In the process of struggling with Australia's past I had already developed a strong sense of the sad disorder of the country's early life. I was trying to juxtapose my own realities to the realities of Lawson; for although he had written of what was hopeful and confident, most of his material dealt with the 'inexpressiveness' of the bushies, the illnesses without doctors or remedies, the deprivations, the hidden malice, the arson in the night – or even the simple weariness of human beings stretched to the limit of fatigue, the fate of whose who, without enough money 'to see them through,' went 'on the land' in Australia.

Educated by the depression, I thought of the social evils of other lands, the men and women lost to crime and alcoholism, the dwarfed and maimed children, the crowded and unsanitary conditions in old Europe's winter-ridden houses. Yet I remembered, too, being hurried as a child through the streets of Cairns at six o'clock closing time, past the open doors of the bars, some adult hand dragging at mine while the workmen staggered onto the pavements, having drunk as much as they possibly could in the scant hour allowed them, often to reel against supportive posts, or to lurch vomiting to the gutter. This was a sight which children were not supposed to see, but naturally we had seen it often enough, and knew vaguely that it was tied up with that great Australian male world, one section of which drank itself into insensibility evening after evening and then went home to sleep it off. This was not so much an evil drunkenness as a gluttony of forgetfulness, a desire to annihilate boredom, or, perhaps, a need to become part of a more expressive humanity.

The Old World, then, had sent part of its human burden to our own shores. And many of these humans had only half emerged from the swamps of the past. I think that those earlier premonitions we had all had about pioneer life were broadening now to warn me that I, too, must learn to conquer and to endure as had my predecessors.

In my new Australian reading I found numerous descriptions of boredom and monotony, the perennial sense of the vacuum, the longing for the reassurance of a human presence. I brooded over Henry Handel Richardson's description of an outback town ('a couple of banks, a hotel or two, a few mingy [miserable] shops built around the four corners of two cross-roads ... the country ... flat and treeless; the soil so dark as to be almost black'). I read of the children she described – the silly twelve-year-old girl who sucked her thumb in the miserable backyard; the little dead child at the hotel decked out like a bride in white; and the butcher's child, half-Chinese, who in the interests of play would hide inside the hanging carcasses of meat! I read of a country which had not yet come to terms with civilization.

There were other writers. Barbara Baynton's stories dealt with the lowly deformed creatures of the backblocks; they were stories which could strike terror into the heart of the reader. One character, the cruel and ignorant Squeaker, was irritated when his mate was accidentally pinned beneath the tree he had been felling, and told her that he'd let it fall on her again 'if she didn't shift.' He told her that her dress was on fire, but she took no notice, lying there, and he made the tea and ate his dinner. When later she said that she would be up soon, he answered, 'Yer won't. Yer back's broke.'

I read of landscapes where human affection had withered and died – the droughts, the tottering sheep, the tireless sun, the treeless plain, the emaciated cattle feebly bellowing, and, along with such backdrops, the rattle of scornful invective: 'My oath!' ... 'Fair dinkum!' ... 'Stinkin' Roger.'

Sitting in the library, I sometimes felt buried alive in these details, felt them to be inescapable, and knew them to be true. Perhaps this awakening to the Australian reality frightened me a little, for it told me what my environment really was, and it told me that I must function in it as a plant must function in the soil where it grows.

***

And so I proceeded through this last university year, so certain that the library I wandered in was built especially for my tastes that even as the time of the final examinations approached, I was hardly aware that it was not upon these subjects that I was to be examined. I had somehow managed to absorb a little objective knowledge in spite of my habits, and after a parade of frantic days and late nights I was able to make my way, pale and with my head whirling, to the hall where pads, pens, ink, and blotting paper were laid out at intervals along the empty tables, under light which streamed from the windows above as if we were in some Gothic examination hall on that island far across the water. It was good luck for me that I was a reader, because here and there I was able to produce a suitable facsimile of what I remembered from various printed pages. But I groaned in a kind of terror as I tried to deceive the examiners by indicating a knowledge I did not possess, by mentioning names without dates, tendencies without circumstances, results without reasons and as I saw what I had done through three years of my uncle's generosity, my parents' faith, and my own self-indulgence, I was able at last to honestly lament the results. I knew that I could never reasonably pass these examinations, and what would I do then? In this context it would not matter that I was popular at dances; or that I had published a few poems in the Sydney *Morning Herald*; or made friends as callow as I was; or had had a relationship with a married man. What achievements were these in what was generally called 'the world of hard knocks'? How was I to earn a living in depression-ridden Australia? And how far away I was from the overseas opportunities we had all talked of! I turned in my last inadequate paper and left the big hall, where the star students were still scratching busily with their pens, and walked in black depression to the ferry.

Three weeks later the results were posted. I was asked to present myself at the office of the Arts Committee, where I found four of my professors gathered, sitting formally in their robes, and I was told that I had failed in two of my major subjects, and could therefore not be given my arts degree in the usual manner, or with the usual confidence. I was asked whether I had anything I wanted to say.

Pale and swollen-eyed, I tried to explain what the library had meant to me: 'I never saw so many books in my life . . . At home in the north we had few books . . . At school the libraries were very small.'

'And did you attempt to study?'

I lowered my eyes. 'I attempted to study, but not the right books.' My voice fell lower still. 'I was . . . I was unrealistic . . .'

Perhaps it was because I sounded so piteous, or perhaps it was because they had already decided – in view of whatever talent I had evidenced – to give me what was called a 'Pass Considered,' but I overheard an appointment being made for me for an oral examination. I was to be given a second chance – but I felt that I did not deserve it. As I sat there and burst into tears, the examiners rose, and quietly left the room.

14

Queen of the Ferries

We are not only the creatures of our inheritance, and of those years of infancy and childhood which at a certain time of life sum up our experiences; we are also born into conditions which nurture our sensibilities.

It was midafternoon, and with the help of some friends, I had brought my clothes and books and the scanty relics of my university life to a tiny side street not far from the Women's College on Kangaroo Point. The house was wooden, and one side of it was built a few feet from a brick wall, formerly part of an old garage; the window of my new bedroom opened directly onto this wall, which was dirty and stained and half covered with a deteriorating red paint. The brick wall absorbed the heat from the summer sun and reflected it back into my small and stuffy room, turning it into a little oven and causing the veneer of the inadequate furniture to curl and warp.

My sisters had also helped in the moving, and I could see that they did not think much of my choice.

'Why did you take *this* room, Johnnie?' Margot asked.

'Wasn't there *anything* better?' Helen said, staring at the wall, and measuring the bed with her hands in a critical manner.

'I took it because I was tired of looking and it was cheap,' I said flatly. My sisters looked at each other and by common consent ceased their remarks.

The house, a small lodging house, was run by a slovenly woman called Mrs. Angeles, whose favorite occupation was to lean against the doors of the rooms rented to her lodgers – open because of the weather – and to discourse upon

214

all available subjects. She would do this as long and as thoroughly as possible, and when lack of interest became too obvious, would continue such discussions with her husband in the kitchen, where they worked together to produce the inadequate supper which was served each night to their captive boarders.

I may have taken the room partially because I felt some childish reluctance to leave Kangaroo Point, which had become so familiar during my days at the university. On this tongue of land, relatively undeveloped and so handily connected with the center of the city by ferryboat, it was still possible to loiter under the big trees by the river, to watch the sunsets, and to get to the heart of town within half an hour. In all my dreams, however, I hadn't thought of living in so mean a little house, or of sitting down each night to dinner with the vulgar Mrs. Angeles and her henpecked husband, with a strange pallid young man (with whitish hair and eyelashes), as well as with an overactive and over-nervous woman (whose journalist husband was working in Melbourne) and her two small children . . . But this was how it had actually turned out.

I remembered my conversation with Helen about the depression, and rehearsed in my mind our obvious obligation to earn our own livings as soon as we got our degrees; but as with all the lessons of life, such verbal expressions have little in common with actual experience. It had not occurred to me, for instance, that 'earning a living' would mean forsaking the kind of luxury (a view of a tree at least, or a window big enough to let in air and light) which I had so far learned to expect – an expectation nurtured by my early experiences of that harmony which light and space and color provide.

Not until the depression came had it been clear how hard it would be to get a job in provincial Queensland, especially one suited to my few talents – one which paid enough money to live and dress and eat adequately. It had been impossible at the last moment to find a cheaper room, and what little common sense I had told me that, in being independent of

215

one's parents, there were not only basic costs to consider, but many other things such as fares and lunches, stamps and envelopes, haircuts and telephone calls.

Perhaps the days at the boardinghouse, with the opportunity to observe around me the dismal fate of the undiscriminating poor, and to develop a heightened social observation as a result, would do me some sort of good; at dinner each night the subject of conversation was either money or status, or a little bit of both. The talents of Mrs. Angeles were explained by Captain Angeles, and the talents of Captain Angeles were discussed by Mrs. Angeles. She let us know every other day that her husband was related to the great liquor fortune. 'The brandy, you know . . . it's a family secret, and you'd pay quite a few pounds if you had the chance to find out about it, but no one could find out, it's a real secret . . . not even the *captain* knows.' She added that she herself came of a very good English family, the Stokely-Joneses from Stokely. Her mother, she said, had always intended to take 'her two girls' to the 'old country' (England). 'She wanted me and my sister to have a chance outer Australia, overseas experience, doncher see?' At this point she would drink demurely from her coffee cup with her little finger elevated. 'She wanted us to look at how people lived over there . . . Well, along came Derek [Captain Angeles] and that put the finish to the travel. Derek emigrated to South America because of the bizness, see, but when he met me he decided on Australia.' She would laugh and show the dark gap between her top teeth, half hidden by the full and remarkably red lips, and push back her untidy brownish hair, and rescue the slipping shoulder of her tentlike dress; while her husband, a little grasshopper of a man, somewhat bandylegged, but military in bearing, would say in his flat, extremely proper English, 'My dear, will you be kind enough to serve the dessert'; and after the dessert was over, would rise to his feet as an example to the rest of us, and bow to his slumping and by now slightly wilting wife, as if she alone had created this masterpiece of a meal (although we had heard

216

them together in the kitchen for at least an hour beforehand, creating it together).

Mrs. Ryan, the wife of the absent journalist, would always bow in return, and in the narrow passage outside, she would whisper to me, 'Thank you for what tasted like horse's meat, Mrs. Angeles,' and shrug her thin shoulders and draw together the nostrils of her well-cut nose, and do a dancelike movement toward her room, murmuring, 'And thank you, Mrs. Stokely-Jones, for giving birth to Miss Stokely-Jones, and thank you, Captain Brandy Angeles, for marrying Miss Stokely-Jones and making her Mrs. Brandy Angeles. Amen!!' She would disappear into her room, leaving me to the mercy of the white-haired boy, who worked in the Roads Department and was called Bert Wilson, and who would try to suggest that we (he and I) should take a stroll together, or else go to the movies or somewhere, but always putting the suggestion indirectly ('Now, I think it would be nice if Mr. Bert Wilson took a walk down the riverbank with Miss Joan, lately of the Women's College – that is, if Miss Joan would consider the idea . . . In fact, I know where some ice cream is to be had on this hot night, if those two would walk as far as the ferry and cross to the other side . . .'), so that his request didn't really have to be taken seriously. In spite of the dreadful heat, the door of my bedroom had to be shut to prevent Mr. Bert Wilson from coming by later to repeat his offer in some even more fanciful or, as he thought, humorous way.

So fast had time gone by since the final posting of the examination results, and the necessity of moving from the Women's College and offering myself on the job market, that I had had little chance to adjust to the sudden change of scene in my life and fortunes. I had been bitterly ashamed of my failure in the examinations, but beyond talking about it with my sisters and with Norman, I had tried to pretend indifference, explaining to everyone that I intended to write for a living, and that before I did anything else I was going to try out all avenues in this direction. I was relieved to find

217

that most of my friends accepted this at face value, for they themselves were engaged in returning to their homes, or in getting jobs – one with his family's business, one going to medical school, and several to teaching jobs of various kinds.

But a false front, however resolute, has so little intrinsic reality that when at night I closed the creaking door of my new room at the boardinghouse, I would lean against it with my face set – less in despair than in fastidious resentment.

During those days of adaptation I did not look for John, or let him know where I was – I was so ashamed of my situation that I hid from him as much as possible, left his letters unanswered, and avoided the ferries he was most likely to catch. Uncle Tony had gone to Melbourne for six months; Helen had been given further work at her laboratories; and my friend Joan Cue was continuing her work with the Prickly Pear Commission in a faraway suburb. Norman had gone to a research job on one of the small islands off the coast of New Guinea, and although he sent me regular accounts of his lonely life, he was not a talented letter writer, and he seemed very far away. Hazel had returned (temporarily) to Fleetwood, where she and Robin were helping our parents to weather the depression (and perhaps considering how they should deal with it themselves). I did not feel that I should complain to my family about my insecurities and problems. In fact, I don't think that anyone else knew exactly what my life was like, and I didn't want to stress that I had chosen a role (that of a writer) which I scarcely knew how to perform, let alone to perform successfully, and that there stretched ahead of me, unless I could succeed in some way, an enormous space of empty time – a whole lifetime perhaps – in which I might wander forever like a lost soul!

The days were beautiful, but burning hot. My room seemed hotter than the street outside under the midday sun. I was isolated and trapped in a cul-de-sac. The small amount of money I had dwindled, as I struggled to renovate or change my clothes, to mend my shoes, to get my hair cut – and, at lunchtime, to control my appetite. I tried to resume my friendship with the girls I had gone to school with, but found that most of them were already on the verge of marrying and that now domesticity interested them more than old pastimes. Blue-eyed Bet had asked me to bridge parties, but I was as uninterested in bridge as I had always been, and Blue-eyed Bet, in any case, was soon to become engaged herself.

I brooded about this new isolation. What had happened to all those Sunday afternoons on the tennis courts, to the idle and flirtatious conversations under shady trees, to the trips to the beaches arranged at the university when the weather was hot! But the sea was some distance away, and now the only available cars had to be borrowed from fathers or uncles or friends, because the young university men were scattered, and I saw suddenly that the world, even here in provincial Queensland, was a very big place, in which many worlds converged, and that, for reasons which had once seemed good to me, I had turned my back upon most of them. What was there left for me, then, but to become a writer?

I went late one night to interview the editor of one of the local papers, and found him with a green shade over his eyes and brawny arms spread out over a littered desk. Copy editors and messenger boys kept running in and out of the room; a clock ticked ominously on a shelf; the dark pencil of the editor made slashes over the long strip of paper which curled like a ribbon before him.

'So you want to be a journalist?'

'Well . . . yes.'

'You don't seem very sure.'

'Oh yes . . . I'm sure.'

'What can you do?'

'I'm told I can write – that is, I've only written the usual things at school, and at the university, but I would like to try . . .'

'Did you bring something you've written?'

219

Since I had been warned not to be what in Australia is called 'too highbrow' during this interview, I handed him a little piece of light verse that had been printed in the Sydney *Morning Herald*.

After a moment he looked up at me through the green of his eyeshade. I saw that he was a sympathetic man, and trying to help me.

'Don't be a *journalist*,' he said.

'Why not?' I stammered.

'It's not what you think it is. It's hard rocky work, and you do a lot of it at night. There are deadlines.' He handed the clipping back to me. 'It's clever. But we print *hard* news.'

'I see.'

Around me I could hear the pulsing life of the paper, the feet running on the stairs, the copy being typed out on the floor below, the murmur of presses in the basement, the traffic noises through the open windows, the shouts and cries of the world. Dimly I understood that journalism, after all, dealt with the noises I was hearing – with the extended life of the universe.

'Why don't you forget it?' the editor said suddenly. 'You wouldn't be able to meet anyone under the greenwood tree.'

I thought of meeting someone under the greenwood tree. I remembered Norman lifting me over the iron fence of the Botanical Gardens at midnight. I remembered wandering between dances on the university grounds with Freddy as he hummed an old English song. I remembered John embracing me in a eucalyptus bower in the footlands of One-Tree Hill.

'I have to earn my living,' I said.

His face changed. 'All right. I'll give you a try,' he said. 'Women's page. One pound a week. Come in on Monday.' With his long dark pencil he began to slash at the copy again.

I came in on Monday, and I wrote pieces for the women's page, but my idea of what women might like to read was not particularly objective, and since one pound a week was not enough to live on, my mind was constantly busy with possible financial supplements. I wrote a piece on modern furniture, but the editors found it 'too highbrow.' I tried to explore social problems such as were written about in *The Yellow Book*, but the editors found *them* 'too modern.' The society reporting I did was dismissed as 'not chatty enough.' After three months the editor who had hired me took me down to the Newmarket Gardens to 'see the roses.' I wore my best dress (my clothes were wearing out), which was a dark silk cut to show my figure, and he flirted with me a little, and cut off a rose for me with his pocket knife.

Tactfully he asked me what I hoped to do with my life. 'Apart from marriage, I mean.'

'I want to be a writer,' I said again. He steered me gently toward the pavilion, and we drank tea and ate fresh scones with strawberry jam.

'How nice it is here,' he said, stretching his long legs in front of him, and lolling in his iron chair. 'How much nicer than in that office at the rush hour . . . Just *look* at the roses.'

'The roses are *marvelous*,' I agreed, 'except that they're all arranged in beds, to the left and to the right. How much better if they were massed here and there . . . Perhaps an article for the gardening page about how to place roses . . .?'

He lifted one eyebrow. 'Suburban Queenslanders have prejudices,' he noted. After a while he murmured, 'You don't want to be a journalist. You want to write *books*.'

I looked at him in terror. 'Are you going to give me the sack?'

'Yes,' he said mildly. 'But you will get married.'

He drove me back to town in silence; then he said that he hoped to see me soon, that if I got *really* stuck, to call him and he would lend me some money. He squeezed my hand, and dropped me at the ferry.

To think back to my life at that time is to remember a continually escalating sense of my own unimportance in the scheme of things, and to appreciate, for the first time, the role of the family which protects the child, not only by feeding and clothing it but by giving it a sense of world place, and so buttressing its self-image. How lucky I had been, I thought now, to *have* a family; how much I had depended upon it; and in that dependence how ungrateful I must have seemed, and how undemonstrative I had indeed been.

And as if in response to this state of mind, I had an unexpected visit from my father – unexpected because he so seldom came now, or could afford to come to Brisbane, so that I had become accustomed to thinking he didn't belong in the southern environment. Perhaps this was indeed part of the strangeness, almost, I should say, divorcement, I had come to feel about myself since the depression had arrived, and since I had moved from the university to this odd non-world of a cheap boardinghouse. In contrast the world we had known in the north now seemed broader, more attractive, and more 'ours.' I felt almost that I should apologize for this living space – as if it were my fault that I must receive my father in this hot little room, where I could not offer him the kind of hospitality he had offered *me* in the past! As he sat on my narrow bed, and I occupied the single wooden chair, I thought he must feel that I simply perched there momentarily, as if I were afloat on a little raft on the sea of the city. I regarded him attentively, thinking that he looked as he had always looked at home – a handsome older man, with his hair thinning a little on top, and his face weathered by his out-of-doors life. I could feel his anxiety, although he tried to disguise it.

'You must tell me how you are getting on, Johnnie Jones. Don't be afraid.' He glanced around the room disapprovingly. 'Are you so hard up?'

'Yes, but that's all right. I'll manage, Daddy. It'll just take time.'

'Now that you've found out what the city is like, and how it is to live and work on your own, do you find it . . .' He paused tentatively. 'Do you find it satisfactory?'

I felt a pang of disillusionment because of his tone, because it struck me that he, who had always been so powerful at home, and in the surrounding districts, might be – outside that limited area, and now in the depression

– comparatively powerless. For one moment I had a terrible vision of my father, the strong man, growing weaker and older; but I tried to smile and said in a firm voice, 'It *can* be exciting.'

'You girls, all you girls, striking out on your own – how will it be? How will you manage?' He looked at me questioningly. 'Is it *safe*? . . . What's the custom these days? I'm out of touch with what the young do.'

'We don't do so much,' I said, laughing a little, but thinking of John.

'The others – Helen and Margot – have professions of a kind,' he said. 'You are the one looking for a way into the writing world . . .'

'Yes,' I said.

'Letters don't tell us much,' he said. 'Somehow we must get you some money . . . or you could come home?'

'No . . . no . . . I'll manage.'

It was at that moment, looking at the worn surfaces of his quite respectable suit, that I saw the faint gloss, especially on the trouser cuffs – that pink stain of the iron oxide of the tableland soil, which I myself, in spite of many washings, still wore on the cuffs of one of my white shirts – a brand, a mark! The sight of this now encouraged me to cross over to the bed, to put my arm around his neck, and to assure him again, and this time laughingly, that everything would be all right.

I took to walking in the provincial city of Brisbane, as later I was to walk in the cities of the world. I started with the city itself, and then branched out to the surrounding suburbs. I did it as I had always done things, by the method of 'first person' exploration, by the *ambulo ergo sum* method. In the gridiron of streets behind Queen Street, I hoped to find secrets revealed to me, or at least to inspect the brass plates on office doors, and to read the names painted upon the hotels, to wonder at the catalogues of exports and imports in the buildings near the wharves, and to ponder about the *raison d'être* of a ballet school or a design showroom. I answered employment ads and ascended and descended a thousand shabby stairways to a thousand shabby doors, to read there a 'Position Filled' notice, or to knock timidly and get no reply. Sometimes I sat for hours in a long row of applicants, looking at my shoes, and hearing the door behind me open and shut, open and shut. If I passed a drunk in a doorway or someone in the street with one leg and a begging bowl, I paused in dismay, fumbling for a few pence, wanting to know the story, consumed with curiosity about that part of mankind somehow linked to my own fate. Had these unfortunates been abandoned by others, or had they willingly filled the slot meant for them? ... At that time there was little which could not interest me, and interest seemed to be all that I had. As I really looked (for the first time) into the weather-beaten face of the old man who ran the ferry, and who now told me that he had a gammy leg from World War I; as I smiled into the baby-blue eyes of the girl who made change at the grimy restaurant where I sometimes bought meat pies for lunch (the meat pie being a special Australian thing, inherited from England, by no means to be despised, and cheap as could be) – I felt my soul expand. And the girl with the blue eyes said, 'You always give me a real nice smile!'

Now, quite suddenly, through the kindness of a friend of a friend, I found myself employed as a public relations operator in a medical supply company, Johnson and Johnson, at a fixed rate of two pounds ten shillings a week. The proviso was that I should make personal visits to all doctors in the vicinity and try to convince them that Johnson and Johnson's catgut and needles were the best on the market, and the most carefully prepared for minor operations in the surgery. I was told that I must also explain that certain kinds of catgut, such as Johnson and Johnson's 'special' brand, were readily absorbed in major operations. Glad as I was from the financial viewpoint to get this job, I disliked the fact that the firm insisted upon printing cards with my name on them and the words in one corner: 'Special Representative for Johnson and Johnson Co., Inc.' At a stroke my anonymity vanished, and the card itself, printed as it was, seemed like a public denial that I ever intended to be a writer. No longer could I prowl the streets in all weathers and at all times, consumed by dreams, plans, and anxieties. No longer, when I was tired, could I rest for a while in the smoke-laden atmosphere of shabby theater foyers, where advertisements pasted on the doors showed a hand clutching a lighted cigarette and the caption 'Time for a Capstan' – or for that matter sit in the Public Library, where the atmosphere was soothing and aged retirees read the paper under the sunlit windows.

Now I must travel to the suburbs, and sit in the waiting rooms of doctors until the patients had all been attended to; or travel to small hospitals and rest homes, sitting while patients and relatives went in and out, and young interns in dazzling white hurried by me with charts in their hands and stethoscopes hanging out of their pockets. Some doctors paid scant attention to the catgut I was trying to publicize, but involved me in philosophical discussions about 'What do young people think today?' or 'Should a doctor in the colonies first spend some time in London or Glasgow or Dublin?' A few dismissed me with impatient smiles. 'Good heavens, we just boil the stuff up in batches, much too expensive to buy it that way'; others leaned forward seriously to listen to the brief talk I had to give, and exclaimed charitably about the 'great interest' of anything I had to say. One matron at an old people's nursing home became concerned at my traveling around the city all day without even a raincoat, and took me into the cozy nurses' room at the back to give me hot beef tea and anchovy toast. And another doctor, tall and rather handsome, dismissed his waiting and long-suffering patients in a body, invited me into his office, where he seated me in a chair opposite him, maneuvering his own chair so that with his knees he could imprison my legs, and began to stroke and pet me in a way which could have nothing to do with catgut. I was half fascinated by his suddenly pale face and flashing eyes, and thought that he must be taking drugs (in those days I thought that drugs produced an instantaneous interest in the opposite sex); but I was also very angry because I was able to see the indignity of being without money or work, and the fruitlessness of this occupation I was engaged in. My efforts to get out of the chair gave the doctor so many opportunities to embrace me, and I myself was so affected by the intensity of his zeal, that I only escaped in the end, with tousled hair and flushed cheeks, by running wildly through the waiting room and into the street.

That night I sat on my narrow bed at the boardinghouse and wrote a short nostalgic story about an innocent girl from a northern farm who came to the city – a story which was not very good in itself, but which represented, I thought, a practical protest against the foolishness of my present life. And the next day, quite unexpectedly, I ran into John at the ferry . . .

As we turned into the street that led up to the city center, he said, 'Let's walk,' and as we walked I told him why I had hidden from him, and had not written to him; and I tried to describe, in as light a way as possible, the story of my adventures and misadventures since I had seen him last. His face grew gloomy and reproachful; he began to castigate himself for not being sensitive enough, and then added an important corollary to the whole situation. 'Naturally you feel like this in that boardinghouse, and to make it worse, you've got too many ambitions to stand it . . . On top of that, there is my part in it . . .'

At this I tried to protest, but he insisted upon expressing himself. 'I had no right to act toward you as I did in the first place. I had no right to make you unhappy because I was unhappy myself . . .'

'You made me happy.'

Standing in the street for a moment, we watched the tram clanging by, and on an impulse I told him about the doctor. His brow clouded again.

'The blackguard! You must leave that ridiculous job! Why did you . . ?'

I think he was about to say, 'Why did you let that episode with the doctor get so far in the first place?' but he restrained

himself and said instead, 'I know it's ridiculous! But I feel
. . . *outraged.*'

We walked up the street, and he put his hand into the
pocket of my jacket to hold mine. After a while, and in a
sober voice, he said, 'To leave my wife and family seems a
cowardly thing to do . . .'

My heart was beating, but I pressed his hand to show
my agreement.

'It's what they call reality,' he added sadly. We looked
at each other.

'My Queen of the Ferries, you must find someone else.'
He stood and watched me as I went away from him up the
street.

15

The Surgeon's Knife

I do not remember that I was hopelessly unhappy on the day when I walked away from John on a Brisbane street corner while he stood there with his hat in his hand, his eyes serious, and the wind lifting his brown hair. I walked away calmly, because I had imagined this scene long ago – had rehearsed it, because it had seemed inevitable and could therefore be carried out with grace – and because I had even thought of it with some sort of bitter relief, being too weak to initiate it, but strong enough to accept it. The sensations themselves – the sun pouring down onto the back of my neck, the guarded look in John's eyes (as if he were afraid that I might cry or try to resist in some way), the emptiness of my hands, which I had clasped in front of me because he had been holding them in his up to that moment – remained in my memory afterward, along with the sharp, bright corners of the buildings opposite, toward which I had turned as I moved away up the street.

I think, in fact, that I was in a state of shock, and yet stimulated enough to take the first step that came into my head, which was to visit my sisters and to discuss with them the possibility of the three of us taking an apartment together on another part of Kangaroo Point where it was easy to reach the center of town by tram, *without* using the ferryboat across the river. Perhaps I knew that only later would I realize the void in my life created by the decision made with John, and would then attempt to nullify it by contriving to meet him again – for what is love if it is not a need which can only be given in to, or given up?

But in the boardinghouse that night I seemed immune to all outside influences, and was able to make plans for the future as if the undramatic and silent farewell in the street had set free some long-paralyzed energy. I even joined in a discussion about Hitler and the Germans, in which Mrs. Angeles deferred to the Captain, and the Captain deferred to her, and I found to my surprise that there were people within the British Empire who thought that Hitler – this little man whose voice, crude and hysterical by turns, had risen shrieking and shouting on a special radio broadcast a few weeks before – was to be taken seriously.

'So you like him?' I inquired of Captain Angeles as we plowed our way through a well-burned pot roast.

'I think he's going to straighten things up in Germany,' said Captain Angeles. 'Germany needs someone to take hold . . . This is why the German people welcome the Führer. He is smartening them up and putting people to work again.'

'He had to give people *work*,' Mrs. Angeles chimed in. 'People are good when they are busy. Doncher know that? People have to keep busy to keep them off the streets.'

Because I felt pity for those who suffered physical pain and unjust imprisonment, I protested in a quivering voice that Mussolini had used mustard gas on barefoot Abyssinian tribesmen, and that now Hitler was calling the Jews 'beasts' – and how could one hope for anything from sources like this? My voice rose, and tears trembled on my eyelashes, until Mrs. Angeles began to pick up the plates and carry them back to the kitchen, and I became aware, as I had many times before, that it was not enough to be capable of indignation, that one must also be capable of analysis.

Moving slowly, as a reaction to those irresistible waves which were rocking the complacent waters of Europe, political ripples were by now reaching Australia. Something powerful and disturbing was happening. On meeting two students who had shared some of my classes at the university, I realized that young local radicals were talking about the end of 'capitalism,' were rejoicing because 'capitalism' must, according to Marxist doctrine, inevitably give way to an 'uprising of the proletariat' – and it seemed obvious to them that this was a suitable historical moment for the shift. It is impossible to say now whether or not these young Queensland enthusiasts were actual members of the Communist Party – as was, for instance, P. R. Stephenson (Inky), whom I once met and who had been at the university before 'my time'; and others, such as Fred Paterson, a Rhodes scholar and, eventually, a member of the Queensland legislature, famous for the skillful manner in which he made fiery speeches to North Queensland workers while he himself stood on the beaches, just below the high-water mark, so as not to be arrested.

In any case, it was a period of optimism for the left in Australia, and although the dogmatic certainty with which these ex-students talked surprised me, I still had a certain sympathy with them, half guessing that they suffered from what I myself suffered from – a feeling of intellectual loneliness and a sense of the 'vacuum.' I don't remember that they ever shared with me those political doubts which, I learned later, were fairly common among British students. Perhaps they thought me too naïve to confide in. They didn't mention the famines in Russia, or the Shakhti trials, or even the current Stalinist wisdom, which was that those socialists who were not completely *with* the Communists must be branded as 'social fascists' and he treated as prime enemies of the 'Revolution.'

This strange aberration, in a sense the rock upon which Stalinism was built, was probably no more popular in Australia than it had been in the United States or England, but the Russian ukase was still passed down via the 'Control and Security Commission' in Australia, although under utmost secrecy, and so was only indirectly translated into the 'Party line.'

While the Nazi movement in Germany now came to the fore as a focus of anxiety, it was not hard to notice that the Japanese, about whose presence on our northern reefs my father had worried for so long, were temporarily forgotten. They were making progress in their own way – for had they not created a puppet state for Manchukuo, and reached as far as the Great Wall of China? What I didn't perceive was that the time to check the Japanese had already long gone by, and also that German rearmament had been so rapid and so sustained that we would eventually face not only a Germany under the influence of Hitler but an armed Germany as well.

The two students I talked to were impatient with me because I didn't understand that 'Hitler wouldn't last.'

'Why shouldn't he last?'

'Hitler is bluffing,' one said.

'It's not a historical likelihood,' the other added.

'My uncle says that Germany is building planes, a great *number* of planes,' I said.

'I suppose your uncle thinks that we should cross the ocean,' one said aggressively, 'to fight for the British in an imperialist's war!'

My heart sank as I thought of another world war, but I answered all the same. 'Perhaps he *would* think that . . .'

'He'll have to ask the trade unions first,' one of them retorted. But perhaps none of this really mattered to me. These conversations were mental exercises only, incompletely realized, painfully stimulated by the situation in the external world. I needed to think that I was in some control of *my* world, and the loss of John (I thought of it as if some natural disaster had occurred to separate him from me) had half persuaded me that I must prepare for a kind of spinstership, and, with it, a more serious life. Because I was not married to John, I had not been able to live in 'the house of matrimony' – that house with its sheltering walls, its protection from heat and cold, its prepared roles and certain status. It was clear again that I lived in the streets, in the 'world,' and to know this was to be more aware of the need for a 'stable' life. Someone had persuaded me to become interested in the League of Nations (that League which had been unable to do anything to restrain Mussolini, or to prevent Japan from setting up Manchukuo) and I suppose that I made sincere and useless gestures in this direction by

231

collecting books. Ironically, most of the books which were donated to the neglected library in a little suite of badly furnished rooms where weekly pro-League meetings were held were about peace, not war; there was, I remember, *Testament of Youth* by Vera Brittain, as well as some volumes of the 'peace poets' from World War I – Wilfrid Wilson Gibson, for instance, and Rupert Brooke, and Alan Seeger – all books which could be translated into a suitable local idiom because they summoned up spectral shapes from the muddy trenches of the Somme, when Australian soldiers had helped to 'turn the line' in France. While in a lackadaisical way I took part in these pro-League meetings, I began to be aware that the advent and rise of Hitler, the creation of Manchukuo, and the decision taken at an Oxford Union debate '*not* to fight for King and Country' were more apropos than were my rather indolent dreams of peace.

But I longed for intellectual links with the 'real' world. I wanted to know more, even as I wanted to assuage my importunate desire for love. While I had still been a schoolgirl at St. Margaret's, I had made friends with an Englishwoman named Violet Ross, who was married to a large friendly Australian with a service job in a government department. She had, I think, been a post-World War I bride, and sometime after the war had found herself living in Brisbane in a small wooden house set in a garden filled with roses and geraniums, not far from St. Margaret's school, to which she had sent her little daughter Anne. Violet came from a Jewish family, had a pale fine-skinned face, a cloud of brownish hair, skin tightly drawn over prominent features, dark intelligent eyes, and a full figure generally wrapped in black dresses, with which she wore, in summer, wide-brimmed pale-coloured hats.

As I had once been anxious, on those faraway Saturdays, to keep up with and to impress Blue-eyed Bet and the other Betty, I now wanted Violet Ross to approve of my social sophistication – not in this case my physical appearance, but some other nameless quality which I thought of as 'knowing what to say.' As her swaying figure approached with open arms to meet me at a restaurant, her cries of 'Oh, my dear . . . you will be happy today because I have the most charming man for lunch, and he will be interested in you because I have told him all about your talents . . .' made me feel that this way of wrapping up a compliment in a greeting not only negated the cloud caused by those long months at the lodging house but seemed to promise that someday I, too, would know the secrets of being eloquent and friendly.

That day Violet's charming man turned out to be only a few years younger than she was, as well as being strikingly English (and, while having no real resemblance to Captain Angeles, eternally preoccupied with his pipe). Both he and Violet were Jewish in origin, and although Jewishness was not considered a special category in the Australia of those days, this gave them an advantage because they were more sensitized than others to the dangers inherent in Hitler's drive for power. They also understood very well the phenomenon which I had found strange in my recent conversations with the young men from the university.

'It's a convention they have,' Violet's friend assured me, 'it's not meant to be taken seriously, you know; it's impossible, for God's sake, to know whether they believe in it *themselves* . . . it's not in the realm of concrete facts. They think that this wretched Führer can solve their political problems for them. I believe that they think that Hitler will turn out to be so ridiculous that the old regime will fall of its own weight, and that then the Marxists will be able to take power.' He added: 'This is Marxism . . . you know what Marxism is?'

'Don't harass the poor child,' Violet said. 'She only left the university last year!'

We sat there drinking iced coffee, eating a salad of avocados, and extracting with little silver forks the pale flesh of reef crayfish from their shells.

'I want her to understand the Marxist-ridden language of those brats she seems to have come in contact with down at

233

George Street,' he said, sounding irritated. 'Young Australians aren't allowed to take themselves seriously, Violet . . . This only makes life harder for them here in these faraway tropics . . . I want to *reassure* her that she can do this, that she can take a moral stance of some kind.'

As with many other long-ago conversations which vanished into the memory bank, I cannot now remember all of this one, but Violet's friend, who knew something about literature and writing, and a good deal about other subjects, looked at me with a sympathy I did not understand, and tried to tune in to my uninformed mind. As we had more coffee and pushed our plates out of the way, and began to talk of the possibility of war, he said something about how dreadful world wars were, but that the most dreadful thing about them was not the loss of life itself, but the loss of the evidences of history – the destruction of art (spectacle of man's handiwork), the ruin of irreplaceable churches, the obliteration of old buildings, even the complete levelling of cities.

I remember that I was horrified by this point of view and protested; that my face was flushed; and that I argued at length, asking how he could talk calmly about the loss of a whole generation of *men*, my mind filled with the images of the poets of peace and the delicately tinted photographs in Uncle Tony's house – the photographs decorated by emu plumes from the abandoned slouch hats, the faces of cousins who had fallen at Gallipoli, those cousins whom I had never seen . . . Violet kissed me afterward and tried to explain that this was an argument between generations.

In the confusion of that farewell I had not told Violet about Mulford Colebrook, the American Foreign Service Officer I had met at a Sunday gathering in the suburbs – a graceful, very fair young man with blue eyes, and that eager, slightly naïve look which I had always associated with facsimiles of such young men in the advertisements in American magazines.

Although I had had no immediate revelation that my name or fate would be intertwined with this man – only the perception that he wore a seersucker suit (a fabric new to me then) and carried a tennis racquet under his arm, transporting me to the tennis courts of my school days – I did know that this man, Mulford Colebrook, demanded nothing of me, either then or later, and that his direct blue gaze expressed only an anxiety to serve me. His figure was willowy and agile, his smile without guile. I felt at home with him at once, not only because I saw that he tended to approve of me but because I knew that he was unlikely to be intimidating, for he came from a less critical culture – a culture that was more pliable and easygoing than ours, but also more enterprising and hardworking, and, especially, less hemmed in on one side by the British hierarchy and on the other by pioneer coercions.

Our first social outing together was to the Kangaroo Point tennis courts, where I scarcely acquitted myself well; after several sets he simply allowed me to watch him play singles with the coach, while he darted rapidly about the court, and also demonstrated a special maneuver in which he scooped up the ball as it approached the back line, and, making a half turn, returned it over his shoulder! He was also a confident partner on the dance floor, and we spent a number of evenings at Lennons Hotel, where the dance space was walled in with dark glass out of which flat geometric designs had been cut in a style considered up-to-date in the Brisbane of those days. It was only on that evening, which happened to be extremely hot and humid, when by common consent we finally left the hotel and drove down the narrow highway to the sea, that I discovered other things to the credit of this man who was to be my first husband and the father of two of my children.

In the joy of life in the tropics, being courted by a man who was attractive to me and *not* married, who indeed seemed to see life as an open highway on which we could both proceed together without any possible hindrance, I was released to assume my naturally cheerful personality and to forget the instinct I had seemed to have for false sexual appropriation. What was happening now was at least happening on a realistic basis – and for a long time, in any case, I had been preparing myself for marriage.

Not that my feeling for Mulford was as automatic as that, but by the time he actually proposed to me I had already decided that I would marry him. I think that, although I thought I was in love, I was so occupied with the arduous process of finding out more about myself that I didn't try to find out much about my new 'loved one,' and I studiously avoided comparing him with John, whose person was packed away with my memories, as if all that was associated with him was part of a language I would never use again. Whatever my real state of mind, I now seemed to want only to indulge in motion – the kind of automatism with which I had experimented during the period of my joblessness. Mulford had bought a small car. I learned to drive it, too, and we explored points north, west, and south – the coast, the nearest mountains, the upper reaches of the Brisbane River. 'I travel for travel's sake,' said Robert Louis Stevenson, and it seems that in this interim between our formal engagement and our marriage we covered as much new territory as was humanly possible. We got to know all those drives to Sandgate and Redcliffe, where the sea met the river, and that part of the old settlement of Petrie where farms had flourished in convict times. We took a boat to Moreton Island, and with masochistic effort, under a blistering sun, we climbed hills of sand that were said to be the highest dunes in the world! We swam on the south coast, which was being labeled the 'sun coast' by publicity agents, and where pale beaches stretched in perfection for miles down to Tweed Heads and Coolangatta, and north to Maroochydore. We even went up onto the Lamington Plateau to a primitive resort, where we slept in a tent on the very edge of the cliff, looking down into deep green stretches of jungle, and were awakened at dawn by the kookaburras on the nearby trees.

I had moved from the Angeleses' as soon as we decided to get married, not because the lodging house was much worse than several of the odd half-furnished apartments I found afterward, but rather because I wanted to rid myself of unpleasant memories. And it was in one of these new half-empty apartments, and just before we went north – where we were to introduce Mulford to my parents and to get married at the same time – that I realized suddenly that Norman (who had communicated regularly, but whose last letters I had delayed answering) was due to arrive the next day from New Guinea on his way south, and was expecting to see me when he stopped off in Brisbane.

As I stood in the apartment on one of those last days, holding several of Norman's letters in my hand, and thinking as one does on such occasions of what might be irrelevant but in this case centered upon Norman himself, I visualised his erect figure and grave face, and imagined him finishing these closely written pages in a little wooden house on an isolated island so close to the equator that it might just as well have been on top of it – writing about the progress of his insect research, and about his simple charming houseboy, and about the calm island bay with its low tides, and about the evenings which were so lonely because he was the only white person on the island . . . His letters always included references to the stupefying heat and humidity, and to the fact that while he wrote them, his boy stood nearby and fanned him slowly so that too much perspiration would not drop from his forehead and leave great stains on the pages before he could get them safely into the envelope. He was not always successful and the letters were marked by the tears of the tropics, so that as I reopened the last one, the sheets had a strange wrinkled appearance and I had to struggle to decipher the date of his arrival and the name of his ship.

I had not been paying attention to the letters lately; scarcely reading them perhaps; acknowledging to myself that for all his sterling qualities, Norman was not a good letter writer; and that if he was expressive as a man, it was

237

only because of a certain expression in his eyes or on his face, and because of his talent for transferring emotion silently in gestures and attitudes.

In the room in which I was standing, Norman's letters in my hand, there were several half-packed suitcases on the floor. On the dressing table there were the roses Mulford had brought me the day before. And on my finger a slender little ring which signified our engagement. I realized that the news of this engagement would reach Norman as soon as he got off the boat, and I knew that he would be surprised that I had not bothered to tell him about my plans for marriage – it would seem to him that I had no regard for him at all. I stood for a while at the window, watching the branches of a tree waving against the sky, and I wondered about human relationships, thinking how difficult and perhaps impossible it was to emerge from our own lives and into the lives of others. I tried to think of Norman – and failed. I tried to think of how he had lived on the island. I wondered whether he had had a native girl there, but for some reason I thought that this was impossible. I wrote a little note to him, and then managed to find one of his old friends in the Biology Department to take it down to the wharves and to see that it got into the ship's mailbag for the following morning.

After I left Australia, Norman wrote to me sometimes – always the same rather formal inexpressive letters, and always signed in the same way: 'Yours sincerely, Norman.'

And so Mulford and I were married, going all the way north to the tableland, to be united during the mysterious dampness and drizzle of an August afternoon in 1933 in the little wooden Anglican church in Malanda. The hem of my satin dress and the edge of the old lace veil which my mother had worn before me were, in the few paces from the church door to the car, at least dampened by the soft rain, if not stained very slightly pink by the seemingly unavoidable stamp of the earth's color (as had been my sisters' clothes and my mother's, and the fabric of my father's and brother's suits). Moreover, it seemed to me that it was not only under the shadow of the church's tin roof that I took my vows of love and loyalty, but as well under the shadow of those rain forests which had ringed me around since I was born.

When we returned to Brisbane we rented half a house on familiar Kangaroo Point, its veranda looking out across the river where the ferries ran, and its lawn expansive enough to make us feel as if we were in the solitary tree-shaded suburbs ... All through those post-marriage days a lazy sensuality pervaded us, and on many occasions, especially on long weekend afternoons, sometimes among the dunes near the vast Pacific, or in more sheltered spots where the huge pine trees stretched up to the sky, we would make love on a rug in the sunshine, and lie afterward with our fingers intertwined, staring up at the sky across which small clouds drifted into the many-layered Pacific blue. What youth does not want to know, maturity admits with ease – on those afternoons and nights there was no future, nothing but the body, the fatigue of exercise, the burning of the skin, the salt on the lips, and in our ears the roar of the surf or the rustle of tropical trees. I know, looking back, that those days were a banquet of relaxation – not, it is true, without realistic intervals, as when some worldly or material difficulty faced us; or later, on my side, in adapting to pregnancy and motherhood; or, more unfortunately, when I sensed some deficiency in our relationship that I did not really understand, and felt a sudden need to search for 'what I really was' or for 'what I hoped to be.' But in general life now seemed open to me and effortless. The tension of survival had lessened and the years in which my role was clearly provided according to Australian standards stretched ahead – years to shop and cook for my husband; to manage our mutual household; to support him in all his endeavors and ambitions; and, eventually, to look after our child. Although I seemed to want all this to be my life, the deeper part of my nature – that part which I had not completely recognized and which, in any case, lies within the mysterious story of the potential growth of a human being – had plans of its own.

Perhaps fortunately, these plans were not then evident to my husband or myself.

Mulford, unaware as he was of the vigorous early training of a pioneer childhood, was astonished at my ability to keep house without effort, and by my frugal use of his money. He was also surprised by the number of books I was able to read in a week, because, not particularly scholarly himself, he didn't realize that I was simply consuming any attractive-looking volume I happened to pick up, and doing it lazily, without particular intent.

Slowly and persistently, however, I was learning to absorb from my new husband some idea of a wider world ... In a way, this happened without effort on my part and was therefore not worth very much. The knowledge we gain so casually from others tends to be inaccurate and shot through with what some scientists might call 'mammalian ambivalences' – so that I learned from Mulford a good deal about the hysterias of his mother, but little of what might account for them; and listened to a sketch of his father's rise from poverty to the comparative luxury of owning a factory, without knowing what it had been like to do this in upper New York State in the late nineteenth century. My knowledge of American life was not enhanced either when, during our honeymoon, I – the product of a horse-and-buggy culture – had to change the tire on our rented car. But I did get a dim and not altogether inaccurate feeling that in America there were a lot of well-off people whose affluence protected them from much practical knowledge.

I listened with intense curiosity and pleasure and a certain innocence to whatever Mulford had to tell me, however, and we studied the world map as if it were the real map of our future, with a view to noting all the places we would visit, and what he could show me, and what we would most enjoy seeing while tracing our way through the United States. Though I sensed my new husband's love for and kindness toward me, I think that I was less aware of his philosophy of life and understood less about his origins than I thought I did.

Sometimes he looked worried, saying, 'I hope I get a post you'll like.' (American Foreign Service officers held dual portfolios – they could serve in either United States consulates or embassies, and although I understood that the one might have more prestige than the other, it did not occur to me that Mulford had already pondered this.'

'I'll like *anything*,' I said. 'Why are you worried?'

I looked into his blue eyes, which occasionally had in them an impenetrable touch of terror, and he smiled and looked away, saying finally, with unaccustomed gravity, 'Some of the posts aren't so good – very hard, and even very dull.'

'But can they be as bad as that? Wild animals? Diseases like leprosy? Servants who steal? . . .'

We would then play games about our future, making up imaginary posts in South America where something close to slavery still existed, and where it was unwise to go out at night; or pokey little towns in the English Midlands; or ports in Arab countries where Americans were not liked, and women couldn't wear slacks. But behind this game there was something real, and I wondered what it could be. I thought that perhaps, like the Americans I had heard of, he expected a certain glossy polish to his life – without illness, disasters, or discomforts. But I was grateful to him for many things, not the least of which was that he did not think it his province to dispose of my time, and that although he was so good at tennis, he did not make me play it; and on his side he was grateful to me for filling in the, so to speak, literary side of his life.

'You will be very popular with the cultural attachés,' he would say with a smile.

Into these fantasy games of 'getting away from it' by exploring the Australian scene and world maps, into our search for history and identity, there now fell a quite natural event – I found myself pregnant. I think that this initially caused us both some turmoil – not because we had not intended to have children, but because we had expected to have them in

241

our own good time, when we were completely and entirely ready. Almost immediately then I began to live through that extraordinary period when the brain insofar as it might be an impediment to the body, seems to shut itself down, and hormones produce a cumbersome contentment in which the waistline swells, the appetite is good, and all is automatically right with the world. I know that if I suffered any anxieties at all at this time, they were separate from the feelings and sensations of the approaching birth. Something told me that nothing could possibly go wrong with that particular slow, inevitable progress toward motherhood. Although in general birth is a violent business, medical authority in the Australia of those days (when young mothers were wrapped up in the somewhat awesome disciplines of a despotic doctor called Dr. Truby King) combined with custom to underrate it; and brought up as I was in the spartan north, I found the actual birth comparatively easy.

In the first days after the baby was born, I was eternally preoccupied with the small, pink, slightly wrinkled, purse-mouthed little face of the creature which lay in my arms. I felt, naturally, that I loved it a great deal, but it was also an object of deep and lasting curiosity, even of philosophical contemplation. For the first time in my life I felt responsibility, a sense not of what I should or could do, but of what I *must* do – a solemn and even somber protective sense which projected my life into eternity. My preoccupation with history now seemed artificial, for here under my hands was a small wriggling piece of life itself – extremely neat, amazingly complete, inscrutable, essential; at once an end in itself and a vision of the future. And from the very moment of its birth, this baby banished the preconceived ideas of excitement, carefree leisure, and endless exploration about which I had so idly conversed with its father. Everything now became provisional. We called the child Jay, because in Queensland there was a law limiting the time that a baby could remain unnamed, so, in haste to come to a final decision, Mulford noted that

Jay had been the name of the first American Secretary of Foreign Affairs!

Each day the baby seemed stronger, heavier, more beautiful, and more fascinating. Each day his eyes seemed to reflect more awareness, the muscles of his back to arch with more power, his hands to reach out further and to grasp more firmly. He slept a great deal. In fact, having a baby seemed to be the easiest thing in the world . . . until everything changed. He became less hungry, he struggled and appeared uneasy, refused the breast, refused bottles of orange juice or water, beat his little hands in the air, wailed frequently, and finally, his face turning from red to white, fell into an exhausted sleep. Mulford and I were desperate; the baby's crib was a source of fear and wonder.

'Is he asleep . . .?'

'I don't know, I've just put him down.'

'What shall we do if he cries all night like he did before?'

'I don't know . . . I don't know . . .'

Mulford peered into the crib. 'Oh, my *God*!' he says.

'What's the matter?'

'He's awake, absolutely *wide* awake.'

'He *can't* be . . . he was just exhausted!'

My weight dropped to a hundred pounds. My face grew mournful, my eyes shadowed. The miracle of having an infant had changed our lives in a way so profound and fundamental that now it scarcely needed to be discussed. Although very soon the child was all right again, all monologues about our future ended. He was there . . . and unless all was well with him, we ourselves were like invalids.

One afternoon Mulford came back from work with the news that an 'inspector' from the American State Department had arrived in Brisbane from Washington and that – naturally enough – he would be sending in a report from the consulate about the work, the status, and the future potentialities of all the officers in the Brisbane office, and also of their *wives*!

'We are asked to have him for dinner,' Mulford said.

243

'Of course; we'll make it as attractive as we can.'

'Do you think you can *manage*?' he asked.

'Why, of course.'

As I said this I realized that here was one great difference between me and my husband – my social training had been built upon my father's expansiveness and my mother's acceptance of people; I was extremely optimistic socially, and hoped for the best in all human encounters. Mulford, however, tended to look upon such encounters with anxiety, so that now he seemed nervous, whereas I was exhilarated by the challenge, and immediately began to exert myself, thinking of how to find the sweetest tropical fruit, the freshest fish, and the most tender meat.

The dinner went off well. Afterward we had coffee outside on the lawn overlooking the river, which glittered under a starry sky. I only remember that the inspector seemed a pleasant and unpretentious man, who asked pertinent questions and listened carefully to the answers. When Mulford went upstairs for a packet of cigarettes, the inspector turned to me and asked me what kind of post I'd like to be sent to.

'London, Paris, or Geneva,' I answered promptly.

But since I had never been out of Australia, and knew little enough about even Australia's urban areas, this preference was only an educated guess. A month later, however, a cable arrived at the office, addressed to Mulford (TRANSFERRING YOU LONDON VIA WASHINGTON. EARLY MARCH), and he returned to the house in the middle of the day with a pleased expression, and a bottle of French champagne under his arm. After drinking some of the champagne, we danced in the kitchen to a record Mulford had brought in his luggage from Haiti, and when the record stopped, and when we had divided what remained from the nearly empty bottle, my husband stood outside on the veranda near the railings, apparently lost in thought.

'Suppose . . .' he began.

'Suppose what?'

'Suppose it's London, *Ontario*?'

'*Ontario*? . . . Where's *that*?'

'It's in Canada. We do have a post there . . .'

'It *can't* be.'

'Well . . . it *could* be. The cable only said London. It didn't say London, *England*.'

When it was affirmed the next day that the posting had indeed been to London, England, we immediately bought another bottle of champagne.

16

The Dream of Staying

In that familiar northern haven, under the red-painted Fleet-wood roof, shadowed by the looming Bellenden Ker Range, our security had seemed endless. We knew by experience the strange upside-down operation of the months – the growth of June and July, the green tasseling of the corn so that Tracey would bring great armfuls of it into the house; the heat of Christmastime, when to swim and eat watermelon seemed the greatest good; and then suddenly some extra moisture in the air, some ominous darkness in the sky, serving as a reminder that the monsoons and the wild storms or cyclones of February and March and April were about to begin again. Then the tablelands would be swathed in a shroud of fine rain, and not until this lifted would the earth be disclosed with its old miracle of emerald grasslands and rich red roads.

In those days changes in the weather had never told us that a ceremony of belonging had been disturbed. It was only later when various members of the family could not gather at Fleetwood at some special time (when Christmas, for instance, would pass without enough people to fill up the places at the table) that there would be some slight sense of unease and melancholy. The economic depression had affected all of us, and it was as if we had adopted unconsciously the nomadic habits of our continent, aping the ancient tribes, and wandering far afield for better 'tucker' and more prolific water holes – with the result that, one by one, we had begun to find our way into the outside world. This had made it impossible, even in practical terms, to keep track of each other's lives. It was not that we no longer knew each other, but rather that our paths diverged, and each of us began to inhabit a country known only to ourselves.

As part of this dispersion, it was hard to find the answers to quite simple questions. What did Hazel really think of the young Englishman of whom she had seemed so fond? Was it serious? And although Helen had had her adventures, was it true that now she intended to marry the man she had first met at the university? Had some loss been involved there, and would it be all right to ask about it? As for Margot, did she ever wish that she had gone to the university, as had Helen, her beloved twin? Did she enjoy her work with the famous brain surgeon on Wickham Terrace, and, if so, how could she actually be talking about going to Malaysia? Tracey, who had given up a scholarship offered him by the agricultural college at Gatton to return to Kureen to help our father – did he feel deprived because of it? And Robin, the youngest, what thoughts passed through *her* head – that head with the formal profile, bound by the smooth swath of dark brown hair?

I myself, who had been the first to marry, felt that I had traveled far from my childhood. It was hard to chart the changes that had taken place, and I had not tried, consciously, to examine them, but rather had taken refuge in that reserve which may have been as much part of an inherited English manner as it was a family characteristic. I was conscious of the distances of the continent and of how it seemed that, as a family, our paths were always crossing and recrossing, and then setting off in different directions – Hazel would be hurrying south to take up a temporary position with a mining company (Hazel was addicted to the 'romance of mining'), while I was planning to go north to Kureen; or Robin would be coming to work in Brisbane just as I was about to leave Brisbane forever.

We, who had always talked of leaving what was familiar, had pacified ourselves with the thought of exotic places. It was a panacea against provincial boredom, but on the other hand there was a kind of fatalism in it – that fatalism which

247

had sent our ancestors out into the backblocks because they knew that they had to make their own opportunities, and therefore were resigned from the beginning to the certainty of long separations from those they loved.

I was beginning to develop new sensitivities, and to find that I did not always like them. My early years had had a certain classic vigor, and they had accustomed me to the fatigue of physical accomplishments. I had been allowed to look down those long vistas marked by the axes of the pioneers, over roots and big stumps, and through mud and tree-covered shade – to the arches of the open sky. Yet already I had had to take to crowds, and to interrelating with men and women whose everyday lives were filled with tensions and difficulties, human beings who – even had they so desired – could never have returned to the country of nature and her humble beasts. Some sense of this made me dwell more than ever upon North Queensland, until I was sure that I was saying goodbye to what I may never have really appreciated.

Mulford and I had many discussions about our projected departure. Sometimes we sat with the baby in the woven hammock on the veranda facing the river, swinging idly to and fro, our thoughts concentrated upon problems we had not yet clarified, our eyes gazing out as if we saw beyond the tropical water the noise and confusion of all the capitals of the world.

'I am not sure I want to leave.'

'What *can* you mean?' Mulford asked.

'I talk about the rest of the world, but I think of my own.'

'Do you know what is the matter?'

'I am not prepared in some way,' I said. 'Perhaps people are *never* ready to leave.'

'I got over that a long time ago,' Mulford said, referring to his two years in Paris before entering the Foreign Service.

'I think . . .'

'What do you think?'

'I think I am going to have to *change*.'

'You're all right as you are.'

'I'm the product of *this* world . . . Perhaps I won't transplant well?'

'You will miss your family.' (To Mulford, who had not had a 'real' family, there was something inexplicable about the strong and tangled relationships we had experienced as children.)

'Yes, but it's so much more than that . . . after all, as long as I can remember I've wanted to leave Australia.'

'Perhaps it was only curiosity?'

'No, no . . . I can't *tell* you how much I wanted to leave.'

'What did you want?'

'I wanted to discover the world.'

'And now?'

I couldn't explain it all to him, and I saw in his vulnerable blue eyes a hint of doubt which probably represented something far beyond either his understanding or my own.

The upshot of these conversations was the decision that I should take the baby and go north on the boat to spend a few weeks with my parents. In this way I could let them see something of their first grandson, while I could see them again for what might be the last time.

'It will help you to acclimatize yourself,' Mulford said, 'to the whole idea of leaving.'

'Do you think . . .?' I asked.

'Do I think what?'

'Am I being romantic? After all, it costs money.'

'Not as much as all that,' he said.

'I don't like leaving you alone.'

He frowned. 'I'll be all right.'

It was true that I didn't like leaving him alone; but it was even more true that I longed to go north again, not only to say farewell to my parents, but for some strange satisfaction for which my reason could find no answer. I wondered whether Mulford understood that his wife, for all her tenderness toward him, was able to forget him for long periods of time. Of this fact I felt somewhat ashamed.

***

This trip north on the boat was to be an interlude of peace and nostalgia, for it was now a long time since I had traveled north via water, which meant being carried from the open ocean through that long and luxurious route that threads the passage between the Queensland coast and the intricate many-islanded sea wall of the Great Barrier Reef.

Nor was this trip to be like other trips which had been stamped with the mark of an earlier time – although the more modern and spotlessly white boat, with its prow forever jutted out above the deep blue of the Pacific or the somewhat shallower turquoise waters of the inner passage, tended in spite of its modernity, to resurrect some half-forgotten memory of childhood. Then I had been carried by some adult along those hushed, warm, paint smelling passages near the cabins, wrapped in one of the khaki blankets embroidered in crimson with the name of the vessel, and placed in a long wooden chair up on deck. I felt again the thrilling sense of that strange voyage long ago, the wonder of rails and stacks and funnels, and, above all, the great throb of the ship like the heart of a beast. I thought that Jay would like the ship as once I had liked it, but some definite masculine bent kept him occupied for long minutes trying to turn a valve used by the sailors to water the deck, or tottering with unsteady gait and shrieking delight toward the dangerous unprotected railings which hung over the sea. I knew, as I watched him, that on this voyage, at least, he would act as a deterrent to the carefree trip I had dreamt of as we boarded the boat.

In the cabin itself, with its neat bunks and leather seats, and its bathroom and basin, luxurious with porcelain and shining chrome, with its little round porthole through which the moist breeze caressed our faces, I remembered again the freedom associated with the sea. It was possible to sense in this interim of travel the hours which could be given over to that most priceless of all occupations, the simple process of 'thinking' – a habit which seemed to be stimulated by the mere movement of the boat itself, and to draw its inspiration from the very air. As soon as the boat made any speed, most of the other passengers were at once drawn into a new kind of time scale, so that they leaned their arms upon the broad smooth ledges which finished the railings and, like so many seers looking into the future, fixed their eyes upon the horizon, with its many levels of shining light.

For me the trip meant a chance to read a little more than usual, to copy down the thoughts which swam into my suddenly receptive brain, to meditate – not upon the nature of goodness, which might have been the tendency of more religious or philosophical natures, but upon the nature of intelligence itself, and what such human intelligence could mean for men in the future. I was interested in my own life – not, I told myself, to the detriment of my husband and child, but with the aim of understanding existence more perfectly. That hunger to understand, which I had known long ago, had a habit of intruding its claims whenever the ordinary struggle of life ceased its activity. I think that I was interested in life as a scientist might be interested, as Helen might have been in her laboratory, or Margot in learning from her doctor the different functions of the brain. I had not yet found out how to conduct my experiments, but I was certain that such experiments existed.

It was true that a boat of this size, with all its accompanying social events, its deck sports and swimming pool, its card games, its dressing for dinner, its dancing under the moon, presented not only the opportunity to think and dream but also an aspect of worldliness which couldn't help but be attractive. Now and then – even when I sat with Jay asleep on my lap, or paraded around the deck with him in a slow, halting play session – I was flirted with by one of the white-suited officers, his bronze and pink complexion well set off by his uniform; or by one of the passengers – for instance a young rather plump squatter with an amorous manner, who was on the first stage of his journey home to a property near Normanton, and who seemed to have a close to religious obsession with young wives holding babies!

'If you only knew what you look like with that child . . .' he would say.

'What *do* I look like?'

'You look absolutely *bonzer.*'

His serious tone and wide-open eyes would prevent me from laughing, but it would affect me a little all the same and even appeal to my vanity, as he continued to profess himself enthralled by each pose he found me in, whether peeling an orange in a deck chair and sharing it with the baby or holding him when he was asleep and I almost asleep myself, in that drowsy after-lunch time when I had pushed the chair into the shade, and the heat of the day had swum up from the decks to relax our positions, and to flush our cheeks. It was, however, the first officer on the boat, wearing his white uniform (and well practiced in seduction), who represented any danger which might exist that I would be unfaithful to Mulford, and it was this tall erect young man who made a habit of tapping discreetly at my cabin door after the baby was asleep to invite me to meet him at the bar, or to see whether I was ready to accompany him to the Captain's table for dinner.

Willing as I was to accept the interest, I don't think that I welcomed its practical application, and only once did I allow myself to notice the power of the young officer's strong arms as we danced together, and to listen to his insistent demands that he should show me the moon from the bridge deck. Sexual desire without the accompaniment of love and knowledge frightened me, and intruded into a privacy which I didn't want to share.

Soon the odors of tropical vegetation drifted from the nearby shore as the boat, under a concentration of dazzlingly pure moonlight, steamed slowly up the channel toward Cairns. As the boat approached the waterfront and we all stood at the railings under the overshadowing coastal cliffs – dark and forbidding but touched with the silver moisture of the rain forests – the rank smells floating up from the wharves (an aroma of rotten fish and coastal mud and heated sugar) mingled with the flash of color from the golden shower tree.

So it was that while I stood holding Jay, and trying to pick out my parents down below on the wharves, I stood engulfed, in dreams as in reality, in the colors and scents of my childhood.

For the next days it was a great relief to be at home, to be received, as it seemed, into the worn wooden arms of the old house, where the floors sometimes creaked a little, as if protesting their separation from the rain forests from which they came. It was in the evenings, soon after I arrived, that I found myself looking at my father and seeing him as I had seen him long ago. It was not my father's concern with what 'was' that had been so vital to us all, I understood now, but rather his idea of what 'was to be' in the future. All those pioneers – purposeful and determined – who had come up the coastal ranges to develop farms and look for minerals, had been intent upon making the future happen. They had wanted to get land, to collect stock, to find silver or tin or gold, to build houses for their families. But some of them had also wanted to build a community, and my father, a natural visionary, was one of these.

Now I seemed to understand better the expression which had so often been on my father's face in the past, a half-compassionate, half-disapproving expression, which meant that he knew people were bound by their experiences.

'They come from cities,' he would say of the immigrants. 'We must teach them about *Nature*.' And listening to tales of industrial problems down on the Cairns wharves, he would laugh and say that the primary producers needed someone to be compassionate about *their* problems, too.

Once when I was quite small (it must have been in the very early twenties) I had been allowed, as a special treat, to go with him on the train to Cairns, and I had heard the farmers on the train boasting that they were going to show those 'wharfies' what they could do and what they couldn't do.

It was at the end of a very dry period, and the wharf lumpers at the Cairns waterfront had been engaged in a series of bitter clashes with the recruiters, who tended to claim freedom to hire efficient loading gangs and objected to the rotary system which was supposed to provide work for all members in turn. The tableland farmers knew that the rotary system sometimes worked against them, and they had tolerated it. But now, after the bad season, aware that perishable products from their own farms were rotting there on the wharves, while the loaders sat around idle, the farmers resented the system with all their might. They had had, they said, 'enough.'

On that particular day, the tall, thin, sunburnt farmers stopped by our carriage to drink water from the hanging canvas water bag, and remained to pour out their grievances to my father. I remembered especially one weather-beaten old man who curved his crooked clawlike hands in front of his face and said, 'It's *our* butter ain't it? I'll load it myself, every pound of it.' We reached the Cairns railway station at dusk that day, and took a horsedrawn cab to Hides Hotel. I remembered the hot dry smell of the leather flaps on the sides of the cab, and the drumming of the horse's hooves as we bowled along from the station to the hotel. After that there were excited conversations at the front desk, and the hotel manager said that the mayor himself was ready to lead a procession up the main street in favor of 'law and order' and 'the survival of North Queensland.'

There were more conversations the next morning, when various local citizens drifted in to talk and to drink tea, and the rumor came that two hundred and thirty farmers were en route down the ranges on a special train they had hired, with the intention of seeing that their products got onto the boats, and that four hundred more men were pushing up to Cairns from the sugar coast to load in person a thousand tons of sugar. The timber men (of whom, of course, my father was one) were declaring that the ramps all over the northern area were filled with waiting logs, and that, come what may, and at whatever cost, 'that timber had to be loaded onto those boats!'

254

At night the town was alive with shouts and cries. Although I wasn't allowed to leave the hotel, I hung over the railings upstairs, and saw the crowds and the banners drifting slowly by toward the wharves, and heard the shouts – 'Knock out the Communists!' and in reply, 'Kill the scabs!' I knew that my father was down there somewhere, and that if he was needed, he, too, would help to load the boats.

All I remembered afterward was that the farmers and the men from the canefields won – or at least they won for the time being – and that the produce was loaded onto the boats and sent south. The farmers and the other primary producers were pleased by what they had accomplished; they felt it a triumph over an obvious injustice. They returned quietly to the tableland, saying, 'We did it! Too right we did!'

Now, sitting on the veranda at Fleetwood, a young married woman returned momentarily to the old homestead (while my child played around the feet of the grown-ups, as once I had played), I began to revise my view of my father. Once I had thought that he knew everything, and was even remotely in tune with the 'Heavenly Father' whom our grandmother so exalted. Although I was wise enough now to know that this wasn't the case, that he was a human being like the rest of us, and had another side to his nature – a more difficult side, despondent and sometimes frustrated – I think that I wondered for the first time how often he himself had felt discouraged. Scenes from the past returned to me for reevaluation, and I saw, or thought I saw, how great a gap existed between man and his aspirations. Was this, I thought, why the concept of God was so much needed?

All through my childhood I had been aware that the strikes on the often sweltering Queensland waterfront – where formerly it had been thought impossible for white men to work – had disrupted the normal flow of goods and transportation, and I had come to comprehend the complexity which governs the human side of industrial affairs. I remembered my father admitting of the unions: 'They've got to *fight* but they've got to *think* too.' In some strange way I was part of the state's noisy, rambunctious, and distinctive history. I was proud of this. I was proud of the widespread union membership, proud of the fact that Queensland had had the first Labor government 'in the world' (even if that particular government had lasted for only seven days), and I was even proud of the wild and sometimes violent organizers who fought the police on so many occasions.

I was proud of my father in a more complete way, but now I wondered if he had always been sensitive about his political role, which must sometimes have been hard to manage. He might have been thought of often as being on the 'other side' – that is, as an owner of property and an employer of men. I knew, as I had known long ago, that my father was a brave man. But now I wondered if he were not also a prophetic man, and whether in the future others might agree with his concept of struggle, but struggle with compromise. I remembered that men died, that little remained of their efforts, that their reward was only life itself.

In all the small details of our brief weeks at Fleetwood, it was clear that the depression, with its attendant evils, was not yet quite over, that perhaps Fleetwood itself would never recover from it. On those last evenings, we were all, my parents and I, avoiding the problems of the immediate present and seeking refuge in the past. I asked my mother whether she remembered how once when we were all small and at Double Island, our father had had to go into Cairns for a meeting, and she had refused to let us go swimming unless we all wore a rope around our waists – which she herself, tiny and thin as she was, then held at the other end. And we talked a good deal of Cape York and of the early days there, and of my mother and father's knowledge of its inhabitants. That area of Cape York Peninsula which stretched upward toward New Guinea was, speaking poetically, the logical extension of our own land on the tablelands – a wild world upon which colonial culture had scarcely put its imprint, a two-hundred-mile-wide finger pointing up from Princess Charlotte Bay to the very shores of the Torres Strait. This land held scarcely a thousand people, along with a number of wild cattle, a few groups of government workers, and a policeman or two patrolling with Aboriginal offsiders. It was really the epitome of northeastern isolation, and in 'the wet' all the tributaries of its rivers – the Mitchell, the Kendall, the 'terrible Archer,' the Stewart, the Pascoe – spread in flood as far as the eye could see (as had the Burdekin when we went south on the train to school). The expanse of water left only here and there small islands of higher land.

During my early years I had never gone as far north as Somerset, which was the original tiny government outpost at the very northeastern tip of the continent, but I knew something about the southern area of the Cape, and had heard of the groups of full-blooded Aborigines still existing there (sometimes living in a close-to-nature state, the men hunting with spear and knife and boomerang, the women bare-breasted and in blue lap-laps, gathering wood and digging roots and caring for the children). Now Tracey and my father described the kind of land seen farther north, the rivers of gold and brownish-green, their banks marked by water stains from the wet, by dark feverish dead-end pools, and by the claw marks of crocodiles. In this country men were lost forever, hunted perhaps for months by the single policeman and his tracker, through sodden roadless wastes where the giant pitcher plants (*Nepenthes gigantes*) grew. There the explorer Kennedy had been speared and killed almost within sight of the sea, while his faithful Aboriginal companion, Jacky-Jacky, buried the notes and maps of the expedition and walked all night up to his waist in water to elude the myalls . . .

'It might seem,' my father said, 'that living as we do down here on the safer tableland, we had no more to do with the isolated peninsula than Uncle Tony had to do with New Guinea when he went there, but it's all part of the battling north, you know, and those men would come down to us here, especially in the old days . . . There was the Jardine family and there were men from Coen and from Laura . . .'

He explained that old John Jardine had been a magistrate in Rockhampton before he was named as government resident up there on the outpost right opposite Albany Island, and that the fact that Queensland should concern itself with a faraway beach on the Strait had alone been a sign of progress.

'It was the most dangerous place on all the coast,' he added. 'It's an Empire habit to guard a channel, and you can imagine that there was a need to monitor the Strait, to give help to marooned vessels, sailors who'd been shipwrecked, anyone in distress . . .' He began to talk about John Jardine's two sons, Frank and Alex, who were only boys but who overlanded like men.

I was transported to my childhood, for we had always heard about those two boys who had fought their way north with horses and cattle to their father's post at Somerset, and I had heard again and again of how they lost their spare clothes in a campfire, and had made cloaks and caps of emu skin, and wrapped their calves in paperbark, and crossed rivers, and slept in the rain, hearing the long-drawn howls of the natives, sheets of bark curved over their bodies; how they had lost their cattle not only to the spears of the natives but to the smothering bogs of rank mud.

I told my parents that I had gone to the university with Frank Vidgen, who was the grandson of old John Jardine, and the result of a long-ago union between one of the Jardine brothers and a South Sea Island girl.

'His skin was a golden color, and we all liked to dance with him because he danced so well, and I think he represented something which especially interested us.'

After I went to bed that night I read for a long time, as I used to do in the past, and once again I listened to the sounds of the night – to a possum on the roof, to a frog in the pawpaw tree, to an occasional cow cropping the grass outside the window. While Jay slept in the little bed nearby and the electric light flickered in the old way – so that at last I had to light the oil lamp – I read an old account of Cape York, which described the beauty of these maritime provinces, the heartbreaking adventures of castaways, the stories of cannibalism, and the descriptions of a moonscape of stunted shrubs and sandy swamps, with red and sometimes curry-colored or black termite mounds, and vast watery distances. The characters in this dramatic scene were not British buccaneers but the offspring of convicts from the hulks, and Aborigines and mixed-bloods from Southeast Asia – for this was scarcely the land of good taste. There were stories, too, of loose unions between invading white males and darker women, and one story of a captured white woman who 'ran with the blacks,' as it was said, and was encountered from time to time by explorers and officials. Another such woman, found near Cooktown, pined away and died when she returned to white society. And I thought of older stories still, of the faraway legends of an ancient dark race who lived in trees, and ate what they could get, and had no knowledge of fire, and were perhaps ancestors of us all. There was something unforgettable about such stories.

Now that I felt myself being transported to that other technological world, which I sensed might be alien to me, I was haunted by the northern land which represented the part of myself I didn't know. These lands of freedom, as our grandmother said once, were not those known of 'in our Christian education.'

The day before we were to leave for the south, my mother came into the room where I was dressing the baby.

'You don't mind going, darling?' she asked.

'Going to America and London? Going so far away?'

'Yes, going so far away'

'Yes, I do mind.'

'There'll be a whole new life for you,' she protested.

'I know.' I looked into her dark eyes, which had seen so much more than I had ever seen, but which were also the eyes of hope and belief.

'I suppose I will get used to it,' I said doubtfully, smiling

259

a little. 'I suppose you will *all* get used to it, and forget me.'

She went out for a moment and brought back a scarf she had made of batik silk, a delicate, strangely colored scarf which was at variance with the sewing she was generally forced to do – turning sheets, or mending socks, or putting up hems. She had always made beautiful things, sometimes sewing whole dresses for breaking-up ceremonies when we were at school – sitting up for half the night to embroider and beautify as many as three dresses at a time. I looked down at the counterpane, tears in my eyes.

'Your father has something for you, too.'

My father came in weighing in his hand his grandfather's heavy gold watch, the watch we had seen and wondered about in our childhood. He put it on the bed.

'I thought Jay should have it. After all, he's the first of a new generation.'

The watch glittered on the white counterpane, and it seemed very rich against the familiar worn furniture and the faded walls. Jay, who did not yet know what gold was, stretched out his babyish hand toward it.

As well as leaving behind the north, and these two people who could never be replaced, I was leaving the innocence of the environment into which I happened to have been born. I was leaving the broad horizon, the crudity of spontaneous action; in a sense I was leaving the very power to live.

17

Departure

When I returned from the north, I was more than ever conscious of this natural and resolved Australian world, and more than ever sorry to leave it. For some reason the particular Australian essence is hard to describe; it has in it both a sweetness and a terrible desiccation, a nothingness and a rocklike reality. Australia is a place where the stars seem to hang low, and where men feel close to a long-ago spinning of the planets. If this heightens human endurance, it also makes demands upon human strength.

Mulford and I were to say goodbye to Brisbane in a few months, but I could still not believe that I would ever go. I felt it necessary to remind myself that there was something undone, unfinished, unrealized about this departure, that some final decision had not been made. In the few short hours I had to myself, I walked a good deal – passing along the cliffs of Kangaroo Point high above the river, walking back past the Women's College and the shabby front of the Angeleses' boardinghouse, and past the end of the street where John had lived – and, as far as I knew, lived still. Sometimes I went toward the ferry (which, because of the car, I seldom took now) and even further to a little peak of land opposite the city proper, where across the water I could see the end of Creek Street, and the dark blot of the old fig tree which seemed, among the buildings, like an encircled relic from the original forest.

I thought of my past and drew no conclusions from it. I was reading *Lady Chatterley's Lover*, a book in a plain brown-paper cover, which was passed around clandestinely from hand to hand because it had been printed in Italy and banned in England, and even in Australia was considered contraband. For some reason it was not the sexual element in this book which influenced me so much, but rather the exhortation to live for the inner self, to resist decadence, and to stress the philosophical 'essence' – an urge which somehow related itself to the whole question of the departure from primitive Australia. It seemed to me that our parents had lived not only for their children but also at the command of the earth from which our nourishment came. The earth was simply there, and our parents had bent before its relentless will.

As I walked the rough asphalt of Kangaroo Point, I murmured the litany of that old life of the earth – the dark inscrutable jungle, the timber cutting, the clearing and plowing, the rain, the rough roads, the mud, the animals, the long hours, the unspoken demand, always the demand: our father, known for his 'probity in public and private life,' chairman of this and member of that, speaker, inspirer, leader of shire and council, supporter of hospital and butter factory, Milk Board and Harbour Board; our mother, wife and worker of many years, carrying on her own private battle with nature, absorbed into the stream of my father's life. Both of them were sacrificed, used, worn by work, allowed – according to my egocentric view – only the merest modicum of self-love. Our parents, separate and reserved as they were, joined hands with the other pioneers. They belonged to a communal time.

But the rest of us belonged to a new time, to the time of 'liberality' and 'sensibility' and 'lonely freedom.' I had advertised myself early as 'restless.' I had assumed, as my sisters had, our right to 'strike out for ourselves.' Didn't it imply that we declared our right to an almost sacred individualism?

But what did I want to do? Did I *want* to leave Australia? Of course I did. Yes. Yes, I must leave. I might be a wanderer, an exile, but I must leave all the same. I must leave, leave, leave . . . I walked myself into a fury. And why *not* leave? Wasn't

262

Australia a cultural cul-de-sac? A great empty space on the map? A pink space taken over by the Empire? Tyrannized over in the calm, orderly British way? We had cities, yes, but so few of them. Were there not many vanished towns, many houses with steps fallen in, many chimney spaces from which trees sprouted? Australia – the lost and discovered and lost again! Somewhere Australia had a house of bottles, a house in a tree, a house stitched out of kangaroo hides. I stopped to look at the glittering water, and to breathe in the ozone from the sea. Australia had a monument to a dog, to an insect, to an alcoholic. There was a town where the goats had eaten a whole church!

I went to bed that night and dreamt of Cape York and woke uneasily to remember a nightmare-like effort to build a raft to cross a river. It was one of those dreams in which one tries to take responsibility for something, and fails, but in some anxious way keeps on trying. In the dream I struggled and gasped, and Mulford murmured, 'Are you awake? It's nearly morning.'

'I was dreaming.' Outside a boat was chugging up the river, its subdued hoot sounding mournfully through rain and mist.

'When you were in the north did you decide why you were so reluctant to leave your native land?'

'Perhaps I did,' I said uneasily.

I thought of the north again, of the tropic fever which I would always have in my blood, of the wild country, of the islands beyond where we lived, inhabited by the mixtures of so many tribes – a world removed from the disciplines and taboos of that other overseas world I was about to enter.

'I think it was because I didn't want to become respectable,' I suggested. A sense of sin oppressed me. And gropingly I wondered about forgiveness.

Mulford was lying beside me in bright blue cotton pajamas. In the early light his eyes were also blue, as blue as those small flowers that shine among the grasses in full summer. His boyish face was overshadowed by the thin fair hair which fell across his forehead, and I was filled with tenderness for his presence, and the rather gentle kind of masculinity he possessed. I put up my hand to caress his cheek, and saw his eyes change like those of a relieved child.

'If only . . .' he said.

I felt that he wanted to say what he had sometimes said before – 'If only you loved me as I love you' – but I tried to prevent his saying it. It was Mulford who had preserved my equanimity and made it possible to give up John, and so to understand those broader possibilities which we also call love.

'Are we lost?' I said.

'Don't you trust me?'

'Yes, I trust you. I trust you only too much.' He drew me to him.

The next evening Mulford brought home our passports and traveling papers. He also brought a letter from my mother, which I took out onto the veranda and read while the sun fell lower and lower in the heavens, staining the river water with orange and red. It was a long time before I understood what the letter was saying. My father had had premonitions of a heart attack: 'He was trying to help string wire through a fence post . . . the man helping him had been inexperienced, and your father was straining to tighten the wire . . . the doctor says that these were the pains of angina . . . a warning . . .'

While I packed and sorted, and made lists, it seemed that voices came to me, penetrating the new world I was building up for myself, voices which spoke of guilt and loss. Sometimes the figures of my mother and father appeared to me to be fading away, fading away, just as the jungle trees were being cut down, one by one. I realized that for a long time inside our family circle we had sensed the future – not as children might sense something vaguely frightening, but rather as adults feel a recurring fear of the inevitable. We had feared that our father might not be able to pay his debts, for instance, and what he called the 'D.O.' – that is, the 'damned overdraft' – and that then he might have to sell the property; and we feared that the burden Tracey carried – nearly as heavy as our father's – might be too much for him.

And there was more than this to be conscious of in those days of pre-departure. It was as if events had been foretold in a pagan temple, so that we colonials, as adjuncts to the West, experienced a generalized and primitive anxiety concerning the future the Fates might have in store for us. History accelerated our understanding – warning, hinting, stimulating, repeating, urging what was unbelievable and inexplicable. Mulford came home from work one afternoon with an article about Nuremberg and its great rallies – an article illustrated by numerous glossy pictures showing the massing of swastikas, the dipping of what were called 'blood flags,' the glare of lights, the smoke rising from braziers, and the accounts of the great continuous roar: *'Sieg Heil! Sieg Heil! Heil Hitler!'*

March came – the year was 1937. It was on the night before we left Brisbane for Sydney, on the first stage of our trip across the seas, and when it seemed that nothing would happen to prevent our departure, that on some pretext I slipped out of the house and – leaving my husband, who was trying to pack up his papers, and my son, sleeping in his crib – walked down through the bushes on the banks of the river, to a big patch of bamboo, to say goodbye to John. The huge moon, aureoled with gold, hung over us where we pressed against the dark bamboos to avoid identification; the river lapped at its banks as rivers have always done, and an occasional mosquito whined in the air nearby. It seemed to me that mosquitoes had always haunted those dark tropical paradises where, in the past, we had wanted to make love. The wind blowing up from the distant sea, where once it had filled the sails of offshore vessels looking for a suitable depository for convicts, now suggested the whole Pacific Ocean, which I would eventually cross in one of the big white ships already carrying tourists to and from Australia. I did not know then that someday – in fact, after we had lived out more than half of our lives – John would come to the United States and would try to find me. Now, thinking that I was to part with him forever, I felt not only that old mysterious eroticism but something closer to fear of my own fate.

He put his arm around my shoulders. When he asked, 'Do you believe that if we had been married . . .?' I knew that he felt somewhat as I felt. Our words drifted away in the darkness of this last, unsatisfactory rendezvous. It was as if we asked useless questions of the mysterious book in which our lives were written.

We left for Sydney the next day, where we were to catch the boat to Perth and, from there, to San Francisco. I remember how excited I was, and also how beautiful the city of Sydney seemed, how green the gardens were across which we walked to the golden sandstone buildings, and how water from the sprinklers glistened on the warm bark of tropical trees and upon the hairy stems of giant tree ferns. I remember also how beneficent seemed the outstretched arm of the statue of Queen Victoria, as if, having blessed the sometimes rebellious subjects of her dominions, she now welcomed them to the kingdom for which we ourselves were headed.

Although I could not look into the future, I seemed to know that soon my father would be ill again, and that he would not recover, and that when I finally reached London, Robin would write to tell me that he could not breathe properly, and that she was having to give him injections – and that he would die. 'It seemed to me that the world stopped with his death,' Robin wrote in September of 1937.

On that hot brilliant day in Sydney, I stood on the crowded deck of the S.S. *Monterey* – my arms tired from holding the heavy baby, my mind filled with vague painful premonitions. Then Mulford came up behind me and lifted the baby out of my arms, and with his unoccupied hand held mine, and both of us were caught up in some momentary sense of sadness and rapture.

My memories of that day, so many years later, were more the memories of the moment than anything else. Some friends were gathered on the wharf below, as was Hazel, the only member of the family able to see us off. She was looking up at me, waving her hand, and I was glad that she was there. I did not forget the sad uneasiness about our family and what might happen to it, but at that moment I was aware only of the old images of water so necessary to those who have been born near the Pacific. I heard the sound of the harbor, the chug-chug of the ferryboats, and the murmur of the tides. The ship we were on was only a larger and stronger vessel, after all, and going a little farther than across the harbor. As it moved slowly, slowly away, the faces on the wharf blurred and faded, and colored streamers – pink and red and blue and green – now our only link with Australia, snapped and fluttered around us in the gathering breeze. I was living rather than thinking, using instinct rather than thought. I was dimly understanding that the world which had made me what I was was breaking up and changing, that the water around me could not for one moment remain still, that the water bore me away, that the water was history.

In Australia the British ethos of 'carrying on' was still very strong, and the saga of our family might best be described in this way. As I went to the United States, and then with Mulford to his new post in London; as both Hazel and Margot went to Southeast Asia; as Helen married and went to live in the south – Tracey and Robin remained for a while in the old house. After my father's death, our mother stayed at Kureen, and Tracey 'carried on' at Fleetwood for nearly two more years, until 1939. Robin went south to Brisbane in 1938. In 1939, the year of the Nazi-Soviet Pact – when World War II had begun – a military order went out from the Queensland government for especially tall timbers to be cut in the rain forests of the north. Tracey had gone into the scrubs to supervise a party of timber getters, and the painful story of what happened then eventually reached me in London. Some of the great trees had been cut and were lying in parallel rows – supposedly well buttressed to prevent them from rolling. But this work had not been properly done, and the logs shifted on their base. Tracey, standing nearby, saw them moving and began to run; but his foot caught in a loop of lawyer vine, he fell to the ground, and was killed instantly by the rolling logs.

Robin flew home to be with our mother, and to try to run the property as best she could . . . Long afterward, when I returned to Australia, I went to Malanda and drove past those half-vanished landmarks and along what remained of the old roads, and went down to the railway line where the creek was and where the grass was lavishly green as it had always been. The man who was with me, and who once had worked for my father, pointed out the far-off boundary of the paddocks, and said, 'Once I was over here – in early 1939, it must have been – before the war . . . I remember seeing your brother Tracey plowing the lower field there. He had so much to do that he must have been late in planting . . . Anyway, there he was – it was after dark, and he was plowing that field down there with a lantern tied in front of the tractor.'

I stared at the field, and I thought of Tracey and of all the farmers who did so much, and did it alone, and I thought of my mother, who lost first her husband and then her only son. The field was green, as fertile and as green as a cemetery . . .

After that we drove up the hill again and I stood looking at the Fleetwood house sinking into the earth, its walls buckled, its roof collapsed. Only remnants of the garden emerged from the encroaching soil. There were brilliant begonias where one corner of the fernery had been, and old ferns marked another corner, as if to prove that once a living house had existed there.

THE END

HELEN OF BURMA
by Helen Rodriguez

'As a story of courage, determination verging on pighead-edness, physical and emotional endurance, inspiration, resilience, triumph over adversity, devotion to duty and the human race, Helen of Burma is unbeatable'
Oxford Times

Helen Rodriguez, daughter of a Scottish nurse and a Port-uguese surgeon, was born and brought up in Burma, in the idyllic civil station of Taunggyi. Her childhood was one of intense happiness and, after she had trained as a nurse in Rangoon, she came back to her beloved Taunggyi to work as a matron in the civil hospital. She was there when Japanese bombers destroyed the town in 1942.

From that moment on she worked day and night, tending to the casualties in appalling conditions and under constant air attack. She defused a bomb single-handed; she evacuated the military hospital by carrying the patients one by one on her back over a period of four days. As the Japanese approached she refused to abandon her patients. Bayoneted, starved, tortured, she faced each crisis with fortitude and she describes them simply yet eloquently, even with wry humour. This is a story of the triumph of human will over almost impossible adversity.

'Helen of Burma is an inspiring story. Nobody reading it can believe that women are, except by their own choice, the lesser sex'
Sunday Telegraph

0 552 99305 0

A VOYAGER OUT: THE LIFE OF MARK KINGSLEY
by Katherine Frank

'A wonderful story, funny, stirring and touching ... a worthy tribute to a remarkable, an admiral and, though she never knew it, a lovable woman'
Geoffrey Wheatcroft, *The Spectator*

Mary Kingsley accomplished a great deal in her tragically short life. Niece of Charles Kingsley and daughter of an unlikely alliance between an amateur explorer and a bedridden, cockney domestic, she was born in 1862. Her youth was sacrificed in fulfilling traditional Victorian expectations of a daughter; looking after her invalid mother while her father indulged his pleasure in travelling. Their deaths allowed her, at the age of 30, a few years of freedom. She was able to fulfill her own desire to travel, and ventured deep into the heart of West Africa, into worlds few white men and no white women had seen before. Her adventures there ranked with those of the most intrepid explorers, always enterprising, enlightening and, at times, highly dangerous. Throughout her travels she still found time to write two volumes of thrilling adventure stories, both of which became bestsellers at the time. Mary Kingsley is the model for the courageous Victorian female explorer. Her sad but fascinating life has been vividly and sympathetically portrayed in Katherine Frank's highly-acclaimed and remarkable biography.

'Katherine Frank has written a quietly beautiful biography that reveals not only the outer life of an extraordinary traveler but something of her inner life as well'
The New York Times Book Review

'A fresh, sensitive, vivid biography'
Literary Review

'A splendid book'
Guardian

0 552 99314 X

All Corgi/Bantam Books are available at your bookshop or newsagent, or can be ordered from the following address:

Corgi/Bantam Books,
Cash Sales Department,
P.O. Box 11, Falmouth, Cornwall TR10 9EN

Please send a cheque or postal order (no currency) and allow 60p for postage and packing for the first book plus 25p for the second book and 15p for each additional book ordered up to a maximum charge of £1.90 in UK.

B.F.P.O customers please allow 60p for the first book, 25p for the second book plus 15p per copy for the next 7 books, thereafter 9p per book.

Overseas customers, including Eire, please allow £1.25 for postage and packing for the first book, 75p for the second book, and 28p for each subsequent title ordered.